GW01606545

RAY OVINGTON

HOW TO DRAW AND PAINT FISH AND GAME

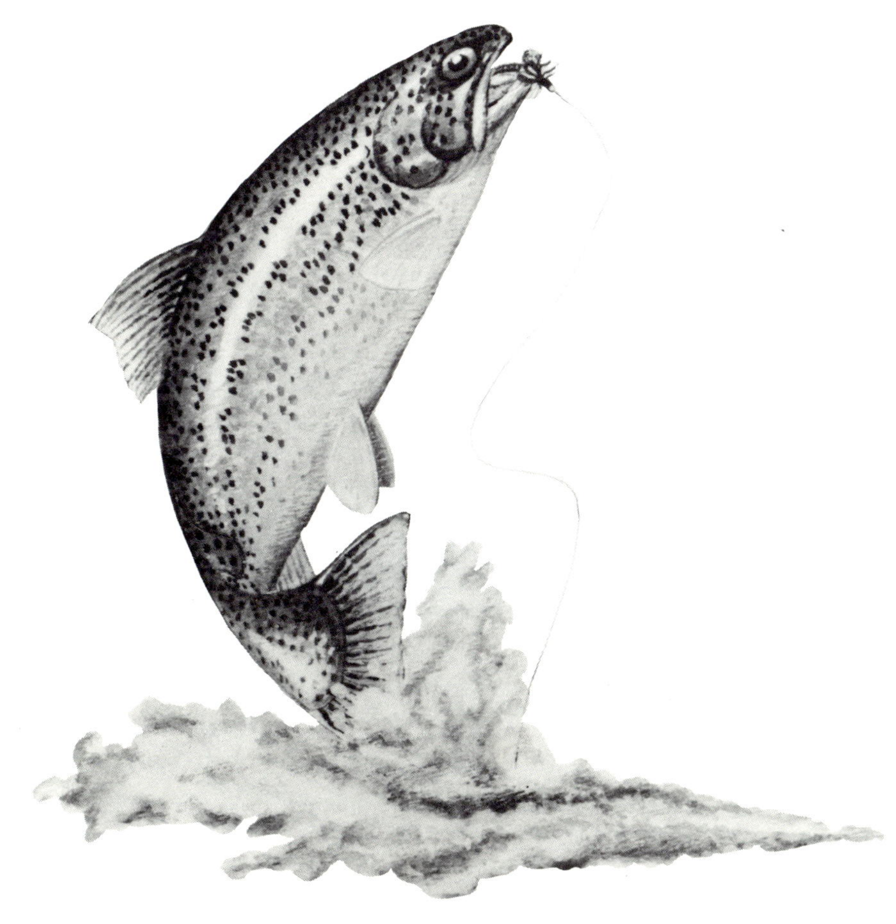

WEATHERVANE BOOKS
NEW YORK

This 1988 edition is published by Weathervane Books,
distributed by Crown Publishers, Inc., 225 Park Avenue South, New York, New York 10003, by arrangement with Prentice Hall Press, a division of Simon & Schuster, Inc.

Printed and Bound in the United States of America

Library of Congress Cataloging-in-Publication Data

Ovington, Ray.
How to draw and paint fish and game / Ray Ovington.
Includes index.
ISBN 0-517-66201-9
1. Wildlife art. 2. Fishes in art. 3. Art—Technique.
I. Title.
N7660.09 1988
751.4—dc19

87-37132
CIP

h g f e d c b a

Contents

Preface

This book on how to draw and paint is designed to teach the art of wildlife illustration using simple tools and simple techniques developed by me over many years. These techniques will enable you to produce a fine work of art.

By following the simple directives and studying the detailed step-by-step drawings, you as a beginning artist or trained professional can learn to draw and paint birds, animals, and fish easily and accurately by first training yourself to see more, thus enlarging your appreciation of nature and consequently increasing your ability to transfer what you see to paper or canvas.

By setting up a routine beginning with the basic profile and filling this in by zoning the physical shapes and forms and then filling in the texture, a seemingly complicated subject is reduced to simple steps in rendering in all media, steps that are seldom explained or detailed in art classes or sufficiently outlined in books. The importance of authenticity is stressed throughout the text and drawings with constant suggestions for gathering appropriate research in the form of photographs, authentic artwork, and the studying of live creatures as well as mounted specimens or museum skins.

This technique of drawing encourages the beginner to proceed despite the fact that he may lack knowledge of biology or be unfamiliar with the skeletal and muscular structure of his subjects, since ample photographic research is readily available for study.

My objective in this book is to teach the art of seeing and observing wildlife, to inspire research in the subjects of interest, and to make drawing and painting an easy recreation, working with simple tools to produce an authentic and exciting rendering of the subject in its appropriate background. You will then become more than just a recorder; you will become a wildlife student and, I hope, a conservationist as well, an appreciator of our natural heritage. By employing the basic techniques outlined herein the artist can grow in stature to produce lifelike, authentic pictures of outdoor life and then branch out into wider horizons using more sophisticated equipment to produce works that can border on fine art as well as inspiring illustration.

HOW TO DRAW AND PAINT FISH AND GAME

·1· The Expressive Field of Outdoor Art

The ancient art of rendering game birds, animals, and fish has deep roots in our heritage, going back in time to the wall paintings of Egyptian tombs and even to the cave paintings of early man at Lascaux and Altamira. The strong instinct for the hunt is deeply embedded in the human consciousness; even today the most popular game species represent the principal foods that early man hunted and fished in order to survive.

In modern times, for at least 300 years or more, the various game species have been the subjects of great artists and illustrators. The word *game* came into being because hunting wild animals for food became a sport, or game, particularly for the wealthy landowners and those who could afford to travel even to distant lands for their shooting sport. For many years artists concentrated on detailed and explicit depictions of dead game hanging on a wall plaque or plank, the significance being to register the hunter's pride in his ability.

In later years, however, the accent shifted to showing the subjects in real-life settings as living creatures to be admired by both hunters and nonhunters. Sporting art, as it is called today, concentrates on living game species, and the primary attraction has been for general outdoorsy people. Gradually, game art has evolved into a unique and popular form of decoration, associated chiefly with masculine qualities or, in the case of certain exotic species, with an almost macho atmosphere.

Game art has always harmonized with the traditional pine-paneled drawing room of yesteryear, where it was the featured decor in the most wealthy homes and offices. It is found today in the waiting rooms of lawyers and doctors and in restaurants that strive to create an atmosphere of quality. The use of game art also develops the illusion of wealth and suggests the feeling of elite forms of recreation in the outdoors.

With the advent of publishing, the sports of game hunting and fishing have been expressed both in glorified text and in lush illustration. In the past, many large-format books and special limited editions with finely reproduced artwork graced the shelves of wealthy sportsmen and collectors. Today's bookstores are filled with books about the sports of hunting and fishing, outdoor adventure, and nature study, most of them well illustrated. Add to this the great and increasing number of monthly magazines that promote these recreations, all with sporting art as well as photographs, and you can see that game art with its implied interest in actual participation in the outdoors is enjoyed by increasing numbers of people. You'll see game species represented on calendars, greeting cards, and advertising art.

Game art is of great interest to nature lovers and conservationists as well as hunters and fishermen. With today's vital interest in ecology, the portrayal of game species rather than songbirds is a very important aspect, since sportsmen contribute, through their purchase of licenses and stamps, to the conservation effort.

Outdoor recreation—whether hunting, fishing, camping, canoeing, or related sports—exposes us to game species and stirs our desire to have samples of the outdoors in our homes in the form of original paintings or prints to adorn our walls, reminding us of our relationship with nature and stimulating further participation in outdoor adventures.

One of the most recent forms of outdoor art, particularly in the game field, has been the duck stamp. Since their introduction, duck stamps, both the national and state annual issues, have helped to spur interest in the preservation of the outdoors but even more have stimulated the production of outdoor art. Close to 2000 artists compete annually for the national duck stamp design. Add to this the tremendous increase in game species prints produced by the growing number of really fine artists, and you have a very specialized art form that has become tremendously important in the art scene.

Although the rendering of game animals, birds, and fish must be called illustration, it can also be fine art when produced to the qualifications the critics have established. Although the difference between fine art and illustration can be hazy, the demand for really fine renditions is steadily increasing regardless of the critic's label.

An artist painting a fine art scene of a woodland path strewn with autumn colors may have his work end up in a prominent gallery. But when the outdoor artist renders a grouse flying through the same scene, it is considered illustration for reasons this author cannot quite fathom. There have been many so-called fine artists who have included game birds in their paintings, and many times the rendering of the bird is atrocious. Many classic paintings of flying mallards found in museums and galleries, for example, show the bird modeled from the ungainly domesticated variety rather than the wild bird. The inaccuracies are intolerable, yet the painting may be classed as fine art.

Today realism—the actuality of the bird with all its physical characteristics, in flight or on the ground—must be rendered with explicit biological accuracy, true in every detail, and the background also must be true to the species and complement it. Whether this be the definition of fine art or of illustration is up to the critics. (The ultimate critic is the one who buys and hangs up the work.) Yet even the beginning artist should be interested in authenticity and accuracy in rendering the spirit, form, details, and esthetic aspects of the subject.

This kind of photographic accuracy is not as difficult to render as it might seem but has been sadly overlooked by many so-called "greats." For example, it doesn't take any more talent to place eleven primary feathers in a duck wing than to draw too many or too few. As to authentic background, certainly a flock of mallards would not be seen waddling around among desert cactus.

Given all the proper elements and the correct research, it is possible to produce beautiful, accurate paintings and drawings, whether called illustration or fine art, using game species as subjects.

The sportsman who really enjoys his sport and appreciates all the nuances and feelings of just being outdoors can add to his involvement with recreation by rendering scenes of his exploits, drawing and painting pictures of his favorite subjects. Creating a piece of art worthy of being hung on the walls of the living room or study, or being exhibited at the local public library or gallery, or actually being sold or given away is a worthy undertaking and one that can offer much indoor recreation in the off-season. The true artist working on a chosen subject puts himself into the picture he is painting; and during that time spent with brush, pen, or pencil, the experience of "being there" is all-absorbing.

There are many excellent artists whose work will inspire you to do it yourself. From the time I was a youngster I admired the works of such illustrators as Lynn Bogue Hunt, Arthur Fuller, and William Shaldach of *Field & Stream* magazine, and Walter Wilwerding, who painted many covers for *Sports Afield* magazine. Milton C. Weilner was another great who inspired me to take up the brush and pen.

The great renderers of animals and birds since Audubon and Louis Agassiz Fuertes have spawned the moderns such as Arthur Singer and Roger Tory Petersen. Today we have excellent artists in great numbers who are preserving the beauties of game species and are thus fulfilling an evident need in the collective psyche of man.

It is one thing to admire others' works and quite another to do it yourself, an endeavor available to all who wish to embark upon some expression of creativity. Whether your works are ever exhibited beyond your own home walls or become the subject of a wildlife stamp or magazine cover is really beside the point. Taking up the pencil, brush, or pen and drawing from your own experiences and interpretations of nature will enhance your enjoyment of your recreation and will be a lasting monument to your own creativity, bringing to all who see it the feeling, the essence, and the values of the great outdoors.

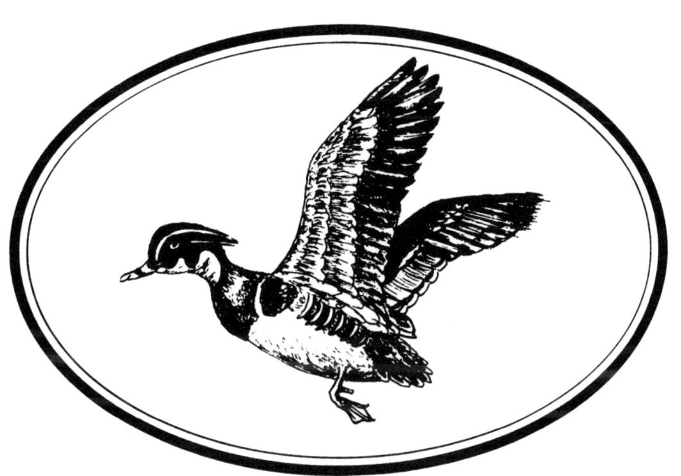

Figure 1.1 This montage of a pheasant, turkey head, brown trout, sailfish, deer, and wood duck gives you a taste of what's ahead.

In this illustration, made with a medium ballpoint pen, the subjects appear a bit rough: They are drawn with the heavier point to show just how the various textures of fur, feather, and scales can be rendered within the limitations of black and white. Although it may look difficult at first, soon you will be able to create similar drawings with ease and confidence.

Seemingly difficult renditions of intricate patterns, such as those of the pheasant, can be broken down into steps so that you actually "assemble" the parts bit by bit, a project which actually requires modest talent and far less time than you would expect.

The squiggly technique used in the gnarled skin of the turkey head is a simple matter of stages of intensity. Start light and open, keeping the pen strokes fairly wide apart and then gradually closing in and intensifying the shadows to set off the highlights and using the gradations to produce form.

The brown trout is possibly the most involved of the trout to render, but when you see the technique broken down later it amounts again to an assembly job.

Direction of pen stroke can help you to define shape, as in the sailfish's body. The light reflections of its big dorsal fin are done by intensifying the darker areas, leaving the highlights to stand by themselves.

The imitation of the deer's fur is easily accomplished with pen stroke direction, and the areas of shadow are merely intensifications, as you will see later.

To create the forms, start working very light to indicate the general look and then very gradually intensify, a technique we pursue throughout the book as we work on the various species of creatures to be created. We'll work in pencil, pen and ink, and wash in this way.

The wash background in this picture is done to show how a setting can accent the figures—another taste of what's to come, this time in rendering a suitable setting for your subjects.

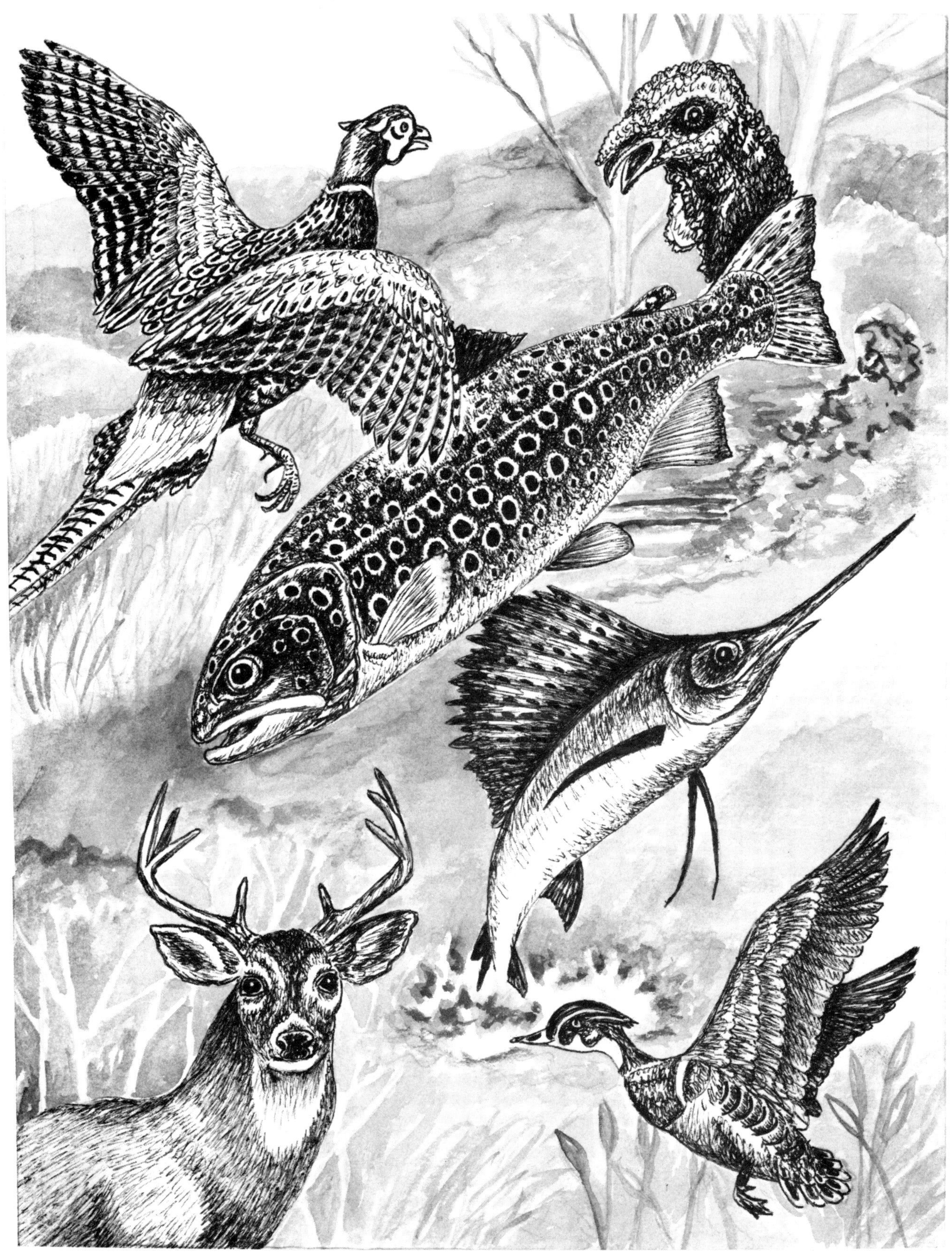

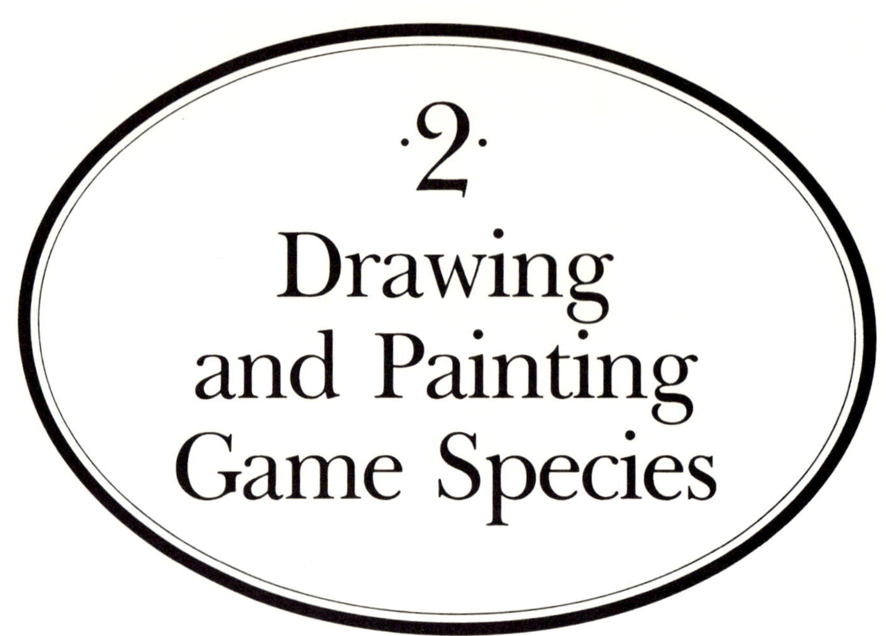

2 Drawing and Painting Game Species

You are fortunate if you have subscribed to and saved magazines that print photos and artwork of birds and animals, or if you have a personal library of outdoor books with fine illustrations or photographs. If not, it is time to start a collection of pictures, even clipping animal photos from the newspapers!

The next best source of reference material is the public library. Most have a full stock of magazines such as *National Wildlife, International Wildlife, Audubon, Bird Lore, Smithsonian, Nature Magazine,* and the like, plus the outdoor recreation magazines such as *Field & Stream, Outdoor Life, Sports Afield* and the many hunting and fishing annuals and monthlies. Pore through these and make copies of the art you wish to save for your research, or ask the library to save the old issues for you when they are through with them. Tear out what you want and file them under species or type of background.

If you are a nature buff and like to take your own pictures of wildlife in action, then a good camera armed with telephoto lenses is needed. Photography is one of the best ways to study nature, particularly for background detail such as old fences, windfalls, rocks, or stumps, which are good to have in your file. If you don't carry a camera, use a pair of binoculars—preferably 7 × 35 for most needs. After spending days behind the camera lens photographing the family life and the growth and development of nesting birds and their chicks, you will feel you know them all personally, having had such intimate views through the power of magnification.

In addition to the casual walk in the woods or the planned hiking trip, birds and many ground animals can be lured into range by devices such as calls, scents, baits, and decoys. There is nothing like the experience of observing wildlife close up to enhance your devotion to creating real-life nature pictures.

Although it is preferable that the artist be completely familiar with the skeleton and musculature of the subjects he draws or paints, this can be compensated by a good eye and by a sense of form and of the relationships of body areas. The artist can also refer to the high-quality photography available today and to the myriad, very fine paintings and drawings by the most celebrated artists in the world.

It is really no fun to copy, however. Just because you are using a photograph of a standing deer, for example, you do not have to render it exactly as it is in the photograph. Play with it a little, staying within the bounds of normal body movements and shape.

To get the "feel" of the subjects you will be painting it is a great help to actually touch the fur, feathers, or scales of the subjects. Note the details of eyes, noses, ears, and tails, of the angles of their construction, and their proportions.

You must have some favorite subjects you would like to start on, so we have included in this book the most popular species of birds, animals, and fish for you to choose from. Don't expect your first drawing or painting to be like the experts'. After some fifty years of drawing and painting these subjects, I am still learning. It was a fourth-grade art teacher who first gave me exposure to the challenges and satisfactions to be found in the world of art. I am indebted to this teacher, Miss Lillian Bain (my first and only formal instructor); through the years her precepts have inspired me to produce interesting and authentic renditions of nature and to capture the spirit of the outdoors.

"The minute you pick up a pencil or brush to transfer something to paper, try to begin to see as you never have before," Miss Bain advised. In that semester we children were taught and trained to use our eyes to note subtle differences in textures and color values, in the relative proportions of objects, in composition. Her advice is as valid today as it was more than fifty years ago, and through the years my relationships with nature in all its forms have been greatly enriched because of her.

True seeing can develop many phases of awareness. We open ourselves to absorb the scene before us, using all our senses—even hearing and touch—to absorb the relative qualities of form, color, light, shade, and perspective. Through our senses we record the "mood," whether cool and blustery, light and warm, dark and threatening, gusty winds or gentle breezes. After absorbing the sight and "feel" of the scene we wish to portray, we can then go to paper or canvas and bring forth a rendition that will have authenticity and depth. The ability to record what you see in this way will have a strong impact on the viewer. Painting—like singing, writing, photography, dancing—is communication. But first you must have something to communicate!

Once you begin to draw or paint, a whole new world of seeing opens up because you will be focusing your attention with new interest. Right from your first attempts, you'll be surprised how fulfilling it can be to really see what is there before you in all its intensity. Your life will be charged with beauty to be shared with others. As you begin to see better, you'll render better; and as you render better, you'll learn to see even deeper. You'll feel the essence of what you see. You then become a true communicator between nature and the viewer, bringing them closer together.

The hawk on the wing, the ducks bursting out from the cattails, a deer eluding you in the alder swamp, a wildflower sparkling with dew, a pastoral farm scene, a blanket of snow, a trout jumping for a fly. Nature! You see it in its honest reality. And when your seeing is clear, you can then transfer it to a picture that you will be proud of. All the training in the world is of little use until you can learn to see.

It is great fun to buy and experiment with all kinds of special-purpose pens and pencils, and various paints and colors. But in the beginning it is better to keep your tools and equipment simple. Learning is easier if you start with the basics.

I like to work in an area that has good natural light and, when the sun sets, an overhead adjustable lamp. I prefer a sloped table that is steady—but I would hate to tell you how many drawings of mine have been done on the dining room table amid the remains of dinner, or on my lap out on a heavily trafficked porch.

For pencils I use the No. 2 almost exclusively, keeping one very sharp for crisp details and another more rounded from use. I include a No. 1 for darker tones and a carbon-black, heavy lead pencil for extremely black rendering. A kneaded eraser or art gum are basic, but the plain old red rubber eraser mounted on the end of the usual pencil will suffice if I can't find the others. An ink eraser can sometimes be used, but you have to be careful not to tear your paper with it.

My equipment for pen and ink is very simple. I use a fine-line ballpoint pen, and a medium ballpoint for darker marking when needed. Neither pen is truly black—such as India ink, or the ink used in professional drawing pens—but the combination of these two points gives me a great deal of latitude. They also reproduce well, especially when reduced for publication—although art directors shy away from them, preferring the real black.

For my paper I like the fine linen type found in notepaper or soft drawing paper. For the illustrations in this book I have used smooth bristol-weight drawing paper and prefer it for all the media I use—pencil, pen and ink, and wash in color and half tone.

A small selection of fine watercolor brushes in small to medium—four at the most—will last for many years.

A compass, a ruler, and a square will have a number of varied uses.

For stippling, the rough style can be done with ballpoint or even with water-soluble tips, but both tend to smudge if you are not careful. The best pen for stippling is the Rapidograph-type pen with interchangeable nibs.

When I am going to do my finished art in either wash or color, I like to simply outline the details of the bird's feathers and apply the color to let the lines show through as they will. This combination produces a beautiful texture. The waterproof ink of the ballpoint will not smudge. Hair, feathers, or fibre markings can also be rendered in fine pencil that will show through if your wash mixture is light enough.

This is the simple approach; you can get more involved and into more sophisticated equipment as you go along. But what I have mentioned here is all that has been used in this book.

The next step is to try out your pencils, pens, and brushes in varied techniques preparatory to rendering form, which comes later on.

In rendering form, which we do by producing dark lines and areas of dark shade on white paper, we are in a sense reversing the process described in the Book of Genesis of the Bible. The first chapter in Genesis is the greatest art lesson ever given. Read it. You begin with the void and add light, and whatever the light shines on is given form. If you keep this simple truth in mind, it is all you really need to be an artist. From here on in, all your work is a matter of rendering—shading to create form—whether it is done in black-and-white pen and ink, half-tone pencil, or wash, or color.

One of the best ways to approach color is to work in black and white and in pencil first, to learn the subtleties of grades of shading. Know the limitations of the pencils you use, and the pens too. When it comes to half-tone wash, that is, everything from black to white with all the gradations between, it is a matter now of starting with the lightest form from your original outline and gradually strengthening the intensity of darkness to create your "world" and the creatures you will bring forth in your work. The transition to color then becomes much easier. Work as dry as possible—conventional wet-paper watercolor is another matter entirely and is not generally used for fine detail work.

Figure 2.1 This wood duck head is one of the more simple subjects to start on, though it is a very beautiful one in color.

Working from your research, you know that its shape is different from other ducks, such as the mallard, and its bill is shorter and stockier than most ducks.

After you have drawn your basic outline in pencil, you will proceed through the four steps shown here to end up with an accurate and pleasing rendition.

During this exercise you will begin to get the feel of your pencil as you explore your outline, beginning to form the lights and shadows. Don't work too dark yet. In step one, merely lay in the basics to indicate the various bill markings, white lines, eye position, and the general shape and form of the markings, the shadows under the chin, and the roundness of the neck.

In step two (the second drawing) we see increased depth appearing, with the needed shading under the chin and the suggestion of feather markings.

The third step is to further intensify. Leave the highlight areas open. And even erase to "bring up" the highlights. Lay in the darker areas that will be refined later.

The last drawing is the final pencil step. You work it over gently and gradually, using the darker pencils for stronger intensifying. Use the eraser if it is needed to heighten the highlights.

Pencil art is a fine way to render your favorite outdoor life. Many artists prefer it, because it doesn't require much equipment and is a fairly rapid medium to work with once the stages of intensity from white to black have been planned out.

Working with pencil is good preparation for the same kind of light and shade rendering to be done in pen and ink, in wash, and in color.

Pencil allows erasing and reforming, a privilege not granted by pen and ink, although with luck and care some changes can be made to correct a goof or create an accent. Wash doesn't allow for much mistake, though there are ways to correct or alter that I will show later.

Note the rendering of the flying wood duck. I have overdone the feather markings to show the method of strengthening. Once you have drawn a good, basic outline form, it is merely a matter of "assembling" the detail, feather by feather.

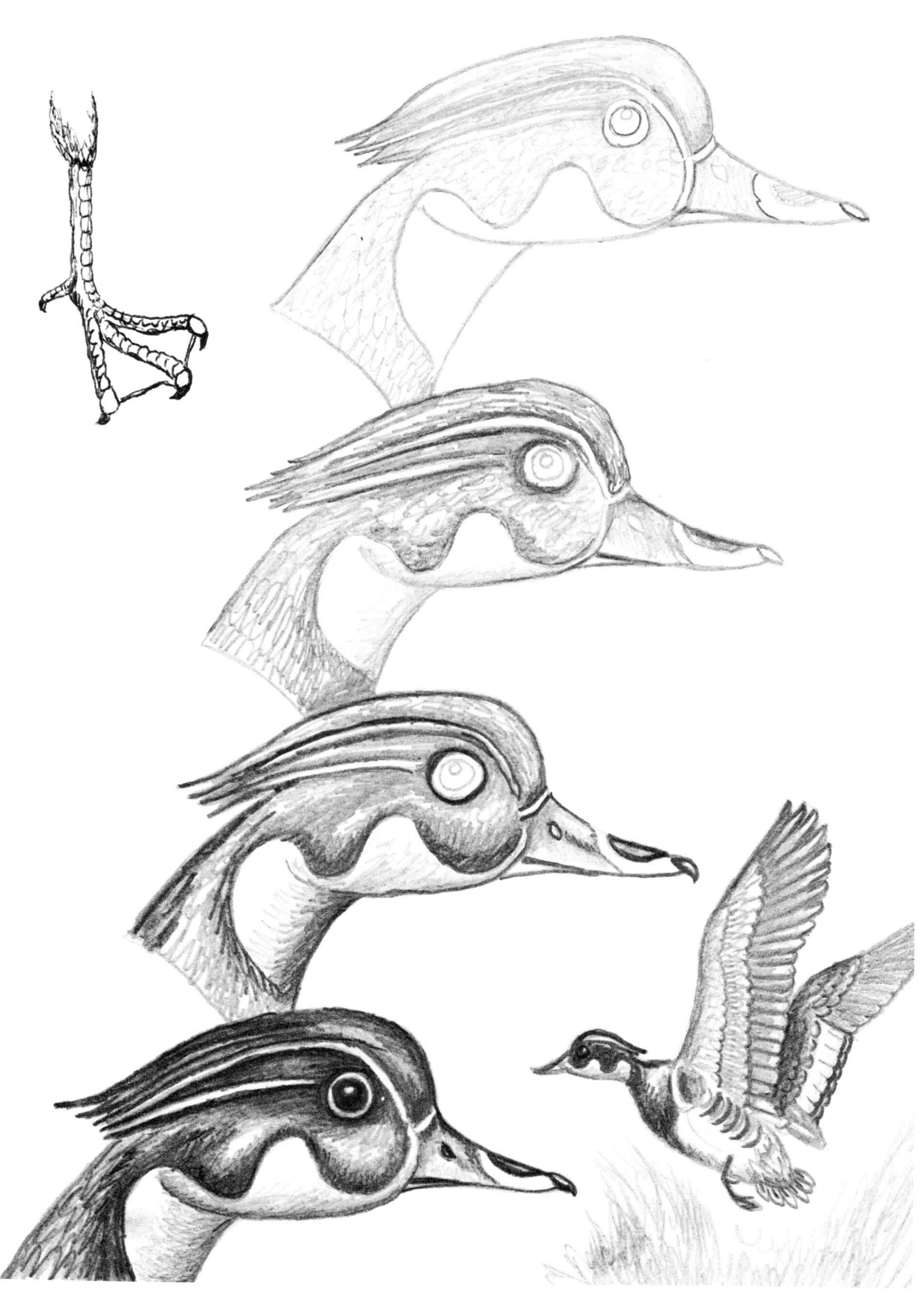

Figure 2.2 Here is the pen-and-ink rendering of the wood-duck head in three stages, similar to the preceding pencil work.

First stage: the all important outline and the important "direction lines" that will ultimately help you to render the finished feather markings along with the shadowing. Work slowly, as I did here, with your medium ballpoint pen.

Second stage: the first attempt at shading. Keep your work light and cover the entire subject in a very general way. The shading of the bill has to take into consideration the color of red at the base of the bill and the shiny black bill tip. The two white stripes on the head, which you have learned to isolate in the pencil work, will really begin to stand out now. The hardest part is rendering the white neck and underside of the head without going too far. This should be very easily and lightly "scratched" in, working up from the outside line to hide it and working toward the open white. In all of your work, try to eliminate the outline by shading, unless of course the white area will be contrasted when it comes time to introduce a background.

As you proceed, remember you have to indicate feathers to a varying degree, so before you go too dark in your "forming," begin to suggest feather markings, allowing some white to show through, which indicates a slight light reflection. At the end, you can go over those feather markings, smoothing them out or accentuating them as needed.

Third stage: Diminish the scratchiness in the final stages of blending, and with a light touch fill in without losing your contrast.

In all your work, take a break once in a while and hold the drawing out at arm's length or hold it up to a mirror. This will show you how the work is coming together, where you are too dark or too light, and what needs to be balanced or intensified. Proceed slowly. Don't go too dark too soon.

This flying version of the wood duck is a preview of what's in store when you begin to work on the whole bird. Note the gradations of "color" on the uplifted wing, the shadows under the bird, and the slight darkening of the flight feathers at their tips—and of course the obvious movement of the form. This bird is really whipping by!

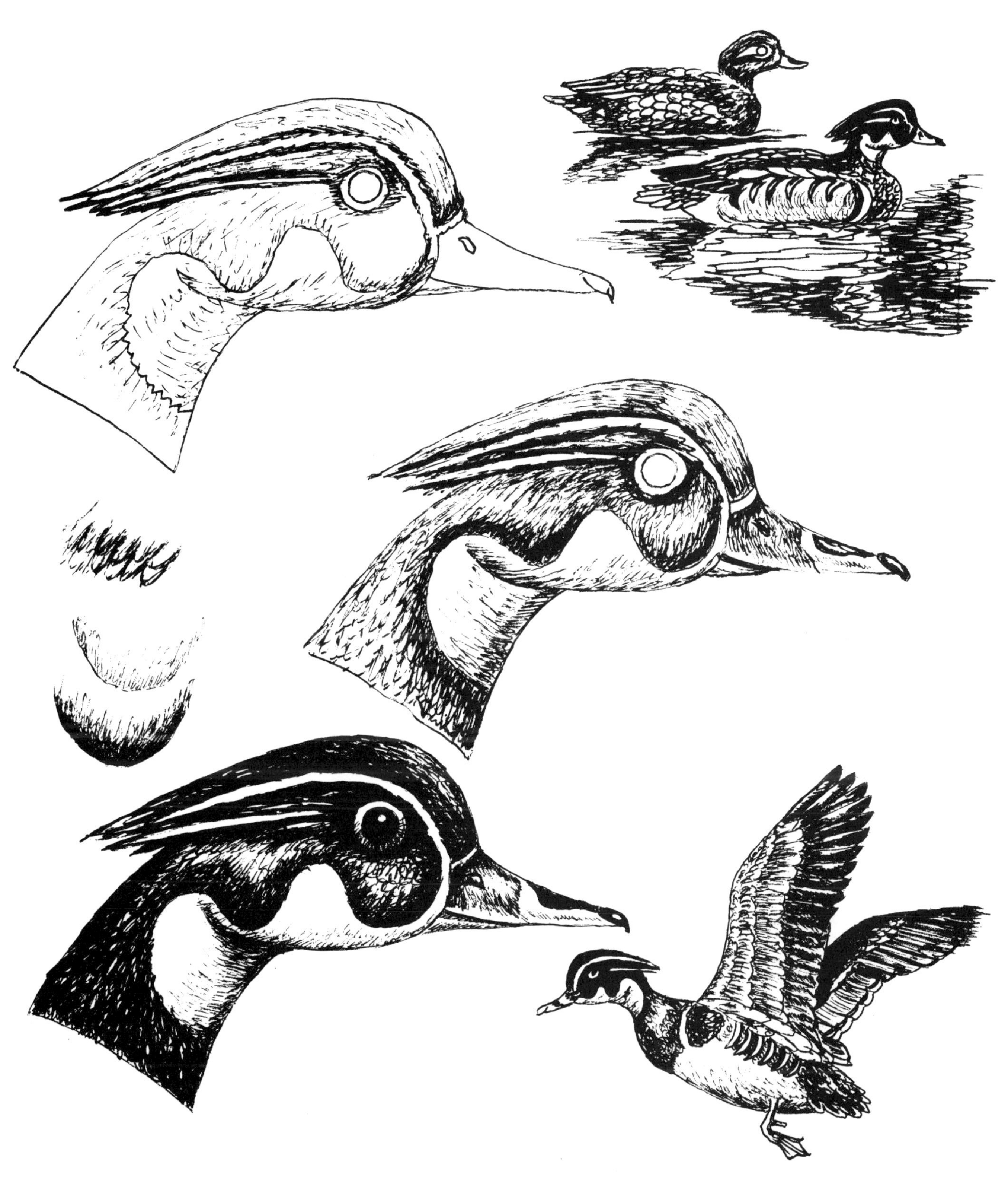

Figure 2.3 Having done your first pencil and pen-and-ink trials, you can begin to see how easy it will be to render in wash and color, which is just one more step in refining the light-to-dark element. It is actually easier than pen and ink.

Start out with the pencil sketch and actually lay in the shading and characteristics of the subject as they will ultimately appear. Working carefully, you can safely lay in the watercolor right over the pencil shadings. In the instances where definition of feather markings should show through to some extent, the pencil lines can be intensified with a very sharp, black point. Later, you can even redraw with the pen where extremely sharp definitions are needed.

Note the gradations in the center of the page to show the stages of laying in the shading and enforcing the intensity.

Start light and cover the entire subject generally, and then begin very gradually to darken, leaving a wide margin around the areas that will appear almost white as highlights. Leave the blending-in for later.

If you make the mistake of placing too dark a spot of paint on the paper, you can "steal" some of it to use elsewhere, gradually reducing it. If you wish to remove some of it, merely squeeze out your brush and place it on the unwanted spot while it is still wet: The brush will absorb some of it, which you can drop in on another feather area. If the paint is dry and the spot too dark, wet your brush, touch the area lightly to moisten the spot, squeeze out the brush, and return to suck up the color as needed. You will then have to exercise some care to blend in what is left.

Half-tone art like this is very simple and fairly quick to perform once you get the hang of it. By the time you finish working the exercises in this book, you will be able to render half tones quickly and well.

Don't be afraid to inject pen work into your color wash when needed, likewise pencil. After you have shaded the neck or back of the bird, or the general fur markings of an animal, you can come in with the pencil very effectively. You can "mix media" at will and even use your finger or a sharp point of cotton to smudge and blend when you want such an effect. Learn to work in gradation levels one by one, and blend where needed.

In this first section, I am merely trying to introduce you to some basics. Further refinements will be taken up when we go to work on the individual species. You will be delighted, for example, to see a ruffed grouse come to life by your own hand.

In most of the art in this book I have slightly overdone the shading and contrasts, more so than I would in a finished drawing or painting I might do for sale. Also, I have had to be careful to strongly define all outside lines because these pictures had to go through the printing, which always robs some definition from the original. The flying wood duck is slightly overdone to show such contrasts. Note the shaded body, and then note the reflection—the bright highlight on the bottom of the duck's breast—which is a planned use of light against dark (that is, the darker markings of the bird's wing). Use your pen for the scaly markings on the feet and legs and for the ends of the wing feathers, to make them ultra-sharp and black for detail and emphasis. Compare this with the drawings of flying birds and you will see that each technique helps the others to aid you in form, contrast, and lifelike rendering.

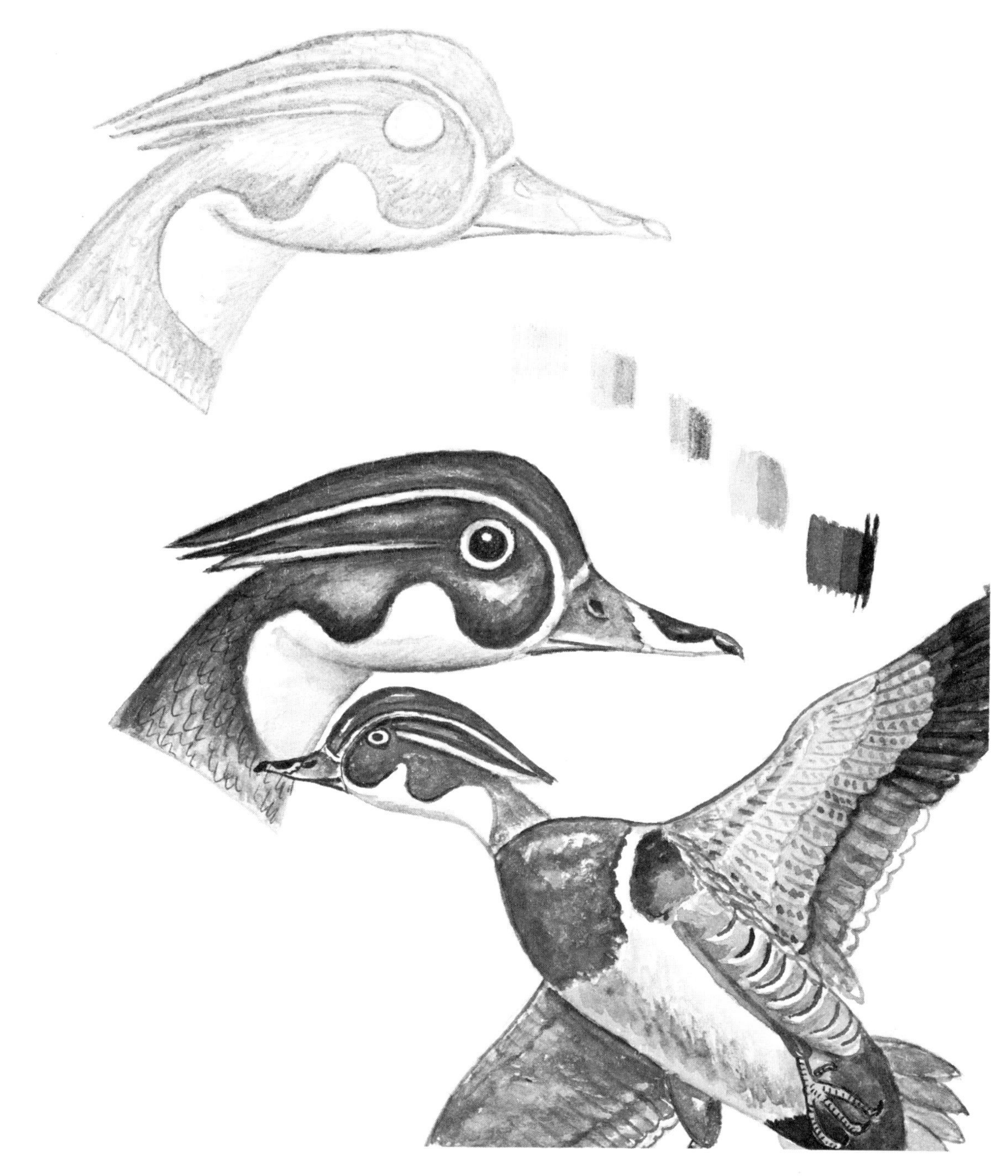

Figure 2.4 This collection of shapes illustrates some techniques you can use to achieve photographic accuracy. Remember: a good artist can be photographically accurate and still be dull.

The split-image drawing of the primary wing feathers is a suggested exercise for drawing all game bird feathers, to show how to shape and shade the individual feathers. Above and to its right, note a group of feather textures that look very close to the real thing. The way they overlap, the white border and characteristic markings, should be rendered to denote the particular species at hand. This technique is used when you are working large enough to warrant it. Incidentally, work much larger than the figures in this book at first, to keep from feeling too cramped. Later, when you get the hang of it, you can scale down to any size you want.

The pencil sketch of the wood-cock head shows how to roughly indicate generalized feather markings that are very light on the actual bird. The long feather belongs to the pheasant. The top of the feather is done in pen and ink only, and the bottom section has a slight water wash added for shading, an example of mixing. Use ballpoint pen; other types of pen will run when you apply water.

The bird head to the right, a quail, requires much detail in the construction of the bill. This example uses pen and ink, and wash. Look at the extended goose wing to see how that particular pattern can be rendered. You can become as detailed as you like. Form made by indication is often just as effective and pleasing as intensely accurate detail, but it must be based on the actual feather construction and relative colors.

The two goose bills show vast differences in bill construction. Don't put a duck bill on a goose!

The pair of feathers at the bottom, one from a female mallard and the other from a female black duck, show the need to see the difference if you are going to render such detail. Those feathers come from the flank of the duck and are very prominent. Take care not to create a hybrid with the head of one species and the feathers of another!

As you progress through the book's exercises, I will acquaint you with many techniques. This introductory section merely suggests some subjects that you can render with your pencil, pen, and brush in your first trials. Actually, this kind of work is really simple, far simpler to do than to read about and show in examples. But, alas, that is the only way I can stand behind you and guide your steps.

Play around with some of these ideas here; don't just pass them by for more interesting things ahead. Yes, even copy them. Make them larger; make them smaller. Play with all three media on these simple examples. Make a pencil drawing of the pheasant tail. Do a pen and ink of the wood-cock head.

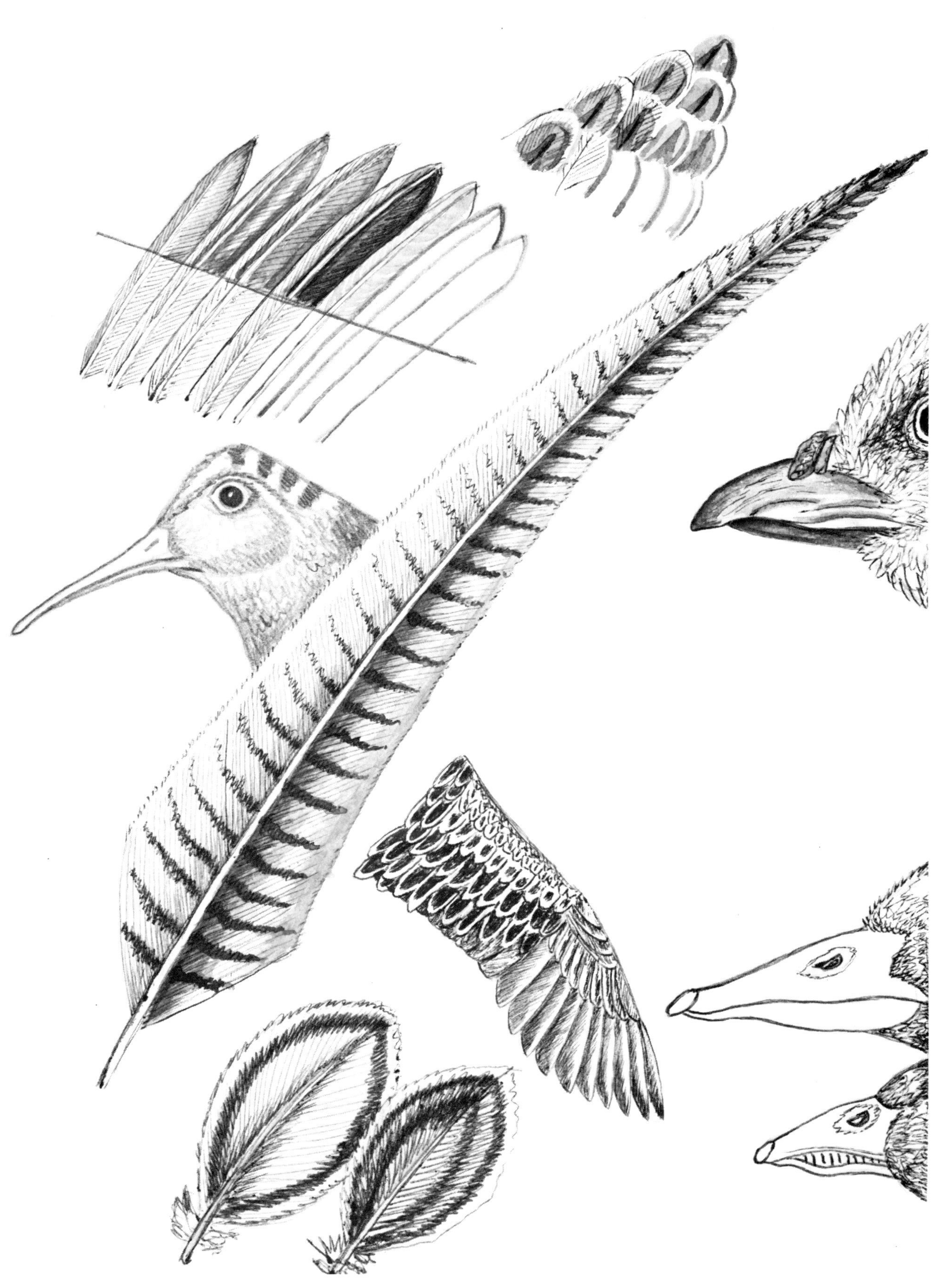

Figure 2.5 Only a few of us will ever see all the species in this book close up. But that fact should not deter you from taking imaginary trips into the woods, fields, oceans, and lowlands through the vicarious medium of your art tools. Given good research—bird books, photos, other artists' work—nothing is impossible. Best of all, the "trip" you go on while making an illustration of a California quail will be exciting, and your imagination will make it so for the people who may see your work later.

Best of all, the skills of "seeing" are brought to light in the exercises here. You will begin to recognize specific characteristics of similar bird species such as the quails or the ducks. You will see that all ducks are not shaped the same. Some have long necks, such as the pintail; others like the wood duck have relatively short necks. Duck heads are different, and in many cases some ducks have shorter, fatter wings and others have long, slim wings. Learn to see and you will begin to bring to life the birds and animals and fish you wish to portray, making your renditions jump out at the viewer with living authenticity.

Although detailing of the species—especially closeups of heads—will be covered later, here is a typical rendition of the familiar turkey done in pen and ink, with open design to show the texture of the peculiar skin of the bird's head and part of the neck.

Note the bill shape is a little different from the pheasant or quail. The pencil rendition of the smooth pheasant's head follows the form and style of this particular subject. It is easier to render in pencil than in pen and ink, and still easier to show in wash (as we do later).

The bobwhite-quail head is easily done in wash by gradual strengthening from gray to almost black; you can work this up from pencil or pen, or both. Note the design of the darker outline against the white cheek line and the throat. Note how the slightly ruffled feathers on the top of the head are done. This can be smoothed out if you wish. Sometimes bobwhite heads appear absolutely smooth on top, but when they are surprised or are about to move around a little the head feathers tend to raise up, showing a sense of urgency or impending action.

Shape and proportion, again, are important. Actual measurements would not help as much as a clear photograph, which can be measured if you like. The idea is to scan the photo and try and approximate the proper proportions and remember them. The bill of a duck, like the mallard, for example, is as long as its head. The feet are as long as the head and bill. As we have mentioned, there is a great variety of wing shapes and sizes. Note for example the chubby wing of the quail in contrast to the mallard wing.

You will "fall in" to a lot of this as we go along covering the various species in this book. Your eyes will gradually open to variations in detail and the need to render them, even in very generalized drawings or paintings. You will find at first that attention to picky detail may be frustrating, but it will become a kind of puzzle or game, and even an obsession, since such detail adds authentic and lifelike attributes to your work.

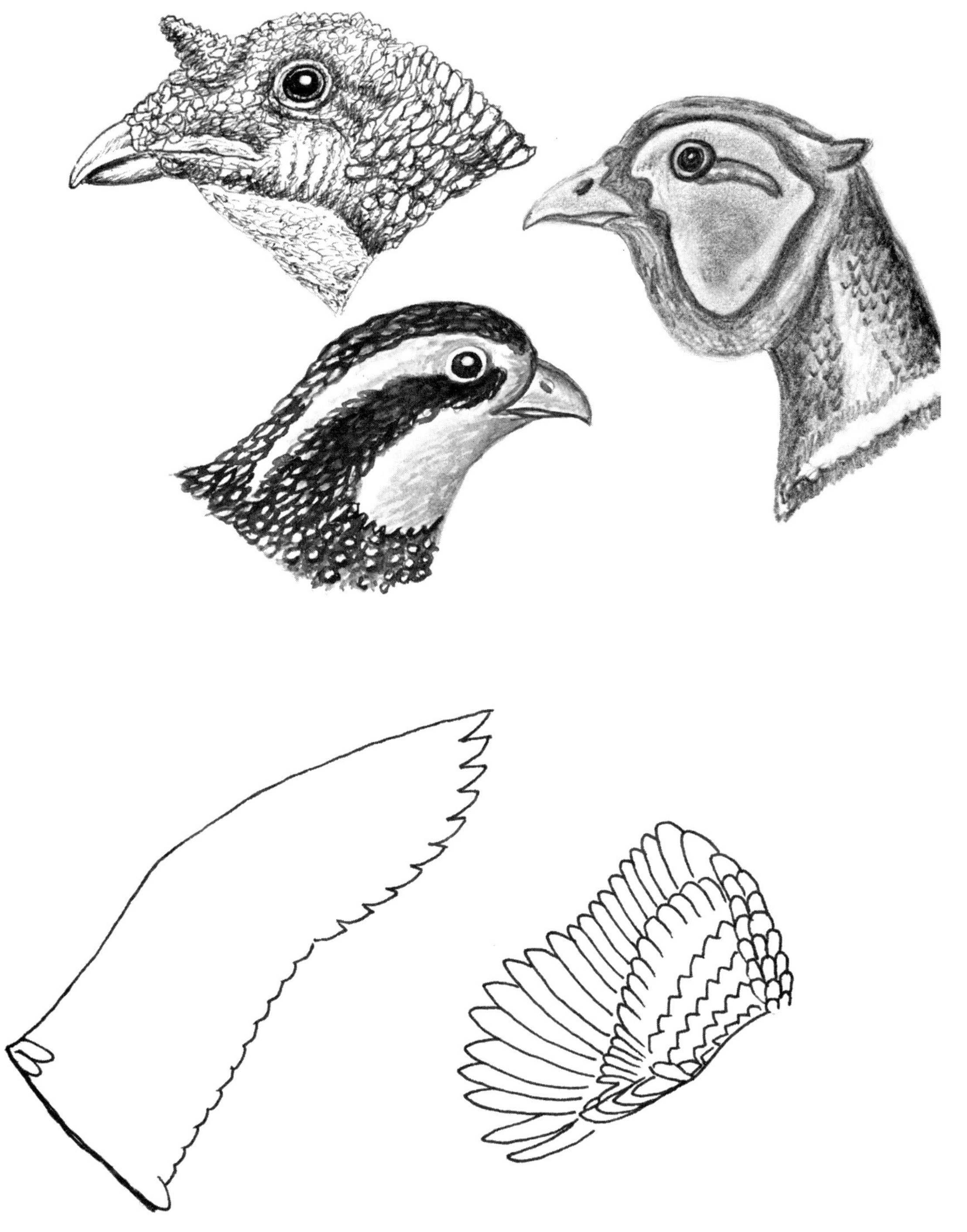

Figure 2.6 As you have probably noticed, the game birds require a good deal of detailing, unless you intend to draw an impression. But even an impression must be based on detail. Accurate detail becomes fun and rewarding once you get over the idea that it is complicated.

When you start on animals such as deer, the accent falls more on form and overall fur texture and the direction of the hairs as they appear in the light and shadow areas of the body. Although it can be helpful to know skeletal and muscular construction, you can work from good photographs, making sure however that the modifications you make fall within believable and natural bounds.

Renderings shown here: pencil, pen and ink, pencil and wash, and the head in wash only. When you are just beginning, it is best to work about twice the size of these illustrations to give you room to express and play around with the values from light to dark.

All animals have an intrinsic structure that you should capture in your work to be authentic—yet try to avoid stiffness and artificiality. As always, once you have an acceptable form to work from begin to fill in slowly, working lightly over the entire specimen, and then go back to gradually deepen the shadows and highlight the bright areas. We'll work over the specifics later.

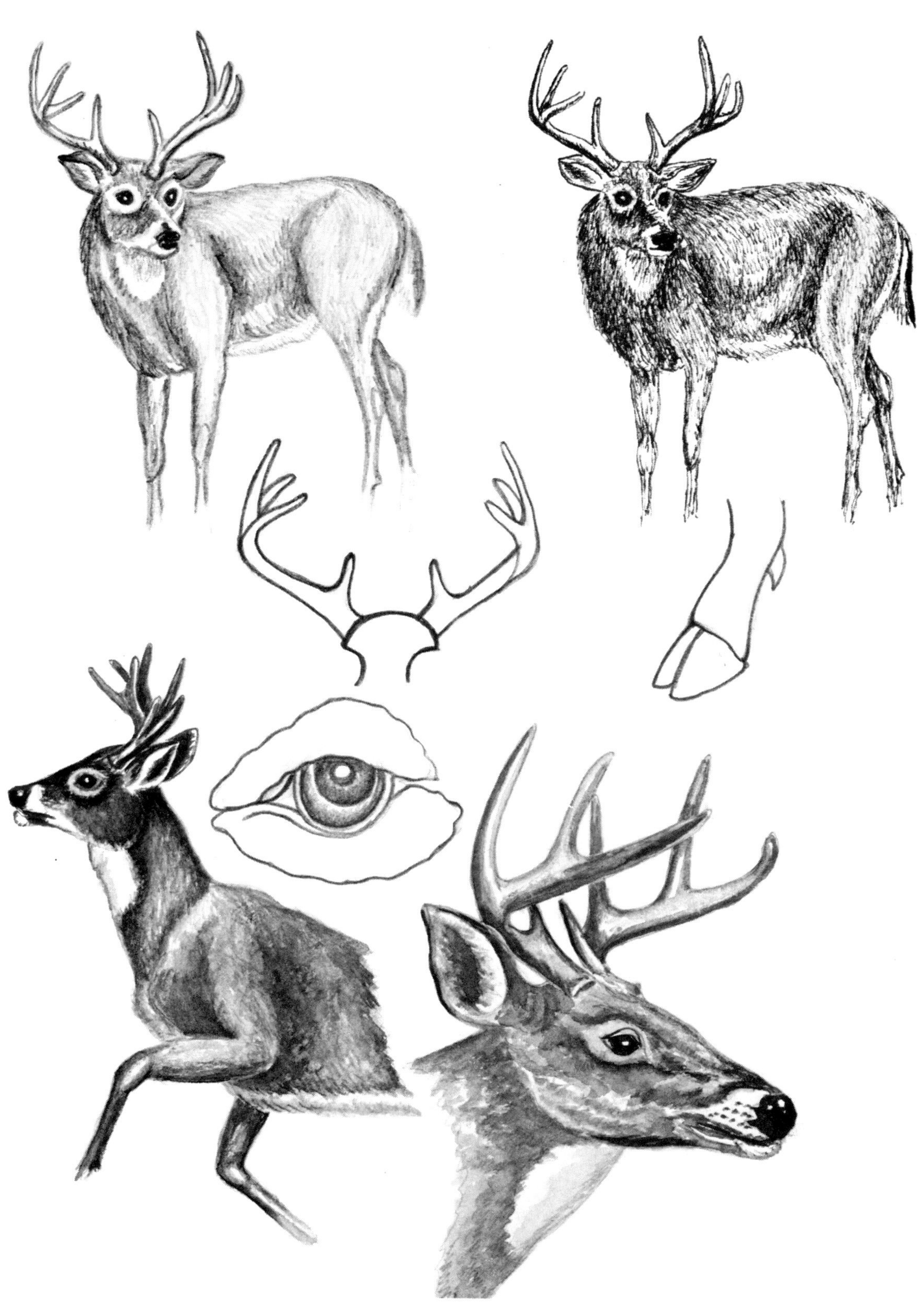

Figure 2.7 The drawing and painting of fish is a constant challenge—imitating on paper the highly reflective surface of objects under all kinds of light conditions. Masters of this form, such as William Shaldach, have done paintings and etchings that adorn the walls of sportsmen's dens, and many have ended up on calendars and greeting cards.

This is the typical pose of a rainbow trout jumping from the water surface. If you like, you can have it hooked to a dry fly or lure, or merely leaping to catch a fly.

First the trout is done in pencil, then pen and ink, followed by pen and ink plus wash, and finally wash only, showing the variety of ways to render it. The big trick is to show the iridescence and reflections while paying attention to the characteristic markings of the species. In Chapter 9 we show how to isolate the fish against a chosen background, and the last illustration shown here indicates this. Remember, we draw black against white, dark against light, always.

Start with an accurate line and use photos from outdoor magazines to enhance details of shape, proportion, and fin shape and angle, paying particular attention to the detail of the head, eyes, gill pads, and mouth.

As you may note in the third drawing—pen and ink, and wash—some of the pen strokes are allowed to show through to indicate scales, but in the wash-only drawing they are not indicated; this is a matter of choice.

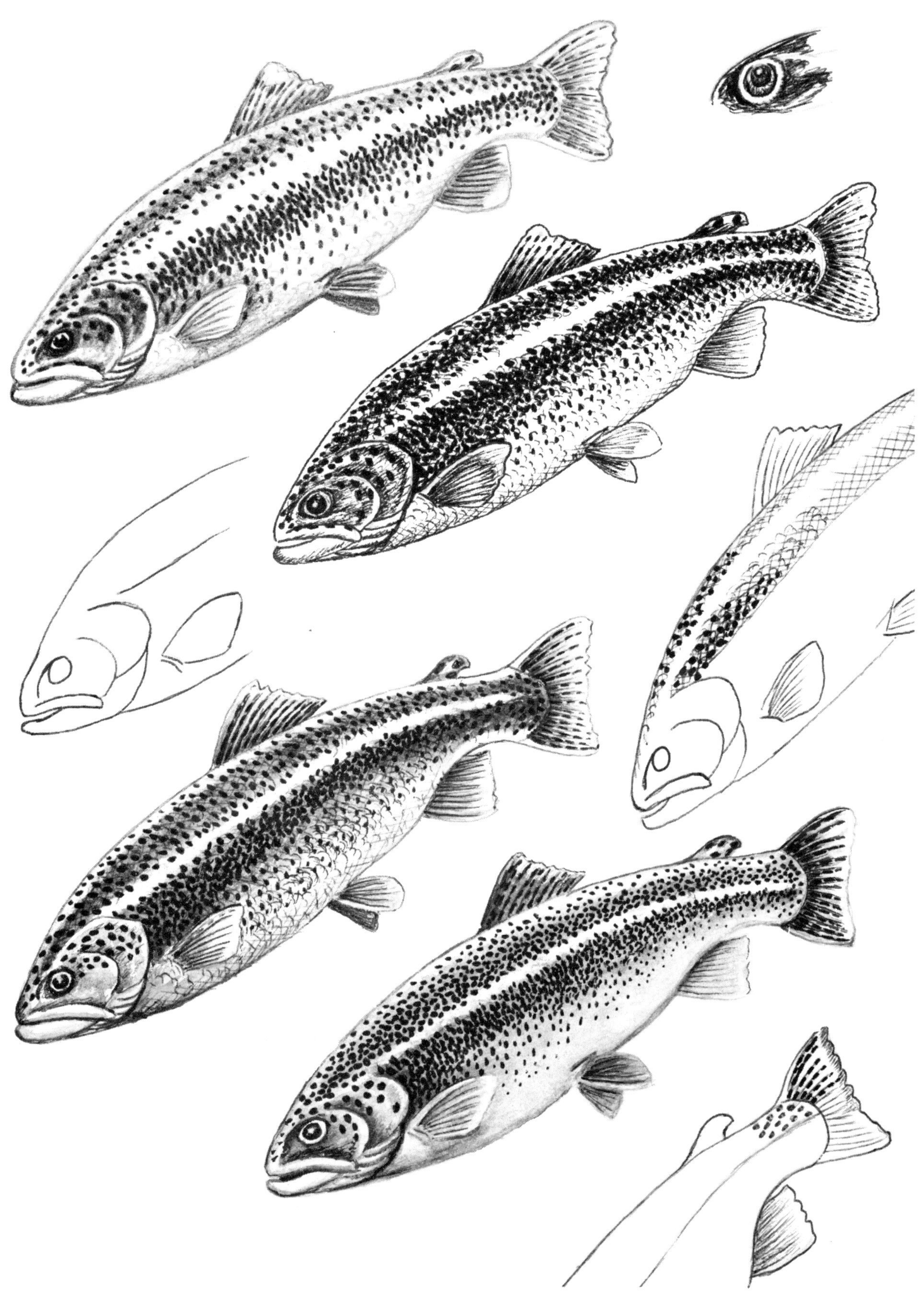

Figure 2.8 This page is an introduction to the many ways of handling contrasts: light against dark, or—in the case of pen and ink—black against white, or white against black. I show them here in pen and ink because that medium offers the most obvious planning challenge and also the best way to produce the needed contrasts. The spot illustrations are purposely overdone and remain rough, lacking the final shading needed for the completed work. The main problem here is always to avoid leaving an isolated outside line on the subject, so think out your entire picture, experimenting with the background in pencil first.

The actual method of shading is simply to use fill-in strokes between your initial strokes to narrow the white space between them. This can be done by inserting more parallel lines or by using lines to cross your first ones at an angle. To avoid having to use awkward hand and wrist positions in making your strokes, turn or rotate your paper to accommodate. (We pursue this kind of technique in Chapter 9, but you need a glimpse of it here as we prepare to work on actual subjects.)

Remember, the setting is very important. It can be equal in significance to your subject—although generally it is better for the subject to have the advantage. In creating your background you will find yourself almost transported there, as you create an old stump, a far-off mountain peak, a rock in the center of a trout stream, or the almost invisible deer antlers in a forest. You will also learn to choose your techniques. Often a pen-and-pencil subject looks great in front of a plain pencil background, or a wash background. A wash subject can be exquisite against a pencil background, or even against pen and ink if the background lends readily itself to it.

(a) Note the dark background for the light wing treatment. When your bird is flying in front of a backdrop of marsh reeds, use it. When the bird is in the clear, cover your wing lines by darkening into them.

(b) Look at the contrast from the dark background to the top of the upper quail's head and how its chin stands out. You taper the shading out to white and introduce the lower quail.

(c) In the case of trout swimming near the surface of the water, you can have dark water against the bright fish, or a dark fish's back against the light background.

(d) Same with fish tails. Make up your mind which way you want to go before starting to fill in, or you will paint yourself into a corner!

(e) Deer antlers are usually hard to see in the woods; you can take some liberty here, as shown. But decide which way you will work: light against dark, or dark against light.

(f) This can be a tough one: The grouse tail has a white border that you must show, so you have to use a fairly dark background to show the tail off or, as in *g,* show the line.

(h) A white tree such as a birch against a dark background, or a darker tree against forest foliage. Work your way around this for a nice blend in your setting, using both types of trees.

(i) Depth in the forest. Note the gradations of light and dark to show the distance and quality of the forest.

(j) The same in reverse.

(k) Folds in the hills. Here you have a chance to really build in form and feeling.

(l) For the sake of depth and perspective, set those hills behind a bare tree.

(m) The mountain behind the trees.

(n) An old stump, a typical "prop" found in the woods.

(o) A rock in the grass. Note that indicating the grass in front of and behind the rock sets it in a natural "pose."

(p) A rotting windfall is a great addition to a picture where this kind of forest-floor subject is found.

(q) The familiar trout-stream rock, which helps show the direction of the current and its relative speed. There could be a trout feeding just behind that rock, if you want to show it there, or you can have it jumping out of the water just behind the rock for a fly.

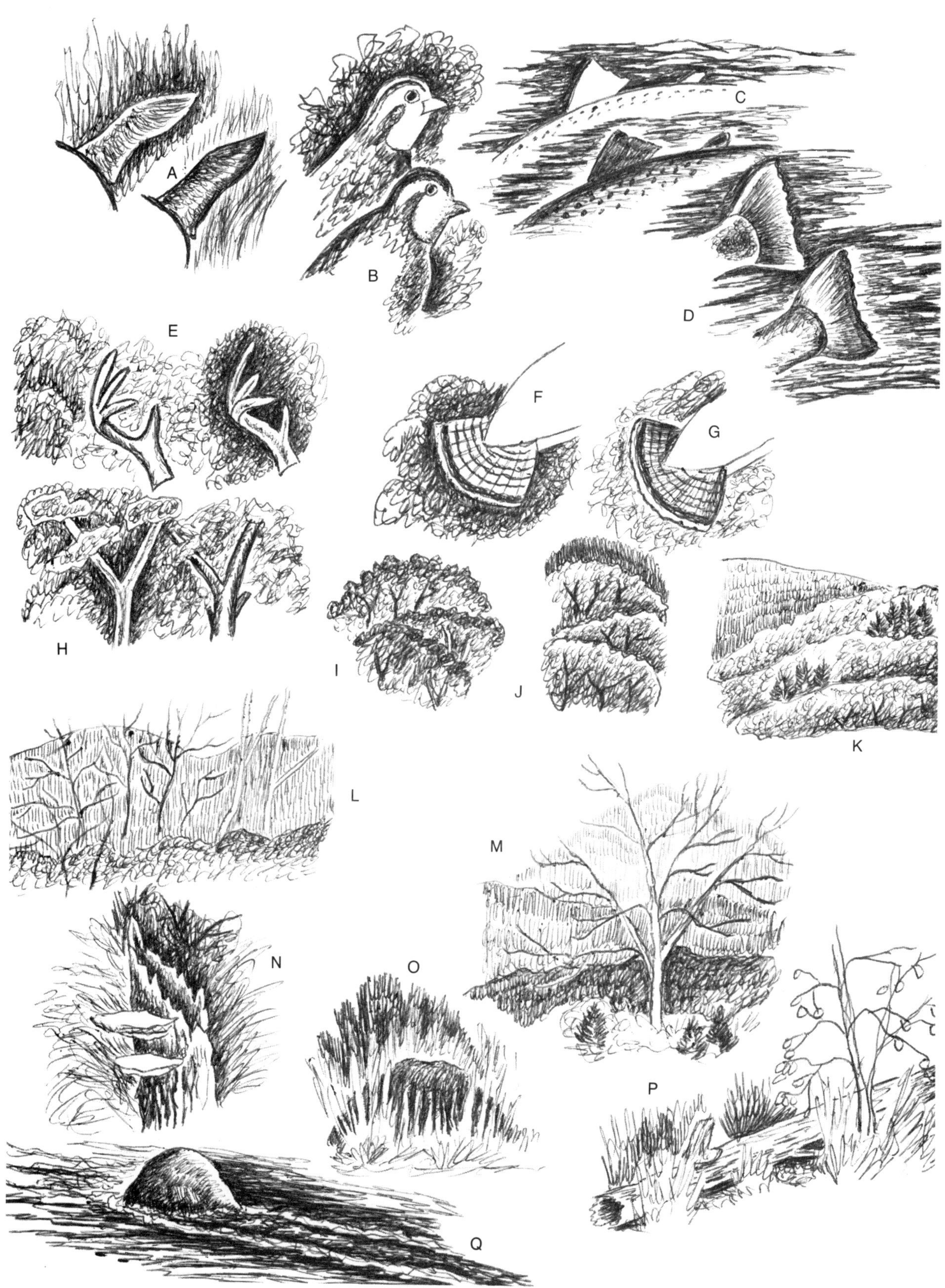
A
B
C
D
E
F
G
H
I
J
K
L
M
N
O
P
Q

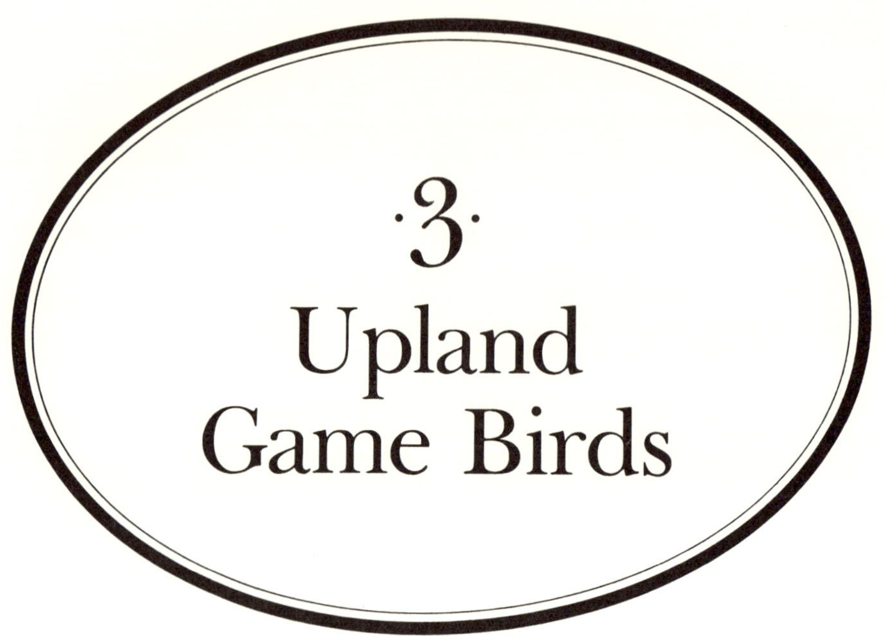

·3· Upland Game Birds

Throughout the book I will give you a general background of each species that will be worked on. This brief look at some of their characteristics will rest later in your subconscious as background reference material while you work. For more information, there are many fine and detailed books on individual species as well as the hunting and fishing magazines, offering extensive details that can add greatly to your store of knowledge.

The packaged, domesticated chicken you buy at the supermarket is the degenerated form of an upland game bird that once, years before ancient Babylon, ran wild. Although it is much easier to drive to the market and pick up a frozen chicken for dinner, the urge to hunt other species of fowl in the wild—grouse, quail, wild turkey, dove—is an expression of the basic hunting urge.

Drawing and painting upland game, whether it be in an overall hunting scene or a closeup portrait of the particular species, is a wonderful way to express the essence of the outdoor experience. Whether you are a shooting sportsman who thrills to the sudden flurry and flight of an upland game bird twisting from cover, or a bird watcher and beginning artist, the study and practical knowledge of the various species of game birds is challenging.

Upland game birds are quite easy to identify, much easier than ducks and geese and far easier than songbirds. Their habits, however, are much harder to study. The sportsman or naturalist who can approach the game bird in the wild close enough for a look, long enough to press a shutter release or trigger, is wise in the ways of nature lore.

Upland game birds are most easily found by pointing and setting dogs such as the English and German pointers, the English and Irish setters, the springer, the cocker or Brittany spaniel, to mention the most popular. These dogs can hold the birds by pointing at them with their nose until the hunter or photographer comes up within range for the "shot."

Game birds can be considered a crop, just as corn, trees, and apples are crops to be harvested in the fall of the year. The once wild barnyard turkey is typical of this tradition.

Since sportsmen have become organized, the game bird crop has been protected with energetically enforced gunning laws and restrictions. Sportsmen's dollars have in large part financed federal and state game commissions and conservation departments, supplying not only game laws but enforcement officers, biology departments, and conservation activities, including the raising of game birds and the betterment of habitat. Thanks to the sportsman, game birds have enjoyed a growth in this country during the past few years that far exceeds that of the protected songbirds.

Upland game birds are classed as such because they inhabit and nest on the land above marshes and fens. They thrive in farmlands and high in the mountains and are never found far from a pure water supply, be it a mountain trickle or a humid swamp. Most of them are seed and grain eaters, although some species vary their diet with berries, fruits, nuts, and insects. They raise large families, sometimes nesting as close to man as possible, and in other cases preferring to be far from civilization.

Many of them migrate each year, though some prefer to reside in one area for their lifespans if conditions are conducive.

The upland game birds covered in this chapter are the most popular to be found in the continental United States and Canada. They are all protected by state game laws and, in some cases, by federal migratory laws set by the federal government and then adapted by the individual states. Limits on birds taken are imposed by the day and the season.

DRAWING THE BASIC BIRD FORM

Before getting involved in specific bird species, this section is designed to get you started in rendering the basic forms of body shapes—profiles, body angles, flying birds, their heads, beaks, feet, and wings—in pencil, pen, and brush.

Game birds, in contrast to the many songbirds, have very distinct forms and coloration in each species, so their characteristics must be well represented. The wild turkey and the grouse both have large and widespread tails. The turkey has a long neck and head while the grouse has a shorter neck and a chickenlike head. The several quails are somewhat similar in shape but have distinct markings. As we go along working on the various species you will begin to see these differences and know how to render them.

In most bird-book illustrations you will find a flat side-view profile, the easiest way to show all of the bird's markings. It is also the most uncreative pose and can seem visually static. It is, however, a good one to start with in order to learn how to render body form. Then you can turn the body in any direction, also twisting the head and neck and tail into new positions, to produce a work that will catch the eye and interest the viewer.

Body proportions are very important. The head and neck must be of proper size in relation to the body. The feet must not be too large or too small. The actual shapes must be accurate. Although this might sound difficult, it really isn't. To draw a house or a person, you would have to account for dimensions and proportions in the same fashion. Good research is all you need, whether from observation of the subject or from the works of other artists or photographers.

To render form you must indicate light and shadow within the bounds of the bird's colorations. Once the bird's pose is established, you decide from what direction the light is going to come from and proceed to build the form from this perspective. It is amazing how many artists fail to shadow the body under the wing when the bird is flying, for example.

There are several light angles to be considered. The simplest one is direct light on the subject, coming from above and behind the viewer. This allows a fairly flat rendering of the subject with the top of the bird lighter than the bottom. If, however, the light is going to come from the side, light and dark should be well indicated, an element that must also be represented in the background. Backlighting—light coming from behind the subject—is the most tricky, but it is also the most interesting and dramatic.

The point to strive for is action of some kind: the grouse about to take off from its hiding place with wings raised, head and neck stretched out; the pheasant streaking out under full power for safe cover; the turkey standing still to remain hidden; the duck coming in for a landing. Show your birds feeding, preening, running, washing, fanning their wings—whatever action is typical. If you have seen them in the wild you will remember them. If not, riffle through your collection of pictures for suggestions and, best of all, invent your own poses to show what you want to convey.

In Chapter 9 you will find just how to render appropriate backgrounds and how to present the bird subject in relation to it. Feather detail—rendering of the actual feather fibers when necessary and the mastering of the bird's colorations—are all demonstrated in more detail in the species covered later.

It is not always necessary to show the entire bird. Beautiful head portraits can be made of a pair of pheasants, for example, and when mounted in an antique oval frame they can be a great addition to the wall decor. This kind of picture can be either a mere impression or a greatly detailed and elegant study.

Bobwhite Quail *(Colinus virinianus)*

The bobwhite is not the easiest of the quail, but we can proceed through the various steps of rendering it to prepare us for the other game-bird species. It is, perhaps, the most popular of the small game birds due to its piercing "bob white" whistle. The other quails have interesting calls but nothing as distinctive as the bobwhite. Of all the game birds of America, the bobwhite is probably the most revered, the most familiar, and a real native—full of craftiness, tradition, and glamour.

Found normally in the fields and brushland from Pennsylvania and New Jersey across into the middle western states and the Mississippi River basin down to Florida and into Mexico, the bobwhite has quite a following among nature lovers and hunters alike. Some subspecies of bobwhite are also found in the western states and into the western parts of Mexico.

The bobwhite sets the standard for all other quail and even for species of partridge, and it serves as a criterion of sport, food value, and overall qualities.

Due to its ability to span a great variety of climate, ground, and cover conditions, the bobwhite has learned to become quite versatile in its chosen environment. It is far different to hunt a bobwhite in the flatlands of Georgia than to hunt one in the swamplands of New Jersey.

Primarily a covey bird, bobwhites gather in flocks in the early fall after the nesting season has long passed. Often the young birds of the season join the older birds to offer a variety of targets to the gunner. During the winter months when the snow is on the ground, the birds band together in coveys, sleeping in a circle with eyes pointed outward so that danger can be seen from any direction. With the deepening snow they crowd together and bask in each other's warmth, taking turns to feed on the seeds and berries that remain above the snow. They often burrow through the soft snow to keep open the feed supplies. Only a severe winter with icy, killing sleet will defeat their bravery, and many birds can then perish.

In the springtime the males call to collect their many hens, and the cocks establish definite areas of their domain. The hens will lay as many as fifteen eggs at one clutch, and the males will help in the upbringing of the young. It does not take much time for the little ones to learn to fly and forage for themselves. Farmers who love this grand game bird are careful in the spring plowing and farming to save the nests that have been made in their fields, for they know that a steady crop of birds will afford hunting excellence in years to come.

Strict state game laws protect the birds from overshooting, and from undershooting, too—for an overabundance can spell disaster to the coveys. More and more areas that have been cleared from the forest have become the haven for quail and as such its range and numbers have vastly increased.

Many years ago the bobwhite ranged into upper New England. Connecticut, for example, used to have good supplies of these birds; today it has a bare minimum. The exception in New England is Cape Cod, which remains a bit warmer than the mainland because of the ocean and the warm breezes that come from the Gulf Stream. Eastern Long Island has many native quail, while the southern Connecticut shore has few.

Bobwhites are the easiest of the quail to raise in captivity. Raising a good strain of wild birds is not easy, however. The best game farms raise the birds far away from the farm buildings, so birds seldom see more than one person. Quite often wild birds are introduced into the main stock to insure the wildness of the strain and to keep it from becoming a soft, pen-type bird, of little interest to the wing shooter.

Bobwhites are also raised by farmers for their food value and have become quite a market commodity in the country's food supply. Canned quail is available commercially.

Many field dog trials use quail for pointing, flushing, and retrieving, and whole strains of fine hunting dogs are raised exclusively for quail hunting.

The bobwhite's identification is easy. First you hear the unmistakable call, then see its small body, plump and round, barred with brown and black markings on a white or off-white color. The female is usually a browner cast than the male, and the male sometimes shows a slight crest. His white bib is a sure identification.

Although it is good to draw a single bobwhite, a pair is always better. If you can spread out in a larger picture, try to place as many birds in the picture as possible, showing them in different poses. Bobwhites like to cluster together, much more so than grouse or even turkeys, so get the covey feeling in the picture if you can. Place one bird on a stump or tree branch or rock, anything that puts it above the covey. This is the lookout bird, the watchman, and makes a center of interest in your picture.

If you like, you can overlap the birds as they work the ground for food, or are flying away or across the picture. Overlapping is tricky, but you can make a very good overlapping picture by using cutouts and moving them around as you sketch in your thumbnail or work on the final drawing outline.

Mountain Quail *(Oreortyx pictus)*

The mountain quail, Gambel's quail, and California quail are three beautifully marked western quail that are a delight to hunters and nature lovers alike.

The distribution of the very popular mountain quail is from California to southern Colorado, New Mexico, and Arizona, and down into the mountains of northern Mexico and parts of western Texas. Though its region is almost identical to the Gambel's quail (the two birds are sometimes found together), the mountain quail, as its name implies, is a higher-altitude inhabitant.

A typical quail, the mountain quail is a covey bird building its nest on the ground and raising a large clutch of from ten to twenty eggs. They hatch after two weeks and develop into shootable and eatable birds in the same year. Of the three similar species, the mountain quail is the most striking in appearance, having the longest tassel sticking up from the top of its head. Both male and female bear this marker. Their heads and chests are dun gray in color, offsetting a rust-red bib marked by first a black and then a white line. The flanks are reddish rust with black-and-white prominent bar markings, which can be seen for quite a distance and as such become a great aid in identification. The back is a dull brown and the tail is semirounded even when in flight. (See Figure 3.3*d*.)

Being mountain dwellers, they have access to a great variety of food, from berries and nuts to grains and seeds and buds, not to mention insects of the forest and brushlands.

Because they inhabit a terrain that is apt to be quite varied over a few feet of ground, spotting mountain quail is not easy. Though they generally rise in small coveys, usually in twos and threes, they fly quite erratically in ruffed-grouse fashion in an attempt to put as many twigs, trees, rocks, and brush between themselves and the pursuer. They will quite often run for cover when the terrain suits rather than flush into the open. It takes a very steady dog to pin them down long enough for the hunter or photographer to move up.

Males and females weigh about the same, about eight or nine ounces, and are just under a foot in length. Flight speeds are hard to measure since they fly in quick spurts, but it is assumed that they escape danger at about 30 miles an hour.

Other than the tassel, their body shape is very similar to the bobwhite's. Note the highly contrasting side markings on the flank and white-ringed bib. Draw the mountain quail in a background of cactus or other western mountain foliage. (Guidebooks on plants or photos that show typical California or New Mexico backgrounds can help you with such detail.) Like the bobwhite, the mountain quail is a covey bird, so put in as many as possible in your picture.

Valley Quail *(Lophortyx californicus)*

The valley quail, sometimes called the California quail, is another of the three tasseled species inhabiting western United States and Mexico. Found almost exclusively in California and Oregon and in the more dry parts of Washington, this little bird is more gregarious than the other two, often coveying in bands of four to six hundred birds, making an expedition quite exciting when such aggregations are found.

Quite easy to tell apart from the other two tasseled quails, the valley quail has drabber markings topped by a black head that is side banded with a thin white bandage extending from the eye down the cheek and across the lower throat. Brown and white bar marks are found on the flanks, and spotted breast feathers of brown and black extend down below the gray upper chest. The tail is quaillike, being fairly narrow even in flight. (See Figure 3.5*d*.)

Valley quail have suffered losses because of shrinking farmlands and orchards, but on the other hand residential development and irrigation have broadened their scope. They are plentiful today in some city parks and at the fringe of developments and general civilization.

The hunting season is regulated closely to the supply of this bird and varies from year to year.

The valley quail is a runner and will often travel in groups through the woodlands, well ahead of the dogs that are trying to pin them down for their masters. When they do take to the air their flight is often erratic, although birds of the same flock may try different ways to evade a hunter. Their flight is quick and sudden, and the sight of twenty-five or more birds rising from a single spot in the grasslands or low bushes is one to behold.

Valley quail weigh about six ounces on the average and stand as high as eleven inches. The hen lays from ten to fifteen eggs, and the young quickly learn to fly by the fall hunting season.

They often roost off the ground in trees and bushes, a habit not common to the other two species. Their food consists of grains, berries, fruits, nuts, and they consume a large number of insects during the summer months. They have been known to destroy large colonies of harmful bugs and worms from cultivated gardens and farmlands.

Gambel's Quail *(Lophortyx gambelii)*

Counterpart of the mountain quail is the Gambel's or desert quail, found in the deserts and arid plains of southern California, New Mexico, and Arizona. One wonders how such a delicate bird can survive the alternating desert heat and cold, the lack of food, and evade the many predators that can easily find the bird in such open surroundings.

Spotting this species is comparatively easy because they are found in the open without the added screen of foliage to hide from hunters. They covey in large numbers in the fall, after the young have gained wing. Winter and summer is much the same for them, and their food consists of what the hot, dry climate can produce in the way of seeds, nuts, grain, weeds, insects, and worms.

The hen builds her nest in the open, covering it as well as possible from sky and land predators by sticks and other forms of nature's litter. The nest is a shallow depression in the ground and, after the mating dance, from ten to fifteen cream-white, brown-blotched eggs are laid. In extraordinary times of severe dryness they may skip one nesting period, but as soon as rain comes they will produce a family.

The call of the Gambel's quail is almost as famous as that of the bobwhite. It sounds strangely like a whistle with syllables sounding out chi-ca-go. At one time it was almost named the Chicago quail, but because it is a resident of California and does not get along well in the east, the name and its backers withdrew.

This bird is easy to recognize by its chestnut-capped head under the typical wavy tassel and its black mask bordered by a white band and a black-and-white neck band. The light blue-gray and white back and breast are punctuated by a horseshoe-shaped blotch of black in the lower breast. Flanks are chestnut colored, banded with thin white strips. Tails are semipointed and not flared when the bird is in flight. (See Figure 3.5*c*.)

Conservation agencies have learned to breed this bird in captivity for restocking purposes, and experiments in various other dry parts of the country are going on with the hope that this bold little bird may spread its range and interest elsewhere.

Ruffed Grouse *(Bonasa umbellus)*

"Old Ruff," as the ruffed grouse is affectionately known from coast to coast, is the favorite of upland game bird hunters even though it is not common or easy to hunt or discover in the woods.

A solitary bird, the ruffed grouse prefers the abandoned orchards, fields, and farms that lie near deep hemlock or pine forests. It has learned to be crafty in avoiding the hunter or any human passing nearby. When it bursts from cover at alarm, its wings set up a loud and startling clap of noise. The ruffed grouse's flight path through the woods will be extremely erratic. Fortunate is the person who sees one in detail.

This species is almost impossible to raise in captivity on any large scale, so the cycle of abundance is up to nature—and to the combined efforts of sportsmen and conservation departments, who must see that the species never becomes too crowded or too sparse in any given area.

The grouse is essentially a nut and berry feeder, seldom eating any of the common farmyard grains. Nonmigratory, nonetheless fluctuations during the year will find this bird drifting from one area to another, based on food and cover rather than temperature.

The mating call of the ruffed grouse is unusual in that the bird does not call perceptibly but drums on a log with very fast beats of its wings. This sound can be heard in the woods sometimes for miles when the air is still. During the act, the male spreads his turkeylike tail, raises his cocky crested head, and *brrrrrrrrr* is what the female hears.

Besides its Latin name, *Bonasa umbellus,* other common names for this bird are old ruff, partridge, pheasant, grouse, and wood chicken. Flight speed has been timed as high as thirty miles per hour, but the usual spurts at danger average about twenty. A ruffed grouse is about the size of a bantam chicken. Males weigh about twenty-two to twenty-seven ounces, females slightly less. Two color phases are common and often found in the same area, the gray and the rust red. Identifying colors are the black shoulder ruffs, the black-banded tail feathers on a large, spread tail, and the crested head. Males and females are almost alike in color. The usual way to tell the sex from the plumage is by the unbanded feathers breaking the center of the band of black on the female's tail. The male tail feathers are not interrupted by this.

Hungarian Partridge *(Perdix perdix)*

About half the size of the average grouse and twice the size of the quail, the Hungarian partridge (also known as gray, Hun, or European partridge) has taken a long time to become as established in this country as the China pheasant has.

The first importation of this bird came in the 1800s but was largely unsuccessful because little was known about conservation methods at that time. The bird was not nearly as strong, hardy, and bold as the pheasant, and plans for its propagation were shelved until a concentrated effort was again made prior to and after World War II. Though a few enterprising private gamekeepers imported the bird, it was not generally available to open hunting. It still has far to go in this respect. Today, many of the more advanced commercial shooting preserves are stocking the Hun from pen-raised birds, but little is being done to effect natural propagation outside a few areas. Where the Hun has taken hold it has made great progress against natural elements and enemies. Controlled hunting, mainly for research, has helped to build up a store of knowledge about this great game bird. Eventually this species may serve as a savior to upland hunting where other species formerly thrived.

At present the Hun is found along the southern string of eastern Great Lakes and on the broad grain and corn farms of the upper Middle West and into Canada. A few of the birds have thrived well in eastern Oregon, northern California and Idaho.

Easy to identify, the rust-gray back and dun-gray breast are marked with a horseshoe-shaped band of rust-colored feathers. Unlike the grouse and chicken families the legs are bare of feathers, similar in this respect to the quail. Further identification is the orange-rust colored head. (See Figure 3.7, bottom.)

Quick to fly at the sight of a man or the disturbance of even the best of hunting dogs, the Hun will tend to rise well ahead, seldom running for cover. Their flight is somewhat like the quail, and being covey birds rather than loners like the ruffed grouse, they offer a pretty and tricky target for the hunter or photographer.

Their food consists of grains, berries, insects, and buds. The nest is on the ground in protective grasses and lined with a few feathers and moss. From ten to twenty eggs are laid, to hatch in about two weeks. The little ones quickly adapt to life and are flying in little over a month.

Their habits are more like the quail than grouse. In winter they generally band together in flocks of twenty or more, offering hunters much sport. In the spring they separate into individual mating routines, and the cocks select their harem of hens and go about the business of mating and raising their young.

Unlike the grouse, the males stay near the nest, helping in the chores of bringing up the chicks.

In Europe the Hungarian partridge is an established game bird. Predictions are that it will become the same in this country in the future, for it can thrive in the more northern climate that has proven too harsh for the native bobwhite quail.

Chukar Partridge *(Alectoris graeca)*

Another import from Europe, the chukar is more adapted to the western dry/arid climate and to country that is wide open. In Europe its home is also in the drier regions.

The first importation in the late 1800s was largely unsuccessful. Since World War II, several enterprising owners of commercial shooting preserves and many private landowners have experimented with this species, but it has taken hold only in the sparsely settled and wasteland areas of western Oregon, Nevada, and parts of California and Arizona.

As a game bird it is halfway between the grouse and the quail in weight, size, and flight pattern. Covey birds like the quail, chukars gather in flocks of twenty or more in the fall and spend the winter together; they disband in spring to form families and raise their young. As many as twenty eggs are laid in the ground nest, and a high percentage of the eggs mature into fine little chicks that quickly adapt to their surroundings.

Chukars are quick, erratic fliers somewhat similar to quail, with a bit of the craftiness of ruffed grouse. Often they will fly close to the ground when it is known that hunters are about. They will play tricks on dogs, often walking together for quite a distance before taking wing.

Markings are quite dramatic and quite unlike any other of the small game birds. Basically of an off-white coloration, they are sharply marked by a narrow ring of dark brown running from the bill and eye, down the side of the cheek, and around under the throat. The flanks are barred with equally dark and narrow slits. The back is rust colored in the male and more of a tan in the female. Legs are bright red, with no grouselike feathers. Tails are blunt and narrow even when expanded. (See Figure 3.7, top.)

The chukar comes in three closely related species—the typical chukar, the rock, and the red-legged—all basically the same in markings, habits, breeding, and in environmental requirements.

Ring-Necked Pheasant *(Phasianus colchicus)*

Known as the ring-neck, China pheasant, or English pheasant, this import from China came by way of years of successful trial in England and Europe. The first successful plantings in America were in 1887. Initial attempts prior to that date had no results. The present American variety is a mixture of several strains, and crossbreeding is still going on to produce a sturdy bird able to withstand harsh winters and to resist disease. Natural breeding to "wild" stock is done also to produce a game bird that is clever and fast on the wing.

Identification of this bird is easy because of its long black-barred tail feathers; there is no American game bird with such a long tail. The male's shiny green head and neck banded by a white collar at the base is another identifying characteristic.

Excellent as a table bird, the pheasant has become America's number one game bird. It is stocked in both private and public hunting grounds in almost every state of the Union, save those where the arid, desert climate or frigid conditions are unfavorable.

Commercial shooting preserves raise the pheasant in pens and release the birds for same-day shooting. Many states stock the ring-neck months before the season is open so that the birds have time to grow and get used to the open. Still other states stock the young bird and find that it breeds in the wild, so they merely replenish the stock when needed.

Several varieties of gun dogs are bred for pheasant shooting, and it is a good dog that can handle this tricky flier. When conditions are right the pheasant will prefer to run and hide, often crossing trails in order to throw the dogs off scent. But when pheasants take to the air in a burst of flying wings and loud, harsh cackling, the surprised hunter can be shocked into missing the target.

Normally the pheasant forms small flocks unlike the loner grouse, but pheasants do not gather together in coveys as quail do. Pheasants prefer the nearness of the farmer and of civilization in general, often surviving at the edges of parkways and enjoying residential areas, golf courses, and city parks. Farmers enjoy their presence and protect their stock of birds by leaving the edges of fields to grow into food and cover. In the spring they try to avoid disturbing the nests while working in the fields. Pheasant farmers raise these birds for specialized markets, and canned or preserved pheasant can be bought in most markets. "Pheasant under glass" is a famous mode of table presentation.

In the wild state the hen lays from seven to twelve dull gray-green eggs in a well-concealed nest under a tree stump, in a stone wall, or under a windfall or uprooted tree. In two or three weeks the chicks learn to fly and, by fall, offer the hunter a fast, though often innocent, target. They are grain feeders, once in a while eating insects and tree buds, and as such are far easier to feed through the harsh winters than grouse or other game birds.

Male pheasants weigh about three pounds or a little under and the females slightly less. When sprung from cover by a hunter or a dog, they can make a burst of speed close to sixty miles per hour. Their course in the air is usually straight up to clear the brush and then a low flat glide between the bushes. Quite often they will fly low right over the dog so that the hunter will be unable to fire.

Wild Turkey *(Meleagris gallopavo)*

This largest of America's game birds has been known since the arrival of the Pilgrims, when this country was first settled by Europeans. At that time the wild turkey enjoyed a wide distribution and the bird became a feature in the feast of Thanksgiving.

As man gradually changed the ecology of the land, much of the woodlands became devoid of this species. The bird, however, did become domesticated, and turkey farming is big business today. In recent years conservation efforts have reestablished the wild turkey in its former haunts, and hunters can now begin to harvest the crop as it increases.

The turkey looks like a cross between a vulture and an oversized ruffed grouse—its skinny head and broad-banded tail being its chief identification, besides its great size. Both sexes have a beard, made of hair-like tufts, but more developed in the male.

The only difference between the domesticated turkey and the wild one is that the latter is more slim becuase of its life in the wilds.

Known as gobblers in the vernacular, these birds flock together, usually roost in trees, and generally find locations in the semiopen forest well away from the environs of man and his cultivation. Unlike the pheasant and the quail, the turkey, like the ruffed grouse, prefers to be alone.

The birds generally feed in the early morning and late evening, flying or cautiously walking to and from the roosts and feeding locations. It is along this route that hunters and bird watchers await the wary birds. Due to human pressure and a sort of built-in awareness, they are very hard to get close to, and the slightest noise or movement by the intruder will alert them to danger.

Like the ruffed grouse, their feed consists of nuts, berries, grapes, and seeds, and blossoms of bushes and trees. They also consume large amounts of insects during the summer.

They prefer walking and running to flying when alarmed and, once aloft, can quickly gain altitude, flying sometimes almost straight up in order to wing clear of the brush or tree limbs.

The nest consists of a slightly indented hole in the ground, generally near a clearing in the forest not far from dense protective cover. The hen lays from eight to fifteen delicately spotted, buff-colored eggs, and incubation takes about twenty-eight days. The young are able to fly in about a month.

During the greater part of the season, the cocks band together away from the hens and the young birds. In early spring before the mating season, each gobbler becomes strong and fierce, establishing his territory and mastership over a group of hens.

There are two subspecies of the typical turkey, one in the southwest known as the Rio Grande and the other known as the Florida turkey. But all turkeys are essentially the same, minor technical differences due only to their different habitat.

Male turkeys weigh from twelve to seventeen pounds, the females weighing nearly ten pounds. Males range in length to twenty inches or more, with the females only measuring about half that length. Flight speed has been estimated at close to fifty miles per hour.

The wild turkey is protected by state game laws set each year after surveys of the game bird supply. Where turkeys are being introduced, limited permit hunting is allowed for the prime purpose of collecting samples that can be analyzed by conservation biologists to further assist the comeback of this grand game bird. Conservationists envision the day when this magnificent bird, with its broad tail and iridescent plumage, will again fly in our forests for all to see—and for those who delight in the succulent meat of the wild turkey, especially at Thanksgiving or Christmas.

The wild turkey is now well established from Pennsylvania down through the mountains and forests to Florida, with spotty distribution as far west as New Mexico, and with large flocks in Texas and the south-central states. Some commercial shooting preserves have attempted to stock the wild turkey, and many private owners of large land tracts have their own supplies of wild birds, allowed to multiply for the benefit of the species.

Many of the protected forests and parks around the country have good supplies of these birds where habitat allows.

Mourning Dove *(Zenaidura macroura)*

Over 20 million of this species in its three phases are shot by American gunners each season, attesting to its great popularity as a game bird. They are fast, tricky fliers easily scared from their feeding or roosting locations; when in open flight what is termed *pass shooting* is a very sporting proposition.

Being a migratory species, the dove is protected by both federal migratory and state game commissions, and seasons are set after both conservation agencies assess the quantity in given areas.

They are relatives of the extinct passenger pigeon, and, though great in number, conservationists are careful to avoid overhunting of this bird. On the other hand, it is imperative that their high numbers be controlled, because if they become too numerous in any given area disease may strike and wipe out the entire strain. They are particularly subject to cold and sleet storms.

The mourning dove is easy to identify by its pigeonlike "hook-coo" call and its size and shape. Its tail bears white side bands that flash in the sun when the bird is in flight. The eastern variety is darker and more prominently marked than the southwest or southeastern varieties. Both are distinguishable from the white wing, since the latter has a broad white band extending from the elbow of the wing to the body. All of them have red legs.

In the east mourning doves do not generally flock together until the fall, preferring to raise their families in quiet. In more southern states, they do flock together and nest in colonies. Several broods can be raised in a given year if weather and food conditions are right, but only two or three eggs are laid at one time, in a nest of small twigs in trees and bushes above the ground. In about two weeks the eggs hatch; the young will fly a month later. Their feeding and nesting sites are never very far from a dependable supply of water. Food consists of grains and seeds, but once in a while they will eat berries and a few insects.

Turtle dove, longtailed dove, and wild dove are some other names for the mourning dove. Whatever they are called, they are fine game birds, and also a bird for the naturalist and bird lover. They are easily enticed by placing feeding shelves near cover with a steady water supply, and many suburban gardens seem richer for their presence. (See Figure 3.9*c*.)

They are subject to most predators, such as owls, hawks, cats, rats, and foxes.

White-Winged Dove *(Zenaida asiatica)*

The white-winged dove is primarily a bird of the southwest, being well established in southern California and along the border country of Texas and Mexico. Subsequent stocking has enlarged its area to include more northerly areas of Texas, California, and Nevada.

As game a bird as the mourning dove, this fast flier is a test to the hunter's skill, especially as the western plains offer faster open-land flying and therefore tougher shooting than the mourning dove's hillier east.

The typical characteristics of this bird are similar to all doves. They are extremely subject to temperature. They must have a steady water supply and are subject to disease when the flocks become too large. An extreme dry spell, or wet spell, or sudden cold will kill them off or stop their mating and breeding for the season. They are also subject to predators, and often an entire nesting period can be wiped out by an overabundance of them.

White-winged doves, like other doves, are migratory. As such, they are subject to federal and international game laws that are in turn administered by the individual states. Since the supply of these birds varies from year to year, the season can shift and so too the bag limits.

Unlike the mourning dove, white-wings breed and stay together in colonies, building their nests in trees and bushes and, when these are lacking, homesteading on the ground. They lay only two or three eggs per clutch, and usually only one chick grows to maturity, learning to fly quickly and "earn" its own living. (See Figure 3.9*b*.)

Known also as the Sonora pigeon, the white-wing weighs but five ounces and measures less than a foot in length. They have been clocked at forty miles an hour as they fly past a hunter in pass shooting.

White-wings can be easily decoyed by staking out wooden imitations on the ground near their roosting or feeding sites. Decoys are also set up in the trees near a waterhole. Not quite as tame as mourning doves, they are much rarer in residential areas and city parks. They are a close relative to the band-tailed pigeon, ground dove, Inca dove, and the white-fronted dove—only a few species from the world's total of more than 290 that have so far been identified.

American Woodcock *(Philohela minor)*

Draw a line up and down the Mississippi River and you have the most western area in which the timber doodle, bog sucker, or—as it's more commonly known—the American woodcock is found. The woodcock is a lover of the wetlands, swamps, and abandoned farms where there is water and good pure soil, and large succulent worms to be found. Like the robin, its chief diet is earthworms, grubs, and the like. Its long bill is made to penetrate into the mud and slime in search of food. If the ground is too dry and hard, the woodcock moves quickly away. When seen in the wild it seems never to stop sticking that bill in the mud, constantly feeding.

A grand game bird for the shotgunner, the woodcock's best territory is in the northeastern states and Canada. It nests in Canada, in New Brunswick and Nova Scotia and farther north, and migrates down as far as Georgia and Alabama. Subject, then, to federal and international migratory regulations, its daily and seasonal hunting limit is set by individual states on the recommendation of the federal authorities.

In the fall the migrants blend with the local breeding stock, and it is quite possible in the better parts of the woodcock range to find birds of both varieties in the same cover. A quick flier, the woodcock takes off from the ground rather than running to cover. Flight starts with a burst of speed, and it generally flies straight away, sometimes staying close to the ground, but when cover is dense it will fly almost straight up to suddenly level off and glide to cover well beyond shotgun range. This bird is easy to locate with a good bird dog used to the peculiar scent of the woodcock. Many bird dogs dislike the odor, and as a consequence certain dogs have to be trained especially for this species of bird.

While the woodcock is not a sturdy species able to resist harsh weather conditions, it makes up for this lack in its ability to migrate quickly away from unfavorable feed or weather conditions. Its coloration and ability to hide a nest also help it to avoid ground or flying killers.

It is subject to polluted waters and in many areas its haunts have been poisoned, drained, or cultivated, thereby limiting its forage areas. The woodcock was at one time more plentiful than it is now. Extensive conservation efforts have brought it back in certain flight areas, where sanctuaries have been set up along the migratory route used by all waterfowl.

The woodcock is a good table bird, though considered "gamey" by some. A small bird, smaller than the dove, it weighs only six to seven ounces and reaches a length of only ten to twelve inches. It has been clocked at thirteen miles an hour—although to the hunter its speed seems to be much greater than that!

Courtship at mating time occurs in the evening or early morning when the light is very dim. One male may mate with several females, and nests are started in the swampland. Usually four eggs are laid, hatching in about twenty days. A month later the young birds are flying and will join the parents in the fall migration southward.

Woodcock are sometimes found in company with ruffed grouse and can offer a fine mixed bag for the versatile hunter and for the photographer.

Figure 3.1 To start you on your first drawing of the bobwhite quail, this simple black pencil drawing is an example of a generalized impression of the bird. In further studies you can determine just how detailed you want your birds to appear.

The pencil treatment is done with a heavy carbon-black lead on smooth paper. You can also work on grained paper to show texture and add visual appeal. Experiment with the size of your subjects, concentrating on the accuracy and detail and general characteristics of the bird's behavior.

In this picture I have shown only part of the bird, and that part is relatively large in contrast to the two flying birds behind it. It is not always necessary to show the entire bird unless you are making an exact study of the species. It would have been more effective also if I had overlapped the flying quail to show one behind the other. As it is now, the smaller bird does not look as far away as it could if I had placed it just under the tip of the lower wing of the nearer bird, or put some tree branches in front of it. Experiment.

Note in the foreground I have purposely indicated the overlapping of the grass blades to show one in front of the other. This is merely a sketch and can be shaded in as much as you like in molding.

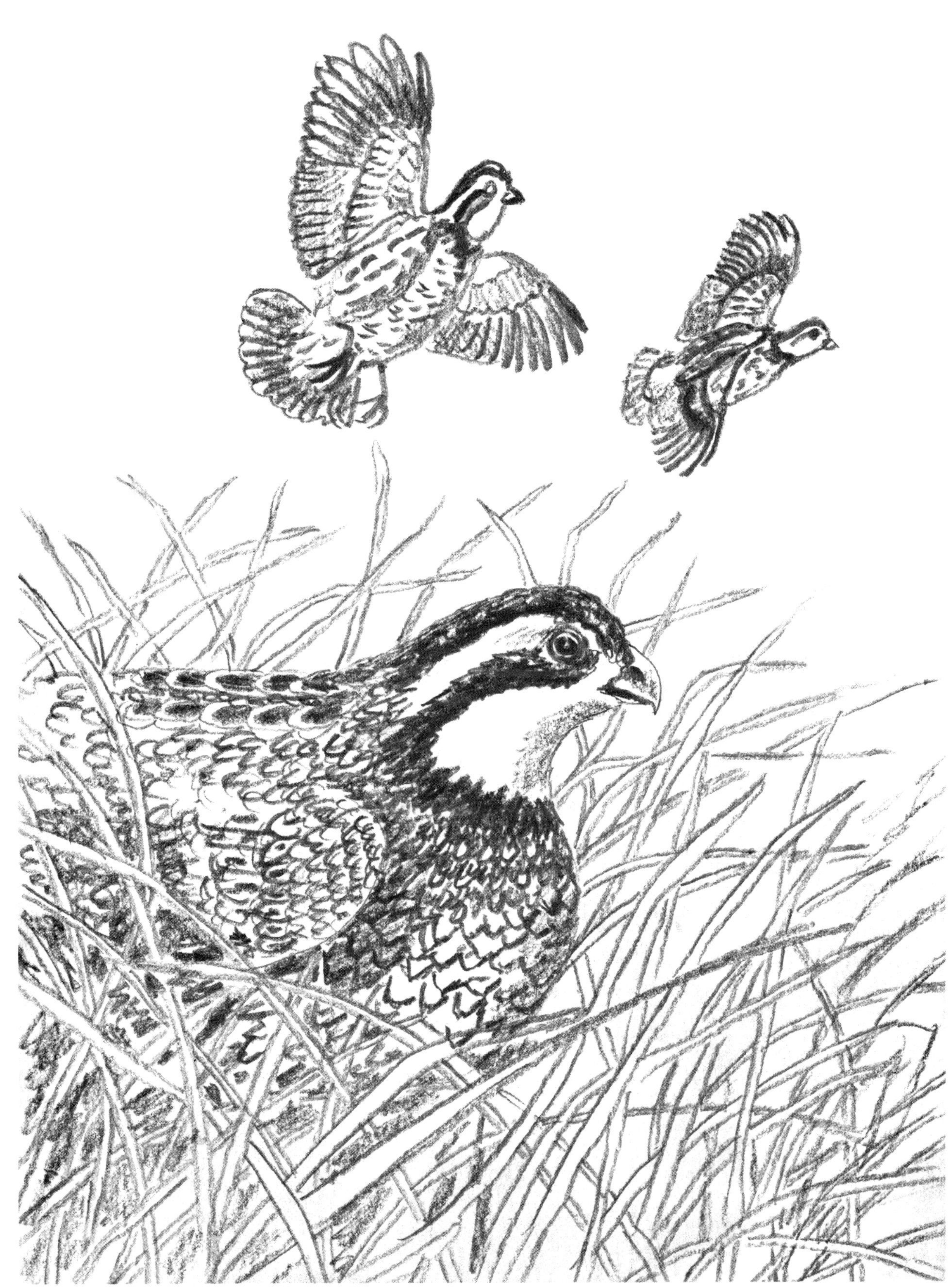

Figure 3.2 The transition from generalized drawing with pencil to rendering the actual feathers and their individual markings may seem like quite a jump at first, but if you work large—as indicated by the outline around the first quail—you will find it quite interesting and fun. Once you have laid out the work map of the bird's outline, the filling-in becomes almost routine. Take it a section at a time and it won't seem too difficult a project.

The second bird shows the pen-and-ink, filled-in version, the next step in the first drawing. Note that the feather fill-ins are very simple and easy to make.

The third standing quail is the same bird as before, but the outlining from the first stage is done in pencil and then gently washed in with a fine brushpoint through the various shades of gray. Note the closeups of feather fill-in technique in a mixture of pen and pencil. After you do your wash, you can come in later with pen or pencil to bring about a special effect or shading accent.

The flying bird is divided into two parts. The upper is in pen and ink only; the bottom section is laid out in pen and ink and then gently washed in with the grays, allowing the pen to show through to represent feather textures and markings. Note the feather detail and how simple it is to fill in.

Once you get to know the feather markings and the various zones, such as the flight feathers, secondaries, shoulders, back, tail and head, the rest is easy. The next step is to move the bird about in various positions and get away from the static profile pose used in bird-identification books.

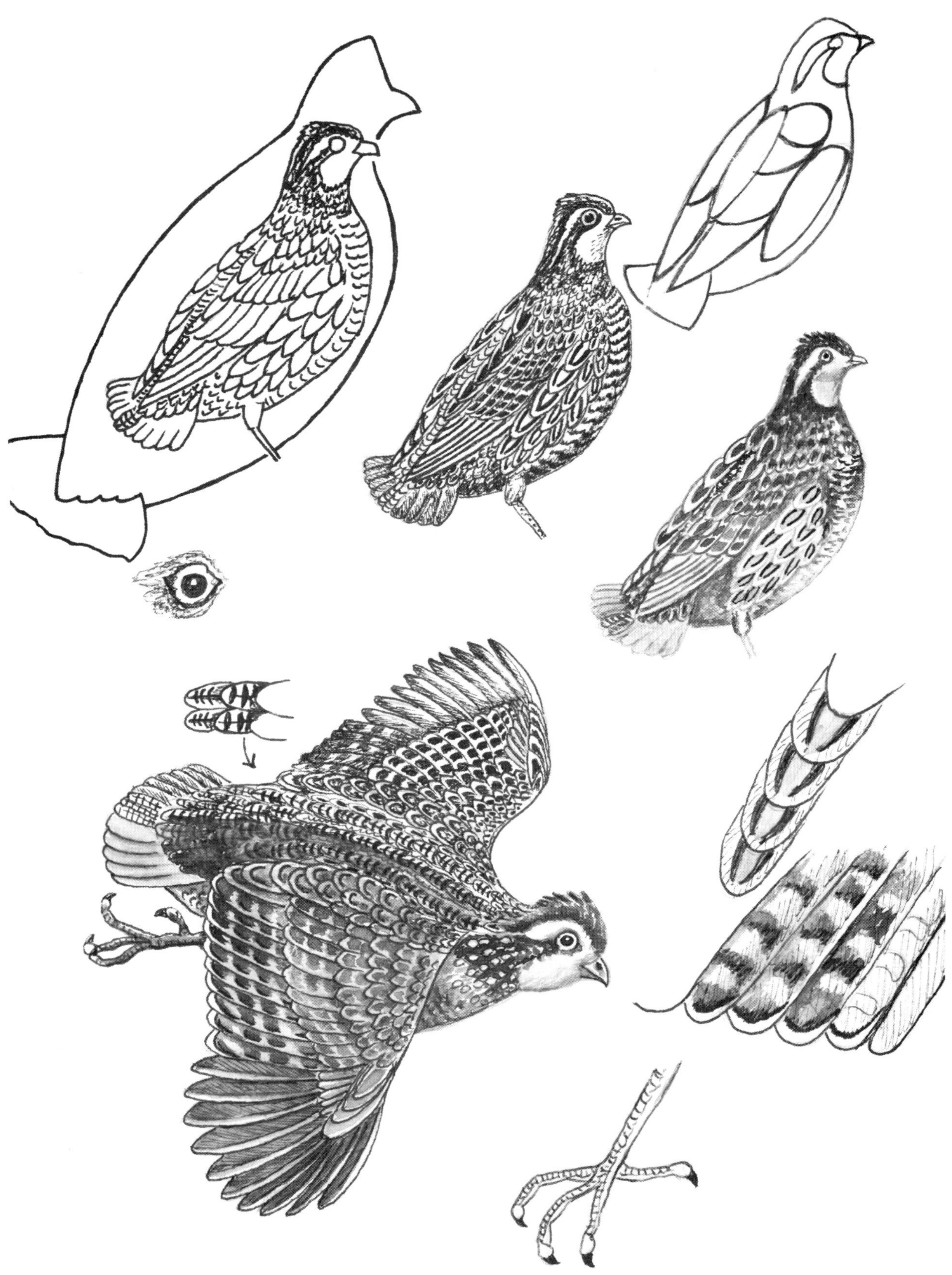

Figure 3.3 Outlining the bird is always the first step, and here you can actually copy from a photograph in order to study a particular bird's shapes and positions. To create your own version, you can begin with the basic egg shape and go from there. Place the "egg" flat to your vision, turn it sideways in both directions, and even reverse it and make your outline. Then you add the head and tail.

Shown here is the flat profile view, the quarter-turn view showing the back, the full back view, and the front view with the head turned. These are examples you can use, particularly when you are going to include several birds in a picture. Quail usually are found in coveys, so you can have a fun time in arranging them in their various positions in your layout.

In the flying stages, you can have one bird flying with its wingtips pointing down, to show the top of the wing, and the other with its wings up to show the underside of the wings and the side-panel markings on the body flank. Extreme angles—such as that shown looking down at the pheasant—are variations of positioning.

Once familiar with the general shapes and markings, your creativity can be unleashed when it comes to positioning the birds on the layout and moving them around into interesting and lifelike poses.

Work from photographs. You can even make carbon copies of the bare outlines from your research and, from those positions, practice moving the heads and tails or bending the wings into various flying positions. Make your subjects live. Study the works of the fine artists and see just how they sculpt their figures and work out interesting angles. This is the creative part of the work. The detailing of actual markings is routine in comparison.

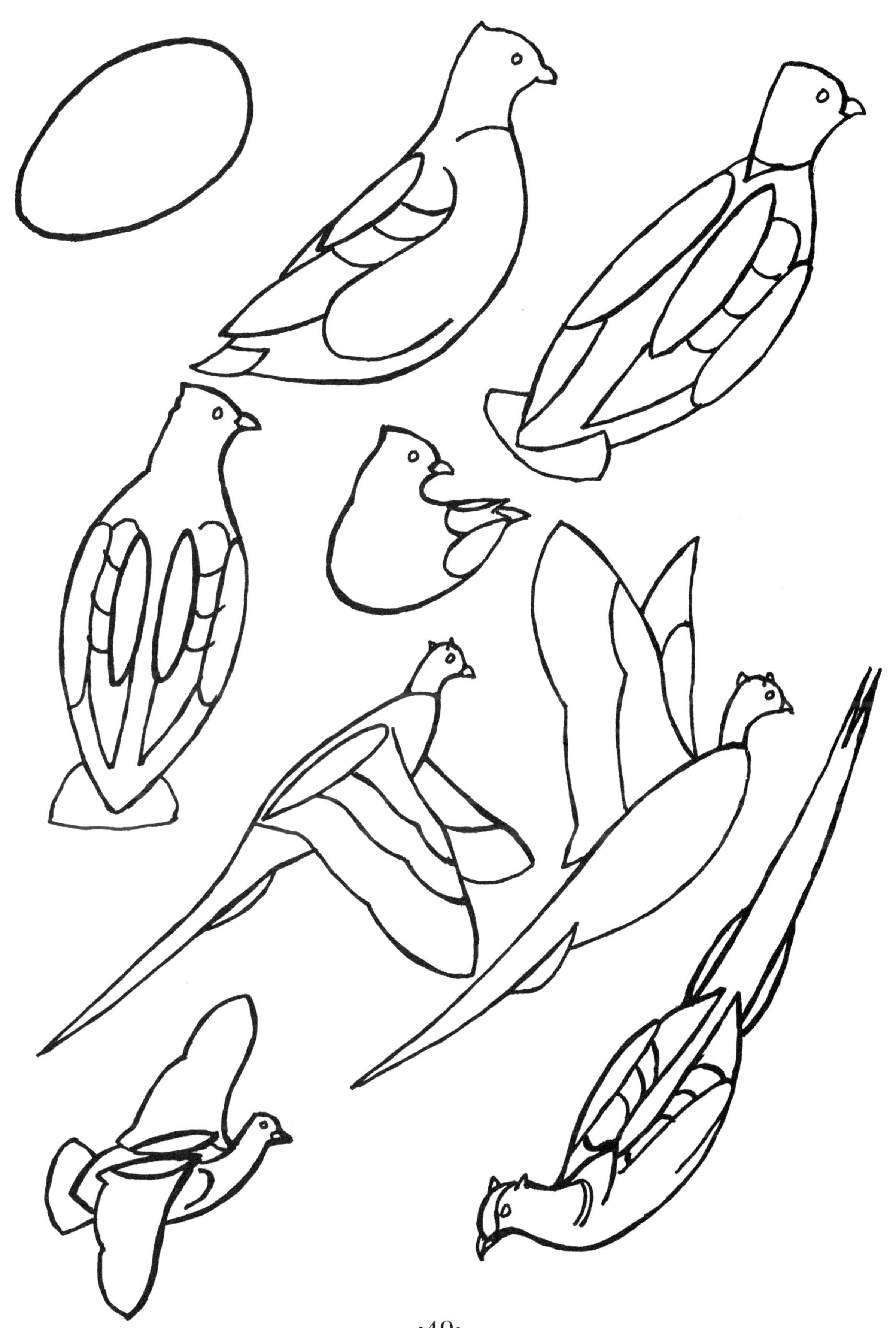

Figure 3.4 Here, four quail species, all different and exciting, offer a chance to study individuality in markings. They are shown in pen and ink, strictly specimen drawings, such as you would find in any good bird book, but they are done in much more obvious markings to show the technique. You will have fun "assembling" the detail once the outline is established. First you divide the bird's body into zones, such as the upper back, the wing segments, the side-flank feather section, the neck and chest, and finally the head. Then you break it down into actual feathers and feather clusters. Finally, you do the shading-in, requiring a detailed eye.

One good way to start on any one of these is to try it in pencil first, indicating only generally the various feather markings and characteristics. Once this is familiar ground, you can go on to pen. If you want to try your own positions other than the flat profile view, begin as before with the "egg" and build from there, drawing your bird of choice and filling it out as far as you want to go. If only a generalized version is wanted, first pencil in the zoning and general markings, then you can add a very effective wash version without the picky detail shown here in pen and ink.

These four quail species offer a great project for experimenting, always staying within the recognizable bounds of feather detail. They will train your eye to see differences in markings.

(a) The Scaled quail of the Southwest—a pretty creation with markings that help hide it in the desert. Check my work against the bird books for accuracy and suggestions for rendering. If you can find actual photos of them, so much the better.

(b) The California quail is a standout with its pretty tassel and prominent flank markings. Zone out the areas and then fill in as much detail as you like. Note the suggestion of feather fibers in the tail.

(c) Gambel's quail. Note the extreme contrast in the flank feather markings compared to the California variety; show this. Likewise, the flank feathers of the Mountain quail *(d)*. The bill shape is the same on all quail, and the eye has a slight suggestion of a lid.

(d) The Mountain quail of the Southwest and California has prominent flank feather markings far different than the other varieties, so make sure of your accuracy or at least give the impression of the correct markings. Put several of these attractive birds in your picture doing various things—bills high for calling, rooting around in the ground for goodies, taking flight, or merely standing guard.

Since each of these quail live in specific locations and habitats, study photos of the various areas in pictures from magazines. Since they are covey birds, it is not necessary always to show the entire bird. Place one coming out from behind a cactus or rock or brush, put one partially behind the other to show depth and contrast.

Do not mix species in the same picture. They are seldom if ever found together. I have shown only the males in this picture. Your favorite bird book will help you with the females. Usually in a group picture the females outnumber the males at least three to one.

Start with the pencil sketch, play around with shapes and groupings until one jumps out at you from your thumbnails, and then proceed to fill in.

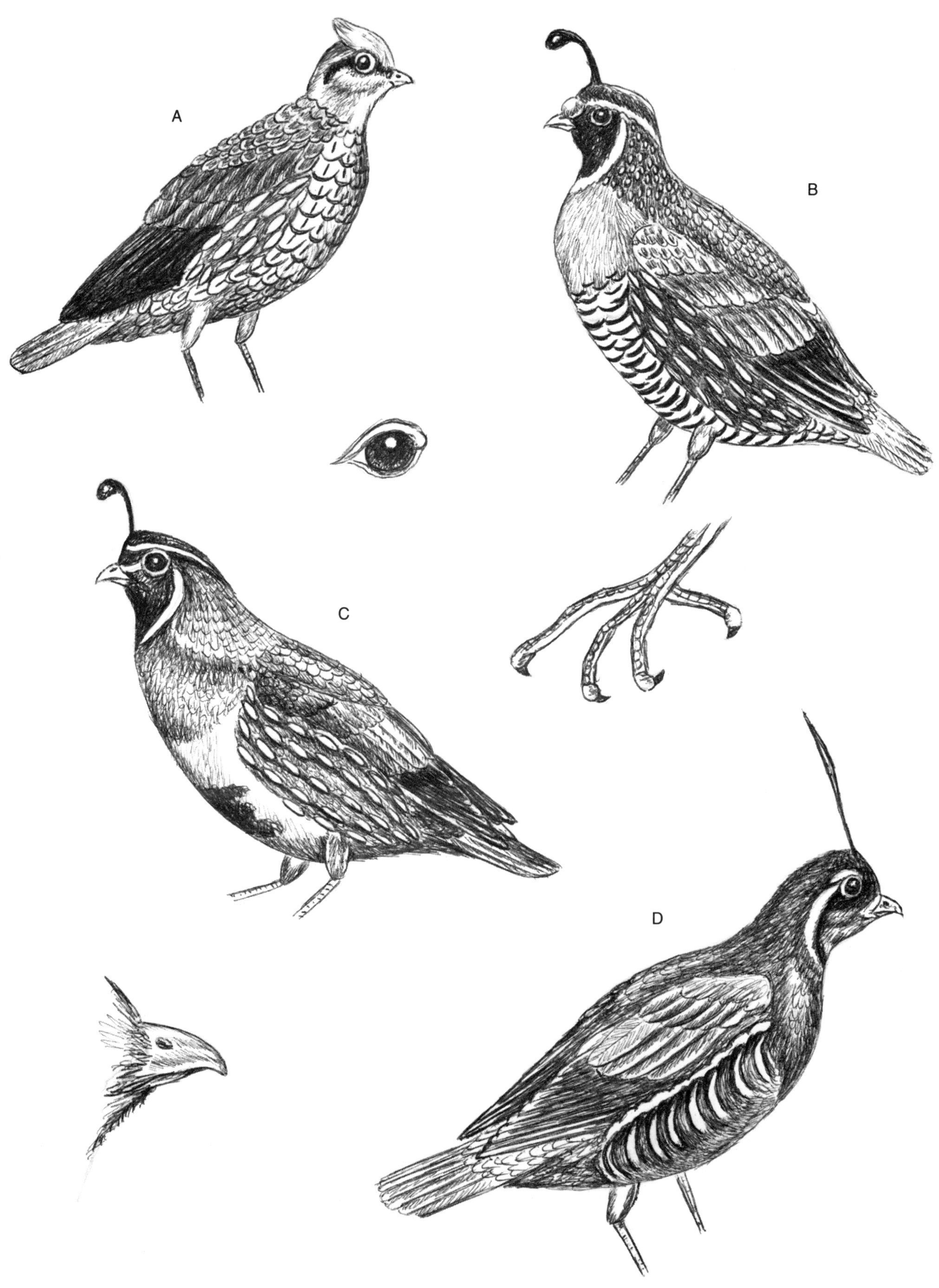
A
B
C
D

Figure 3.5 "Old Ruff"—done this time in pencil both flying and standing, for variety. An impressive bird, the ruffed grouse is somewhat complicated to render unless you patiently zone it out and then fill in the feathers, as you did with the bobwhite quail. In pencil you can work an effective impression rather than adhere to the strict feather markings, but you may find eventually that you will prefer to go into detail, even in a pencil sketch.

The pencil rendering remains unfinished and somewhat rough so that you can readily see the contrasts between the zones and the actual feather-by-feather markings.

Start with the all important form. Play with it, alter it, change it—until it "feels good." Begin with the egg shape unless you are working from the outlines of a photograph and, even then, don't be tied to the photo. Experiment. Although this bird looks like a big project, it's really simple if you take it step by step in the basic layout and gradually fill in as you go along. Sketch in the major elements; detail the strong points of the feathers and later shade in where needed, using hard, medium, and soft pencils to render your effects. Note the four clusters of feathers I have isolated for your study. It is really easy when you break it down to individual steps and specific areas of work. And what a reward when you arrive at the finishing touches.

In Chapter 9 we will detail a background for this bird. Work as large as I have here and you should have no problems. Birds of this size look great in a picture at least eighteen by twenty-four inches, matted, and in a good frame.

Although most artists show the grouse with its tail spread, this is not always natural. Quite often they are shown properly with the tail feathers together, though it is not as dramatic a pose.

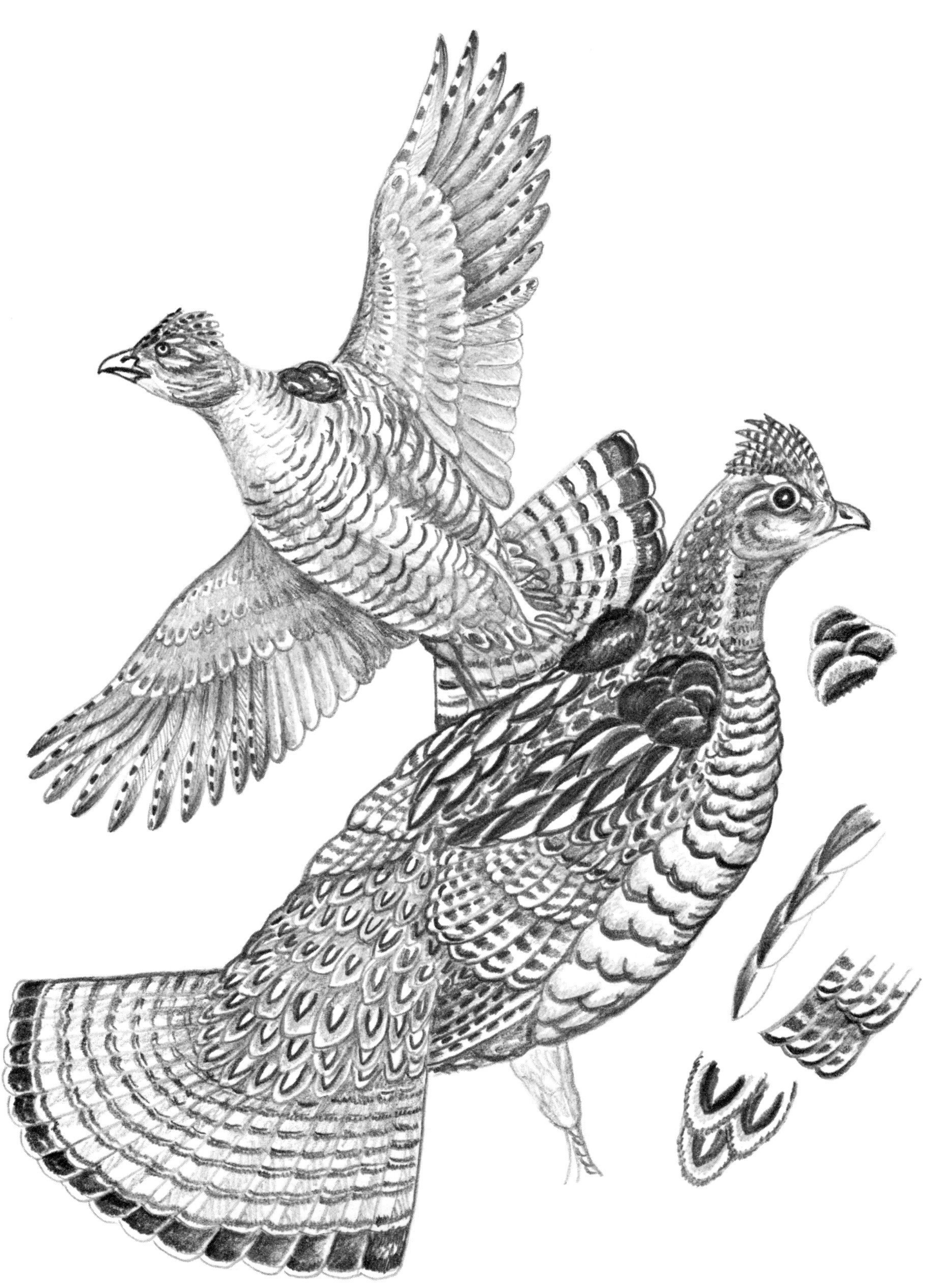

Figure 3.6 Two partridges are shown, done in wash, working from pencil outlines and zoning and feather markings. The chukar partridge (top) and the Hungarian partridge (bottom) are shown in both standing and flying positions for marking identification. Both are beautiful in color, but even in black and white or half tone they offer a gorgeous subject to work with. They are not found together, so don't mix them. The females are not shown here; consult your bird book for them. Also study their habitat for backgrounds, when it comes time to place them in suitable surroundings.

Again, these illustrations are done partially in the rough to show the obvious zoning needed and the feather markings or indications of special feather markings that are true to the bird species.

As always, begin with the lightest touch and gradually strengthen by deepening your grays. This is great training for your future work in color. When working with the brush in the grays, you are learning definition, contrasts, and blends as you work up from the white paper. You won't need to mix colors on the pallette; you'll be able to gradually work the levels of color right on the paper, seeing your work take shape before your eyes.

When you wish to introduce more contrast, especially in the dark area, use the pen lightly to intensify, for wing feathers especially, or for very dark identifying colors or actual feathers.

Move your birds around a bit. Have them doing something. And arrange your layout so that the viewer's attention is always on the birds and does not flow out of the picture.

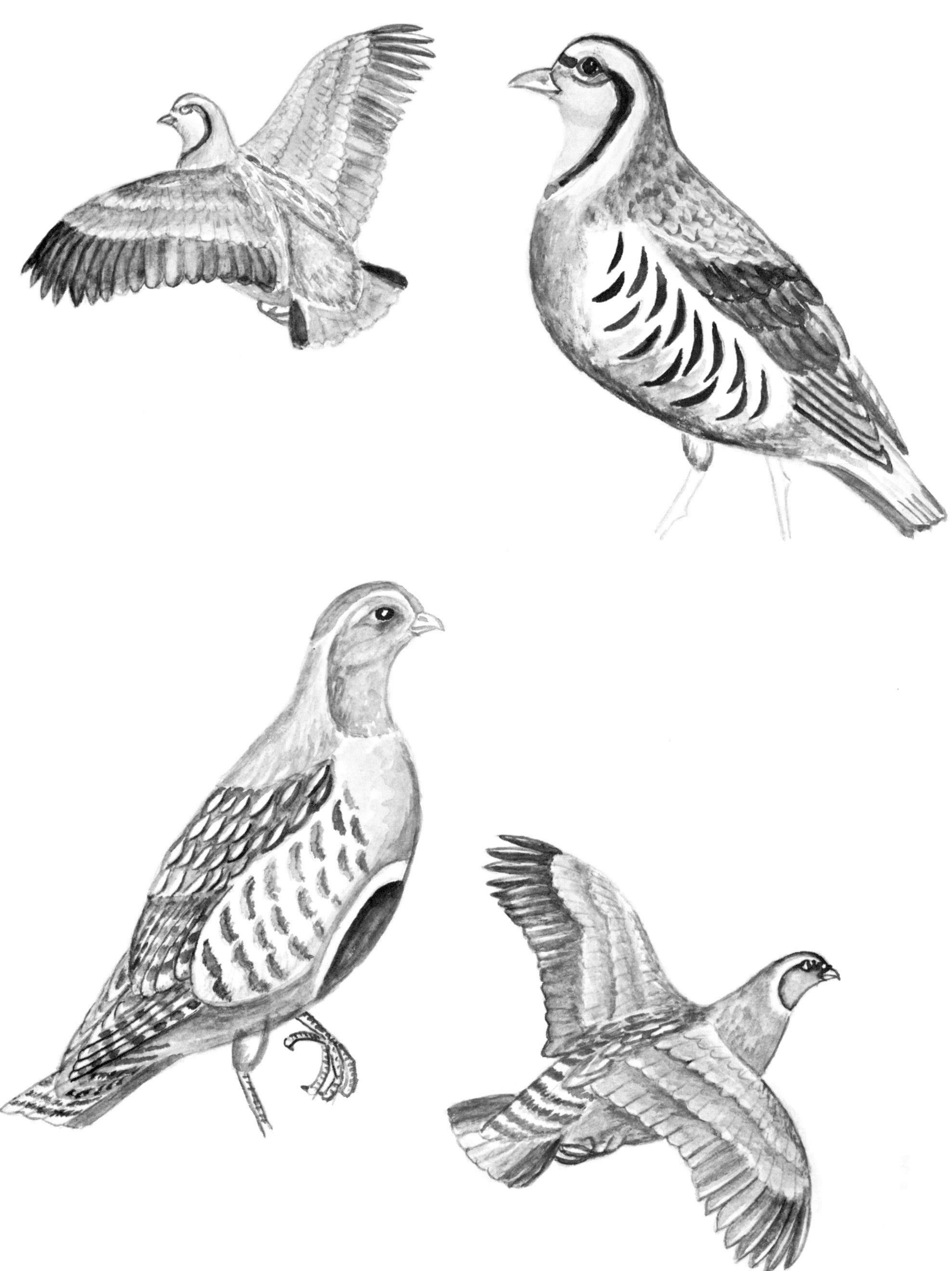

Figure 3.7 Ah, the magnificent pheasant, probably the most popular of all the upland game species. I've seen it depicted as a dead bird hanging on a board, placed on a china platter, under glass, and best of all in the natural state—flying, standing, preening, peacefully feeding, or exploding out in front of a hunter—in hundreds of poses in hundreds of articles, advertisements, home decorations, you name it.

In order to bring out the subtleties of coloration, I have used wash and, as usual, have overdone the effects for instructional purposes. Even so, the cock looks pretty good there with his mate.

Note the difference in the two tail feathers. *a* is the male feather and *b* is the female. You would be surprised how many artists fail to note the distinction when they render one or the other. *a* is shown in two stages of drawing, the right side being the finished rendition.

The cock presents the problem of rendering the green iridescent neck and head in contrast to the bright red flesh of the face. In this case I chose to show the red as a lighter tone than the green.

The two feather tufts are not really ears, but are merely tufts of feathers somewhat similar to those found on owls. Why he has them, nobody knows for sure.

Note the simplicity of the hen's feathers in contrast to the gaudy arrangements found on the cock. Any good bird book will give you the zoning and feather markings of both birds, and you can go from there—once you have decided on the form and position of your bird as done in your initial thumbnail drawing. Subtle shadows will help you to give the bird a rounded form. This is done after the final feathering is completed, by very gently darkening either with light pen or brush, or even pencil.

Get to know this bird first hand. Visit a pheasant farm, do a bit of hunting, and actually feel a real bird. Pluck out some representative feathers for future research and copying. A well-mounted specimen to have before you is also a great help when you are working.

The pen and inks of flying pheasants, shown here for contrast, demonstrate that even in a very small picture it is possible to achieve lifelike details. The upper flyer shows the back markings and the spread tail; the lower flyer is poised with his wings up to display the bright and contrasting flank feather markings.

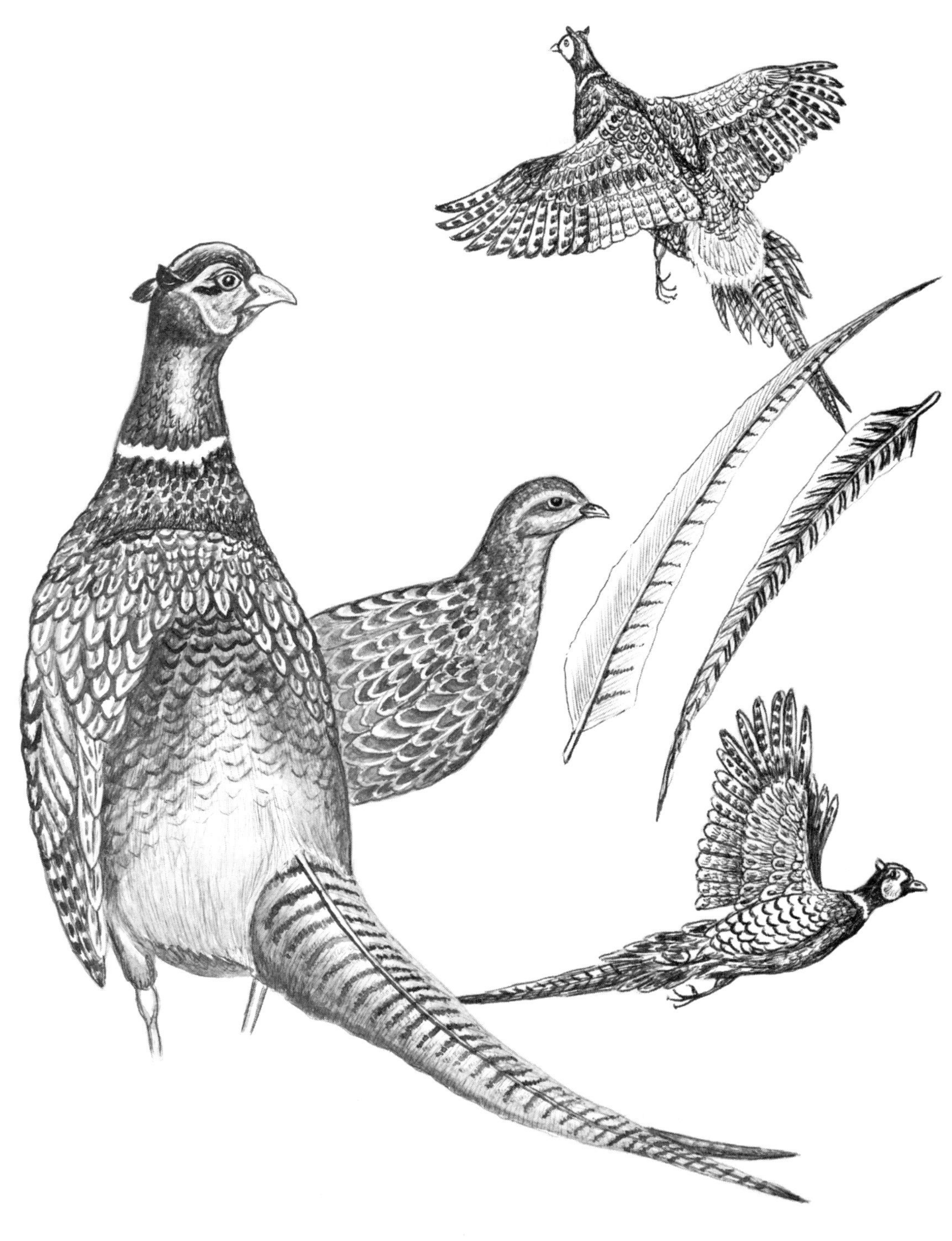

Figure 3.8 Here is old Tom Turkey, just as beautiful in the wild as he is in the barnyard—more colorful than the ruffed grouse or even the quails, but a joy to render—showing his shiny feathers and his gnarley head—even in black and white or wash.

In this case, I chose pencil again to show the subtle nuances you can work into your subject, generalizing yet staying close to the actual feathering patterns that are so important unless a vague impression is all you want. The flyer, with its underwing up, shows the breast feathers and the strong upper leg with its feather overlappings. The inset pen and ink of the upper wing shows the zoning and actual feather indications to be followed.

The standing bird is a typical pose, which shows the patterns and how to render them in soft pencil. The same technique is used with brush and paint. The little sections of zoned bird parts show how to mark out the detail to be softened and filled in.

I couldn't resist a closeup of the head, since the turkey's head is the most fun of all the birds', due to its peculiar texture and makeup. Homely, isn't it? Draw it that way without going into caricature.

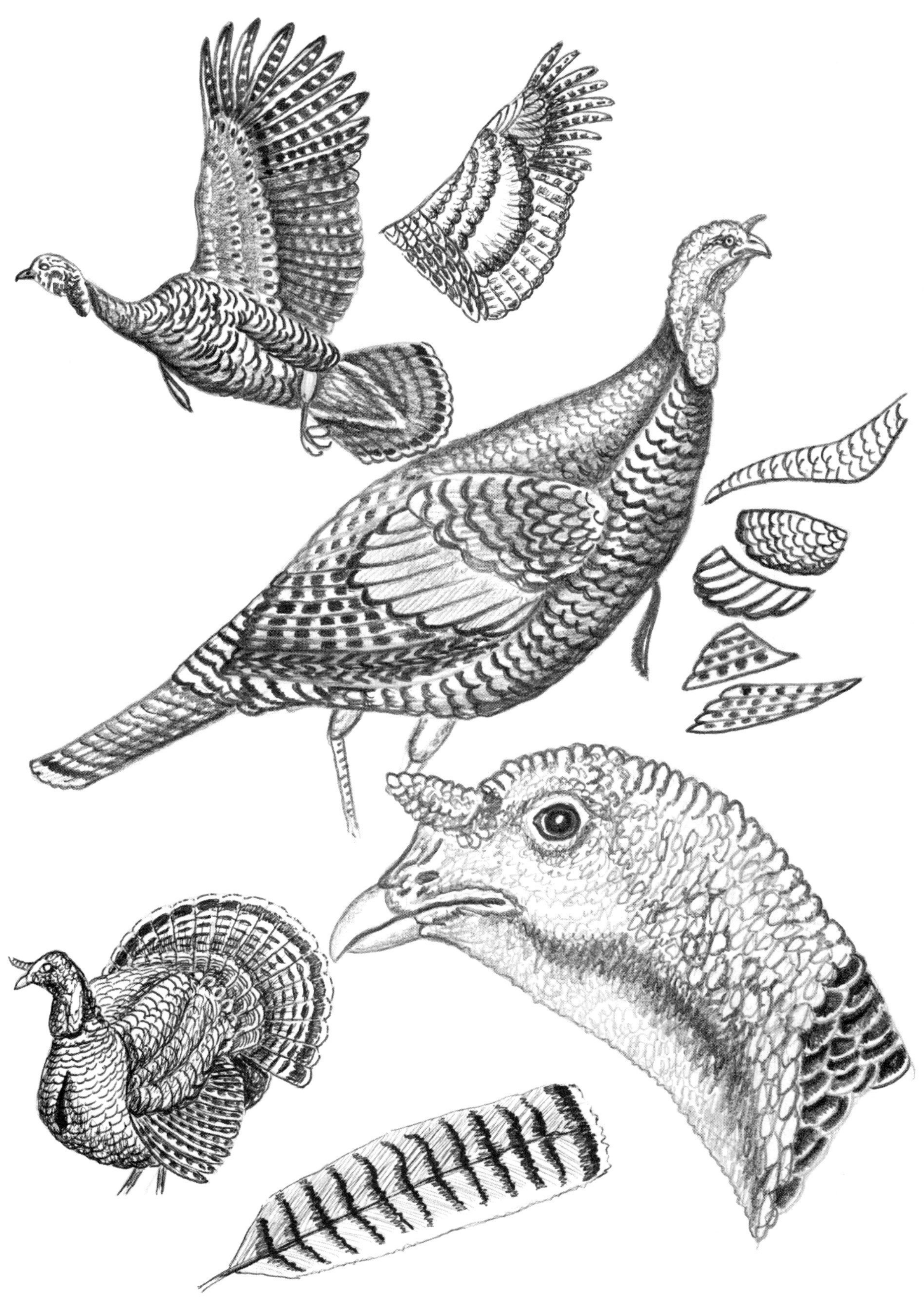

Figure 3.9 Doves are far easier rendered in pencil or wash than in pen and ink due to their softness and lack of detailed feather markings. When considering drawing any species, think it out first and decide which method or medium you will be using. Again, experiment. For the doves however, I chose the wash and, as usual, have somewhat overdone the illustrations to show the markings that are needed.

(a) The common pigeon—a good example to practice on since it is readily available everywhere. The pigeon can aid you in your study of all birds, acting as a model and sharpening your observation, so don't look down on it. Don't render it in a boring position but have it doing something, anything, like carrying a tuft of hair, feathers, or grass to build its nest. Have the male cooing to his mate, or scratching his neck. You can observe them in pairs and arrange a pair in combination that will make the picture not only interesting but emotionally effective.

(b) The white-winged dove of the West. You will note that its tail is similar to the pigeon's, not pointed as in the case of the mourning dove. Softness is important here, but so is shading and the subtle play of light on the body of the bird. The white-lined wingtip feathers are overmarked here and should be shaded when you advance in your technique. The overlapping feathers are details, as is the foot of the bird, a bit more chubby than that of the quail or other upland birds.

(c) The mourning dove. Shown in flight and standing. Watch these fast flying birds as they come and go at the feeding shelf, and make quick sketches of the impressions they make on your mind. Then transfer these sketches to the outline form and gradually fill in as required. Place them in a pleasing background.

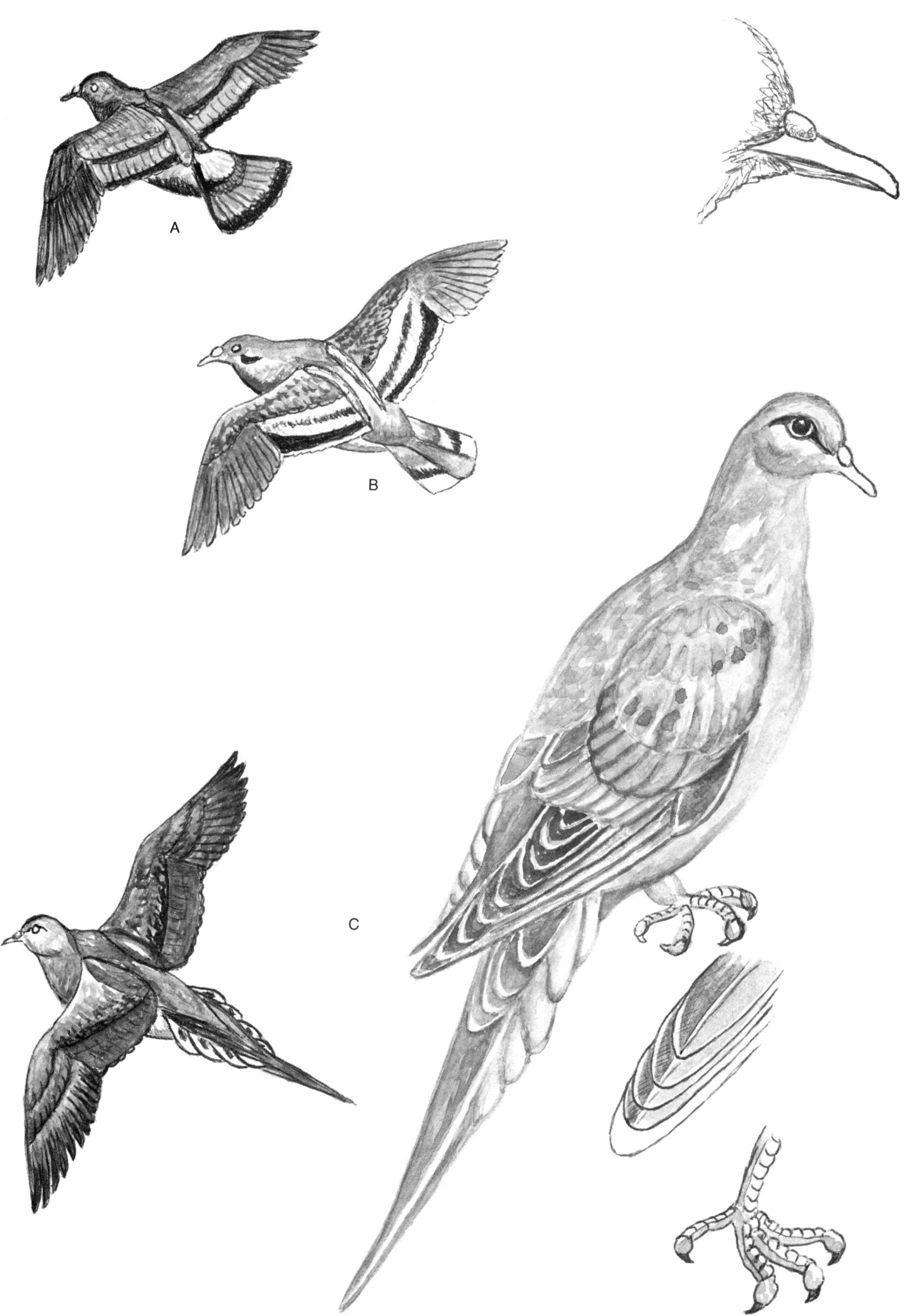
A
B
C

Figure 3.10 Our little friend, the woodcock, is shown here, a bird that Mother Nature played some tricks with. No doubt about it, this bird is strange; and this uniqueness should be brought out without too much exaggeration. A perky bird when seen in the wild, the woodcock never stands still, poking constantly into the mud and leaves in search of worms and bugs. It pops up and down, see-saws on its little legs, whips its beak to and fro—then all of a sudden it bursts forth from the ground in a spurt of flight to come to rest further along the woodland floor, resuming its interminable search for food. So picture the woodcock in motion!

I want you to do a little work on your own here, studying the flying bird first. Note I have left the upper wing entirely open for you, having outlined it for careful detail work. I have also indicated in various zoned areas the fill-in markings to be shaded a trifle later when needed. The lower wing's outer flight feathers are a case in point. Note that I have lined in the fiber markings of the flight feathers, to be shaded in as I did with the first two feathers. Same with the tail feathers. The other wing feather markings are indicated. All you need do is the detail and you end up with the completed bird. If you are interested only in an impressionistic rendition, you should still work from the outline and roughly indicate the feather markings from the layout, as I have done in the small pencil rendition of the standing bird. Note the somewhat exaggerated shading up and down the bird's bill to make it stand out from the body. If you know woodcocks, you know that they have very prominent eyes, a trait not common in other birds, so show them that way.

Have fun with this bird. Show two or three in the picture if you like. They are not a covey bird, but they sometimes are found close together as they work their way like little vacuum cleaners over the forest floor. Show them that way.

Play around with positions, especially for flying. Have the woodcock flying away from you at an angle seen from below. Try an upwing position somewhat similar in angle to the one illustrated here. Point the bird's head further up or further down. Have it fly right at you or directly away. Experiment.

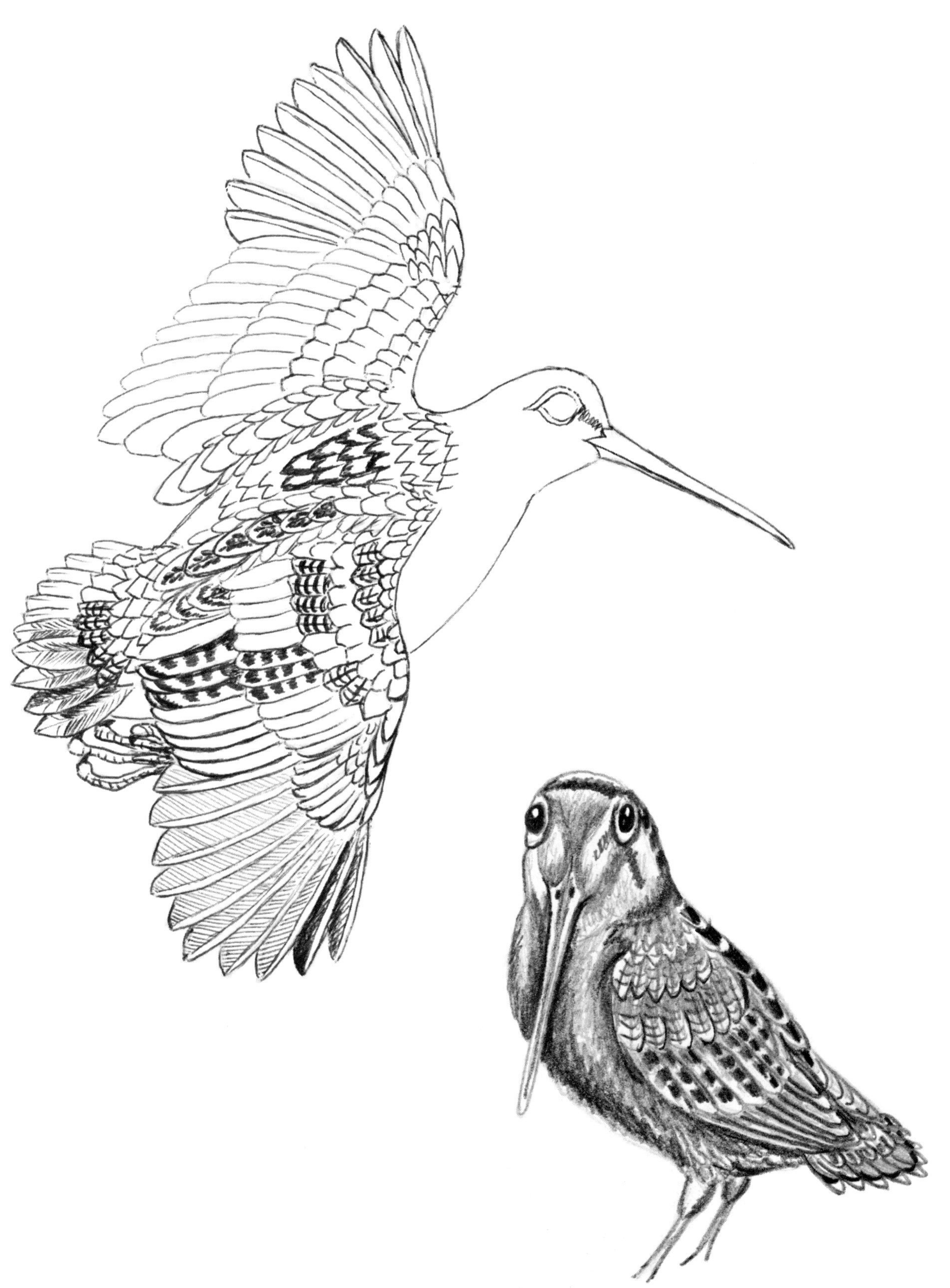

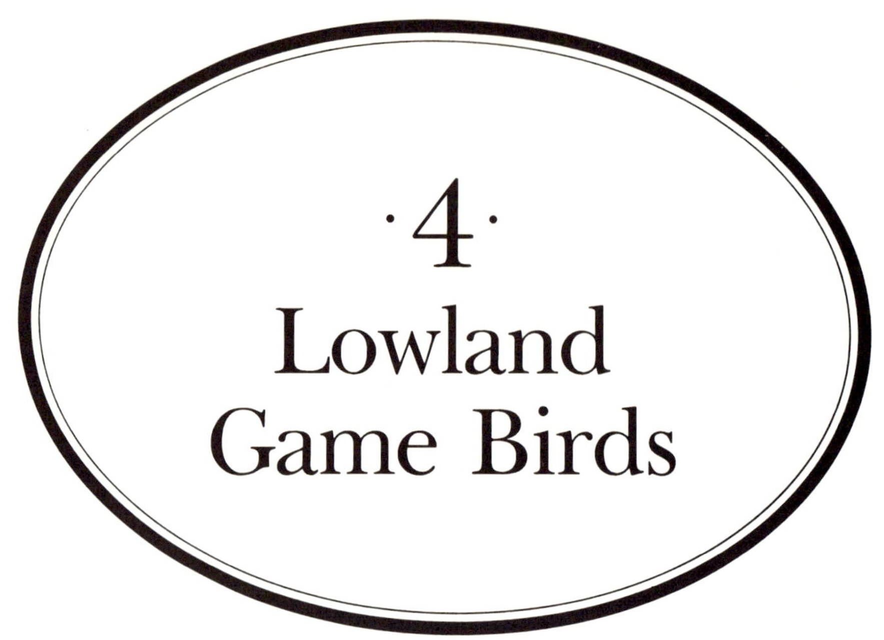

·4· Lowland Game Birds

In the classification "lowland game birds" we find the waterfowl, ducks, and geese that inhabit North America. Though there are many more species than those used for subjects in this book, the ones chosen are representative of the various types.

Mallards, wigeons, teals, and pintails are classed as "puddle ducks," or birds that rise quickly from the ground or water surface in a burst of power. They are called puddle ducks because they feed in shallow or "puddle" marshlands. Canvasbacks, redheads, scaups, and sea ducks are classified as diving ducks, birds that can't take off suddenly but require a long run over the water, paddling their feet and banging their pinions on the water until they obtain enough lift under their wings to become airborne.

Most species nest very far north, as far as the Arctic Circle, so little is seen of their domestic lives. We see them on their north or south migrations near lakes and streams, ponds, swamps, and along the shores of both oceans. Although many species do nest within our boundaries, they are quite shy and sometimes difficult to observe. Try to capture them with pen or brush in flight or on the ground in natural poses. They have beautiful forms and striking colors. Placed in their proper environment they make beautiful and interesting pictures.

Mallard Duck (*Anas platyrhynchos*)

Probably the most painted and drawn duck is the mallard. You have seen this bird on greeting cards, posters, tumblers, neckties, ashtrays, ad infinitum. Along with the Canada goose and the bald eagle, the mallard is almost a national symbol.

And has it been mangled by even the great classical artists! Avoid this by trying your best to render the mallard as it is, a beautiful species second only to the wood duck or possibly the green- or blue-winged teals.

Study the duck stamps of the past and you'll find the mallard. You'll see it flying in the pages of the sporting magazines and books on duck and goose hunting. Perhaps the foremost painter of ducks is Richard Bishop, who worked almost solely from photographs and prints taken from motion picture film. His work was ultra-accurate, even at times to the point of awkwardness. After all, a duck is not the prettiest thing as it puts its flaps down preparatory for a landing.

Paint your mallards in pairs—sitting on the water, preening themselves, one possibly asleep near the shore, taking off in quick flight, or whiffling in for a landing. Make them live and sparkle in their distinct colors.

The mallard is the most popular of the puddle ducks. It rises from the water almost vertically and, because of the placement of their legs, do little actual deep diving, preferring to feed in shallow water.

Also known as the green-head, English duck, or stock duck, mallards are the most prolific and dominant ducks of the country. Males are easily identified by their yellow bill, bright green head, and neck banded by a white ring at the chestnut-colored chest. Black-and-white banded squares of shiny blue patches adorn the secondary wing sections. The female is mottled brown, though bearing the same blue wing patches. Both have yellow-orange legs.

Marsh plants, grain (especially corn), large seeds, hickory nuts, and acorns make up most of the diet whether they are nesting in the far north or in your city park. Though they migrate as far north as central Alaska and travel as far south as Florida and Mexico, they usually stay well within those boundaries and are most prevalent in the central and middle west.

Easily tamed, they have become the domesticated duck of many farms. They are the prime waterfowl bird of the commercial shooting preserve, because they are so easy to raise and produce the fastest flyers that can be raised profitably in captivity. Extensive stocking and conservation activities have enlarged the coverage of the mallard, and today it is found almost everywhere in the country, its weakest distribution found only in the extreme northwest.

Mallards are easily lured to the hunter or photographer concealed in a blind by the use of "blocks," or lifelike colored decoys floating near the cover of marsh grasses. They can also be lured by making feeding sounds with the aid of a duck call.

From nine to twelve eggs hatch into flying birds by the fall migration time. Seasons are regulated by federal migratory laws and state seasons and bag limits. Mallards weigh between two and three pounds and top speed has been clocked at between forty-five and fifty miles per hour in full flight.

Pintail Duck (*Anas acuta*)

The drake pintail could not possibly be misidentified. It is far too distinctive, with its long white neck topped by a brown-capped and bibbed head, and its white tail banded by black borders and spriglike tail feathers that trail out behind. The green and chestnut colored secondary wing patch is further identification. The female, however, is harder to tell from other pond ducks except for the green wing patch.

Perhaps because of its beauty—and of course excellent table qualities—some hunters rank the pintail or "sprig" as the third most popular duck with sportsmen. Its wide distribution helps to establish this enthusiasm: The pintail is available from Long Island down through the central states and up into Washington, Oregon, and British Columbia during the migrating season, and all over the map from the western tip of Alaska to Newfoundland during its summer breeding season. It uses all the major flyways for the migration, both north and south.

Pintails are fast flying birds that are especially finicky when danger is about. They can and do usually warn other ducks of approaching danger, and if they spot fraudulent decoys or hunters during their flight, they can quickly wheel in an instant to veer out of gun range.

The hen lays fewer eggs than most of the other species, but the numbers of these birds have not been affected significantly by hunting or pollution. Regulated hunting has been helped by federal and state laws, and game bag limits vary from year to year according to the census taken of the species.

Although they prefer grains and grasses with available nuts and even insects, mollusks do figure in their diet while on migration. Because long necks enable deeper feeding, roots of grass form a staple of their diet.

They weigh a little over the two-pound mark and reach a length of twenty-nine inches or more. Flight speed has been estimated at sixty miles per hour, with a good tail wind.

Blue-Winged Teal (*Anas discors*)

Fast and erratic flyers, teal fool many gunners. It is not that they fly any faster than most puddle ducks, but their small size is what forms the illusion of speed. They are very wary birds and quick to flip or zoom off course in an instant, even at the slightest hint of danger. They cover the country from east to west, into Central America in winter, and from Alaska to Newfoundland during the summer.

The blue-winged teal male has a blueish-purple head with a half-moon of white running vertically through the eye. The body is cinnamon color, but its main identifying marks are the light blue shoulders and the green secondary feathers separated with a thin white band. The female is drab, mottled brown, but also features the green secondary feathers to separate them from other species.

Teal are excellent table birds despite their preference for mollusks and water insects, as well as grains, seeds, grasses, and the like. They weigh about thirteen ounces, reach a length of not more than fifteen inches, and have been clocked at fifty miles per hour at top speed when alerted.

Green-Winged Teal (Anas carolinensis)

Considered to be among the swiftest and most erratic flyers of all ducks, green-winged teal are a striking sight to see, reaching out on long, zooming sweeps across the marshes; whiffling and dodging, wing-tip to wing-tip, for a touchdown; bursting out of a shallow pond or rising in a thrashing jumble through reeds and cattails to level out in the clouds of a wintry sky. It is estimated that the green-wing can pass the 160 miles-per-hour mark, making it a tough target for the telephoto camera or shotgun.

Teal often fly in tight, balled-up flocks, seldom in the classical V-formation used by the larger ducks and geese. Sometimes a veritable cloud of them will suddenly appear on the horizon like a swarm of bees, weaving a pattern across the sky, often making a striking change of direction en masse and suddenly descending to a compact mass in the reeds.

On the water they float like puffballs, unlike many of the larger ducks that swim and lie almost half submerged. When a group of them settle into a shallow pond to do their "puddling" for grasses (they are strict vegetarians), they will be seen in active head diving, their bobbing tails signaling the activity of their eager bills as they feed on sprouts and grasses under the muddy water. Again and again they will arise with violent wing flaps, as if about to take off, only to resume paddling, "talking," diving, and swimming around each other in endless activity. Teal, unlike other puddle ducks such as mallards and blacks, are excellent divers. They are also particularly agile on their feet, capable of rapid bursts across the ground when danger shows cause to scurry for cover. They are often found at some distance from water, because they will range into the brush and even the woods for forage or escape.

Their natural tameness has been their undoing, and they are easily attracted to a blind by the use of decoys. Decoys can be of any species, for teal don't seem to care what birds are in the area. They are often found in the company of blue-wings, mallards, blacks, and wigeon. Occasionally they will nest and stay near wood ducks, though they nest on the ground, not in tree nests.

Teal breed in the northern states and Canada, all across the map. They follow the established flyways when they leave their nesting grounds in October, or if driven south by an early fall storm in September. They follow and stay in their preferred freshwater ponds, streams, and lakes, leaving the ocean and brackish water to the other species. Teal will go to the brackish waters only when freshwater shallows are frozen over.

Breeding range extends from northern Alaska, northern Manitoba, James Bay, and southern Ungava, south to central California, northern New Mexico, northern Nebraska, southern Minnesota, northern Michigan, southern Ontario, western New York, and Quebec. They winter from southern British Columbia, northern Nebraska, northern Missouri, southern Illinois, Kentucky, and Chesapeake Bay to the Bahamas, West Indies, Honduras, and southern Mexico.

The European teal is similar in markings but does not have the white moonlike marking on the side of the breast.

As a table delicacy, the teal is considered tops. The flank feathers are used by fishing fly-tiers and are considered to be quite valuable.

Wood Duck (*Alix sponsa*)

The most beautiful of American waterfowl, the wood duck—or woody, summer duck, squealer, or tree duck—is fantastically marked with all colors of the rainbow. One would think that this bird would be an import from some exotic country of the Far East, but it has always been a true resident of North America.

The wood duck sports a long hanging crest of blue-green, lined with thin white feathers, a white throat, a chestnut-pink white-spotted upper breast, and gold flanks banded by black-and-white flank feathers (used by fly-tiers for many trout-fly patterns). Its underparts are off-white and purple under the tail. The back is mottled blueish-gray. Legs are pale yellow. Light-blue secondaries mark the wings, and the underwings are gray brown. The female is drab by contrast, although she wears the crest.

This species frequents the river bottoms and marshes of British Columbia, Washington, and northern California, and the same environments starting from the Mississippi River and moving east and north to New Brunswick, Nova Scotia, and the Great Lakes region. They winter in the south-central states and into the Gulf Coast area and Florida.

The wood duck's diet is almost exclusively vegetable, which makes it an excellent table bird. Weighing usually one pound, ten ounces, its length runs to twenty inches, with flight speeds rated in short spurts at from forty to fifty miles per hour.

Hunted for sport, food, and particularly as mounted specimens and for its feathers, the wood duck is favored over most other birds. Heavy shooting at one time reduced the bird's numbers dangerously, but conservation groups have brought it back to sizeable numbers. Some states once closed the season on this species some years ago, but they have opened it again in a limited way.

The wood duck does not generally make its nest on the ground but prefers trees, old stumps, windfalls—anything that can support the nest above the water and offer good protection from predators. Bird nesting boxes designed for "woodies" have been extensively used by conservationists and sportsmen to increase their numbers. Many clubs sponsor bird box programs for them. Usually ten eggs are laid, and in about a month the young leave the box and learn to fly and paddle in the nearby water.

Canvasback Duck (*Aythya valisneria*)

The canvasback is another bird that has suffered recently due to the wrong use of the "pothole" country (small lakes in northern U.S. and Canada) in which its nesting is done. Summering in the west-central plains states and into Canada as far north as southern Alaska, its nesting sites have been subject to farming development and swamp and pothole drainage, not to mention years of either too much or too little distribution of water during the critical nesting and duckling-raising times.

The canvasback has recently been protected against hunting in many states. The future of its comeback lies in man's ability to correct the use of lands where it raises its young.

The canvasback, known as "can" or bullneck, has the same-colored head as the redheaded duck, though the shape of the head is much longer. The canvasback sports a longer bill and a slimmer, longer neck, which is noticeable in flight and when holding its head straight up while on the water. The female is yellowish-tan speckled with white. The feet are black instead of gray, as in the case of the redhead.

Canvasbacks generally stay together even during the fall migration, and, in the past, great flocks covered the sky from end to end and could be seen passing on cold wintry days. Now the flocks are much smaller as they migrate up to their wintering grounds from Washington to southern California in the west, skipping to the Great Lakes region and New England, south to Florida and the Gulf Coast, and into Mexico.

Being diving ducks, their rise off the water is slow and gradual, and by the same token their descent takes a long runway. They usually fly high at all times and come in with flaps down for the landing. When in regular flight they have been clocked at upwards of sixty-five miles per hour—one of our fastest ducks.

Their clutches are fewer than some other species, seldom containing more than eight or nine eggs. Almost all of their food is vegetable. They like wild celery; pond weed with crustaceans and snails are a second choice. On the table they are rated excellent.

Canvasbacks weigh almost three pounds and measure twenty to twenty-three inches in length.

Redheaded Duck (*Aythya americana*)

The redheaded duck, with its near cousin the canvasback, has suffered severely in recent years, and conservation has enforced strict regulations against hunting in most states. Extensive rehabilitation of its nesting grounds in the west-central states and provinces of Canada are hoped to bring about an upsurge.

This bird migrates in long, scattered V-shaped flocks and winters from Washington state south into Mexico and across the southern states into Georgia, with strays reaching into northern Florida.

Easily identifiable by its roundish chestnut-red head, black upper chest, gray back and white belly, the male cannot be mistaken for a canvasback. The female is a drab, buff brown. The "redhead's" flight is long and low in takeoff due to the position of its legs. A fast and direct flyer, it has been clocked at over fifty miles per hour.

This is a diving duck and as such inhabits both fresh and saltwater areas where there is proper food. Redheads are often found in company with other diving ducks as well as pond ducks, their diet being almost exclusively vegetable. They are more able to search out roots and grasses below the water level reached by the pond ducks. At times they will feed on mollusks, crustaceans, snails, and insects.

A good duck dinner with the chief ingredient being redheads is one to remember!

They are easily lured to decoys fashioned to imitate them, though they will sometimes come into mallard and black duck decoys. Generally they fly quite high when approaching their feeding or roosting locations but then will suddenly drop down and swoop in low.

Often the hunter will get straightaway shots or will have to take on these birds as they approach head-on at a fast clip. As such they offer challenging targets. Even when approaching their landing from left or right they offer a fast target, which can confound even an expert.

The female lays from ten to fifteen eggs, and the young hatch quickly and learn to fly south when the parents' migration begins. Adults weigh over two pounds and are usually about nineteen inches long.

American Wigeon (*Moreca americana*)

The baldpate, or American wigeon, is one of the more colorful of the puddle ducks. It is easily spotted by the white patch on the forehead, the green swatch through the eye to the back of the head, and the green-and-white shoulder and secondary-wing feather patch markings, bottomed by a white lower breast. The female is of drab brown coloration but wearing the same shoulder and secondary wing badges of green and white. Often found in their company is the European wigeon, which frequents the eastern shore of the lower United States.

Wigeons winter from Maryland to Florida and Central America, and up as far north as Washington, nesting in the mountain states and up into interior Alaska, with the greatest bulk of nesters staying in the western Canadian provinces.

They are small birds, weighing a little less than two pounds, and can fly almost twenty-five miles an hour, bursting up from cover or the water almost vertically in typical pond-duck fashion, and then zooming away. They fly in erratically shaped flocks of from five to twenty and frequently intermingle in migrating flocks with pintails and teal.

Their food consists of grains such as alfalfa, water celery, and grass roots. This diet makes them a consistently good table bird. They are easily scared but can be lured by decoys and the aid of skillful vocal calling. At the slightest hint of danger they can veer off projected course in a split second, winging out of danger. Because of their small size they appear to fly much faster than the larger ducks.

About ten eggs are laid, and mortality is very low under normal nesting conditions. Conservation efforts for waterfowl in general have helped this species, and no sign of a severe lack has shown in recent years.

Many bird farms raise this species as an exotic to be released in private ponds for decorative purposes. They seldom nest in the wild in the eastern states, however, and almost never migrate into eastern Canada at all.

Shoveller Duck (*Spatula clypeata*)

Looking like a holdover from prehistoric times, the shoveller, spoony, spoonbill, or shovelbill is an exceptional duck easily identified by its oversized spoon-shaped bill in both the male and the female.

At a distance the male might be confused with the mallard since its head is of the same green, but at closer inspection the white breast, belly, and wing shoulders, plus its chestnut flanks, mark it as the shoveller. Both male and female sport green secondary feathers. The female, like most females of the duck family, is mottled brown.

This is a well known and very widely distributed duck. It is found nesting from Alaska to the mountain and central provinces of Canada, and in the northern United States as far east as the Great Lakes region. It winters from the Carolinas to Florida and across the Gulf and down into Mexico and Central America. It is also found extensively on the west coast from northern Washington to the peninsula of Baja California.

Technically related to the teal, shovellers are not too far from them in flight characteristics, though they seem to fly more slowly with less zig-zagging and darting. Like the other shallow-water ducks described, the shovellers rise quickly in an almost vertical flight and then level off straight away. Shovellers quite often tend to stay with their own kind, though they migrate with the blue-winged teal and other species in the fall.

On the table they are considered excellent food due to their love of water plants, but only by those who enjoy a gamey taste. They eat grains and seeds in addition to insect larvae and small crustaceans.

Shovellers will decoy to mallard and teal "blocks," and seldom is it necessary to lure them with an exact replica of themselves. From seven to fifteen eggs are laid in each clutch.

Canada Goose (*Branta canadensis*), American Brant (*Branta bernicla*), and Black Brant (*Branta nigricans*)

The Canada goose has been a symbol of knowledge and wonder for centuries. Just why this is, no one knows; the goose evidently has a mystical kind of aura that brings out admiration from humans. It is a most graceful bird with its long neck, longer than any duck's. And when seen flying in skeins or in the classic V-formation across an autumn sky, it offers a feeling of vastness and strength since it migrates long distances against many odds.

In this bird you have many graceful lines to work with. You can create a form with them that expresses many feelings. It can border on the caricature. Even impressionistic renditions can be made from watching this energetic species as it feeds, preens, plays, and exercises in a nearby pond. Don't exclude humor from your work!

The blue and Ross's geese are included here as variations. They are hunting and bird-watching favorites. (See Figure 4.11, *b* and *c*.)

The Canada goose and its close relatives, the Western Richardson's and cackling, comprise the largest of our waterfowl. The two brants can be classed among them because of generally similar markings and the fact of their popularity as prime game birds for sport and for the table.

All species nest far north, as far as northern Alaska, and migrate as far south as the Gulf of Mexico, thus covering the entire span of North America. They are all ground nesters, incubating from five to seven eggs that hatch into chicks which learn to fly and feed within a month of piercing the shell. The young migrate in the fall with the older stock. They are mainly grain feeders, preferring corn. The brants feed on eel grass and so are found to a great extent in brackish water or saltwater flats and marshes.

All species are protected by international migratory regulations, once again adapted by the various states through which they travel in the fall. The Canada goose and family are better eating than the brants, though all are eagerly sought after by the hunter. All species flock for migration, the Canadas usually forming a V-flight pattern across the sky.

Their prime colors are dark brown on the back and wings, with necks and heads of black—with a patch of white through the head in the case of the Canadas, and just below the head on the brants. Chests are mottled light brown with white underdressing. Feet are black. Canadas weigh between seven and eight pounds, the American and black brants weighing a little over three-and-a-half pounds.

Canadas are reputed to mate for life in the manner of swans. They show a great amount of intelligence and are very brave in the protection of their nests and young.

All species have shown an increase over the past few years due to the great conservation activity on the state and national level. Sporting organizations are largely responsible for their comeback. Only pollution and destruction of wetlands can threaten their supply.

White-Fronted Goose (*Anser albifrons*) and Blue Goose (*Chen caerulescens*)

The white-fronted goose is also known as specklebelly, so named because of the black-and-white splotches on the breast and underparts. The rest of the bird is brownish, mottled with gray. The pinkish bill with its white feather guard just in front of the eyes identifies it with certainty. Legs are light yellowish-orange. White-fronted geese weigh between four and five pounds. They nest in the Yukon, the Arctic, and across to Hudson's Bay and migrate down through California and into central Mexico and the Texas Coast, winging their way in V-formation in the manner of Canada geese. (See Figure 4.11*a*.)

The Blue Goose, known as blue brant, nests in the upper Hudson's Bay region and winters along the Gulf of Mexico, flying down the Mississippi River migration route. Although this bird is not as numerous as the white front, it is hunted widely when regulations allow. The male has a long white neck, and the rest of the bird is a gray-black and white, with pinkish-colored legs and bill. Many of these geese suffered setbacks in numbers until strict conservation laws and migratory sanctuaries were set up for them. They are on the increase now and are easily identified in the spring and fall migration periods, when they arrive at the safety zones to rest and feed up for the next leg of their journey. They feed mainly on roots and sedges, grasses, and other delectables found in marsh and lowlands. Sometimes rice, grains, and wheat comprise their diet.

They are prized on the table, and some farmers raise them for their excellent eggs. When nesting, five or six eggs are laid. The young join the migration southward that same season.

In the family grouping of these birds is the equally popular snow goose, found in the Pacific and the central Atlantic states.

Snow Goose (*Anser caerulescens*) and Ross's Goose (*Anser rossi*)

These white geese practically light up in the sky, their white bodies contrasted by jet black wingtips and bright orange bills. The sexes are alike in coloration. They weigh approximately two-and-a-half pounds and range in length from twenty-one to twenty-six inches.

Like all geese, their food is primarily vegetable matter consisting of grasses, grains, and aquatic vegetation. In company with other geese, they prefer grainfields, marshes, ponds, and lakes and are often found mixing together with the different species—which does not facilitate identification!

They fly in modified V-formation, or in bunches strung out over a long span, and their flight pattern is strong and powerful. This species winters almost exclusively in central California. (See Figure 4.11*c*.)

Figure 4.1 Ducks, especially the mallard, have always been popular with illustrators and artists, and you can become one of them by following the simple instructions herein. After the experience of the very detailed upland birds, many of the ducks will be far simpler, though they demand much more flexibility of expression. Their bodies are more elastic and potentially more active than the ground birds.

Shown here in wash is the typical view of the flying male and female mallard, to show the difference in sex markings. Note I have drawn an enlarged outline around the male. This is to suggest you work larger than I do here. Note in both flyers that you can see the pen-and-ink outlines through the wash covering. I have left them this way purposely so you can see the steps from outline to softened wash. You should carry them one step further to almost, but not entirely, obliterate the lines, keepng them only where needed for accent. The wing example shows its proportions, how it is bent, and the laid-over layers of feathers that make it up. Note the shoulder pad—the brightly colored secondary feathers—which are best shown in color, of course, being normally the brightest part of the bird. Check your bird books for the colors of these secondary bands. Note the direction of the feathers. The eleven flight feathers overlap each other from the body out to the wing tip, but the secondaries overlap in the *opposite direction* leading down to the shoulder pad. Shade them accordingly and, if you work large, include the feather stem, usually shown as a white line. You will note in the duck's head that there is a dark line that usually goes through the eye. This is to show the curving of the head and the pouchy underside of the head as shown in the upper line drawing. The beak detail is enlarged to show the general makeup of a typical bill. The bills vary with the species, so don't get the wrong bill on the wrong bird.

It would be worth your while to visit a nearby park and watch the mallards as they play in a pond, chasing each other and other birds, feeding, washing, sleeping, scratching, and generally cruising about at their leisure. Make quick preliminary sketches of what you see, or better, take lots of photographs for study in the studio. The mallard is so common that everyone has seen one illustrated at some time, and people will be quick to find your flaws. Note how the bird rests on the water or walks on the land. Note the details of the feet. The mallard at the bottom is feeding underwater, a typical pose you can use in an illustration. They are fun birds and easy to study. Bring your visual memories to the drawing table and experiment with them.

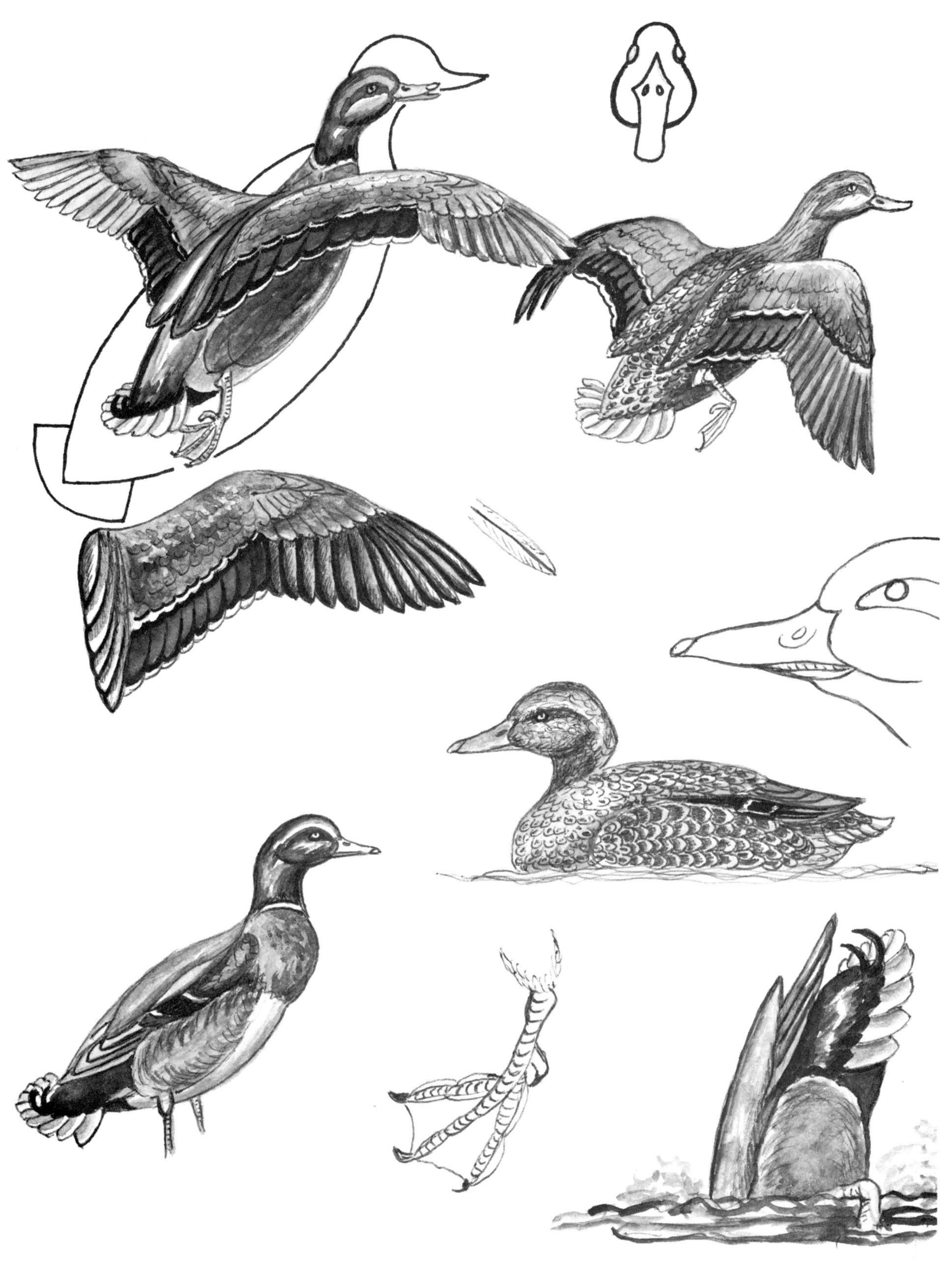

Figure 4.2 The pintail duck is different from all others because of the length of its neck. The pintail's neck is longer, almost as long as some geese, though relatively thin and graceful. Here's your chance to show that grace in the flying or standing bird. You can make it almost swanlike, and its strong head marking will help you to accent it. The wing shape is not as stocky as the mallard, a bit longer, you should note. The female is done in pen and ink to show the detailed markings of the feathers. She requires much more work than the male, but is pretty nonetheless. If you want to be impressionistic, you can merely indicate those feather markings based on the samples shown here. *a* is the feather on the back and shoulder; *b* is the flank feather composition. The closeup of the head is always a good subject for a portrait.

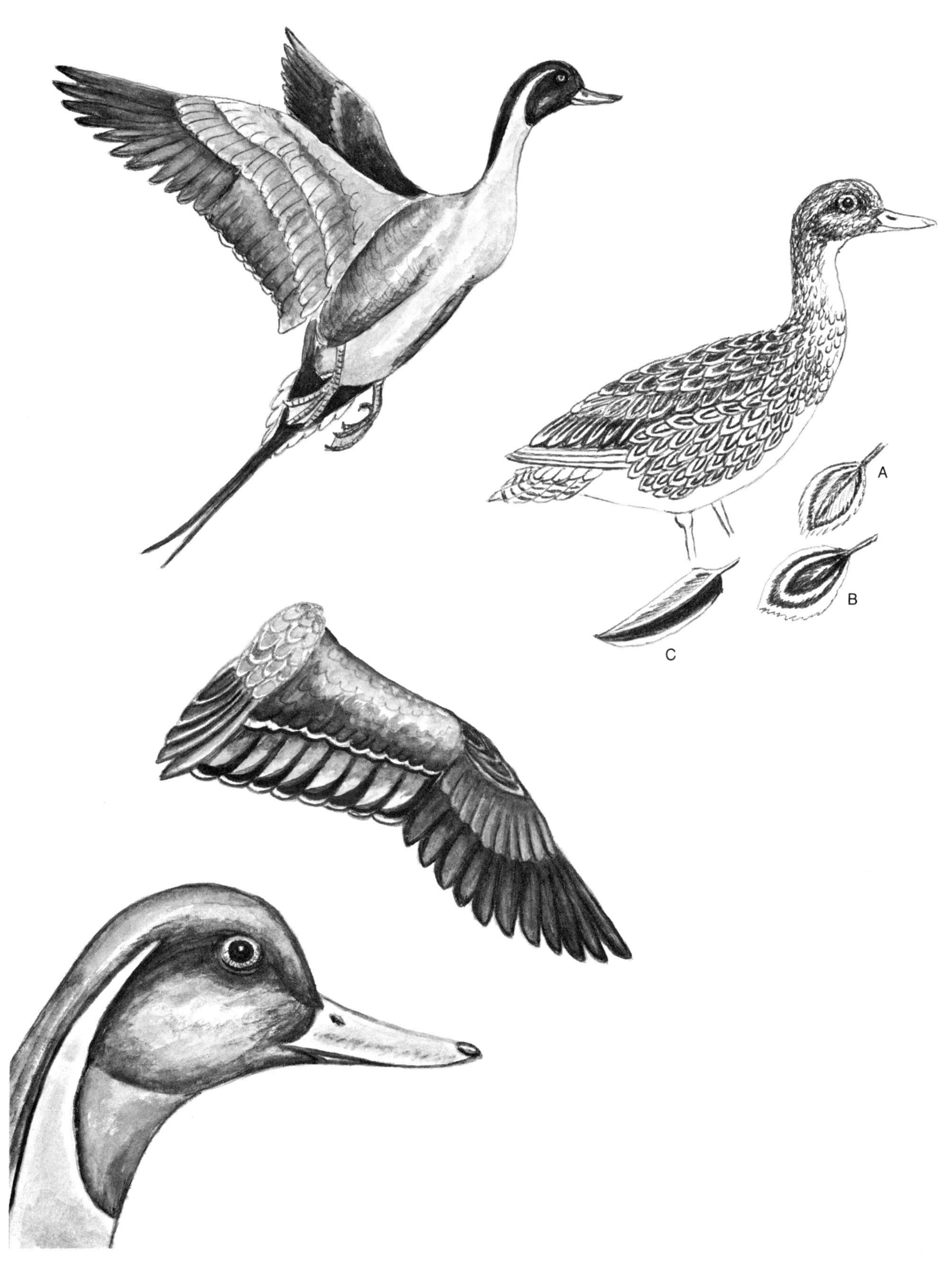
A
B
C

Figure 4.3 To lead off in this lesson on blue-winged teal, note the outlined positions of the ducks from left to right as they appear to be rising up from the water, flying along and then dropping down for a splash landing. Study all these poses and check magazine photographs and the works of other artists for accuracy. You have a great variety of positions to use in your rendering that will produce a mood in the picture.

Mallards, blacks, teal, wigeon, wood ducks, and gadwalls are all "puddle ducks" that rise quickly from the water, as contrasted to the diving ducks such as the redhead and canvasback.

The blue-winged teal is very specially colored and marked. With the detail lessons behind you, you are in for fun rendering the teal with as much precision as you did the upland bird species. The females all have quite detailed and distinct markings, but the males often outdo them in color and dramatics. The blue-wing is noted for his half-moon white band on the head, behind the bill and in front of the eye, and his blue head as well as blue wing patch. The overlapping shoulder feathers are also a distinction of this bird and its cousin, the green-winged teal. Study the detail here, start with your bare outline and then zone in, followed by the placing of the actual feather markings. If you are going to work in pencil, use a sharp point and then follow with the shading. If you work in pen and ink, you will merely pen over the pencil markings. If you work in wash, fill in the pen markings, leaving white or bright areas with a very light touch, if any.

Following the idea of flight patterns, place three or five birds in flight. A good way to do this is to make cutouts and move them around on the paper until you get a pleasing combination. Avoid the flat look of birds on the land. Move them around and, when doing a pair, have them paying attention to each other in some way.

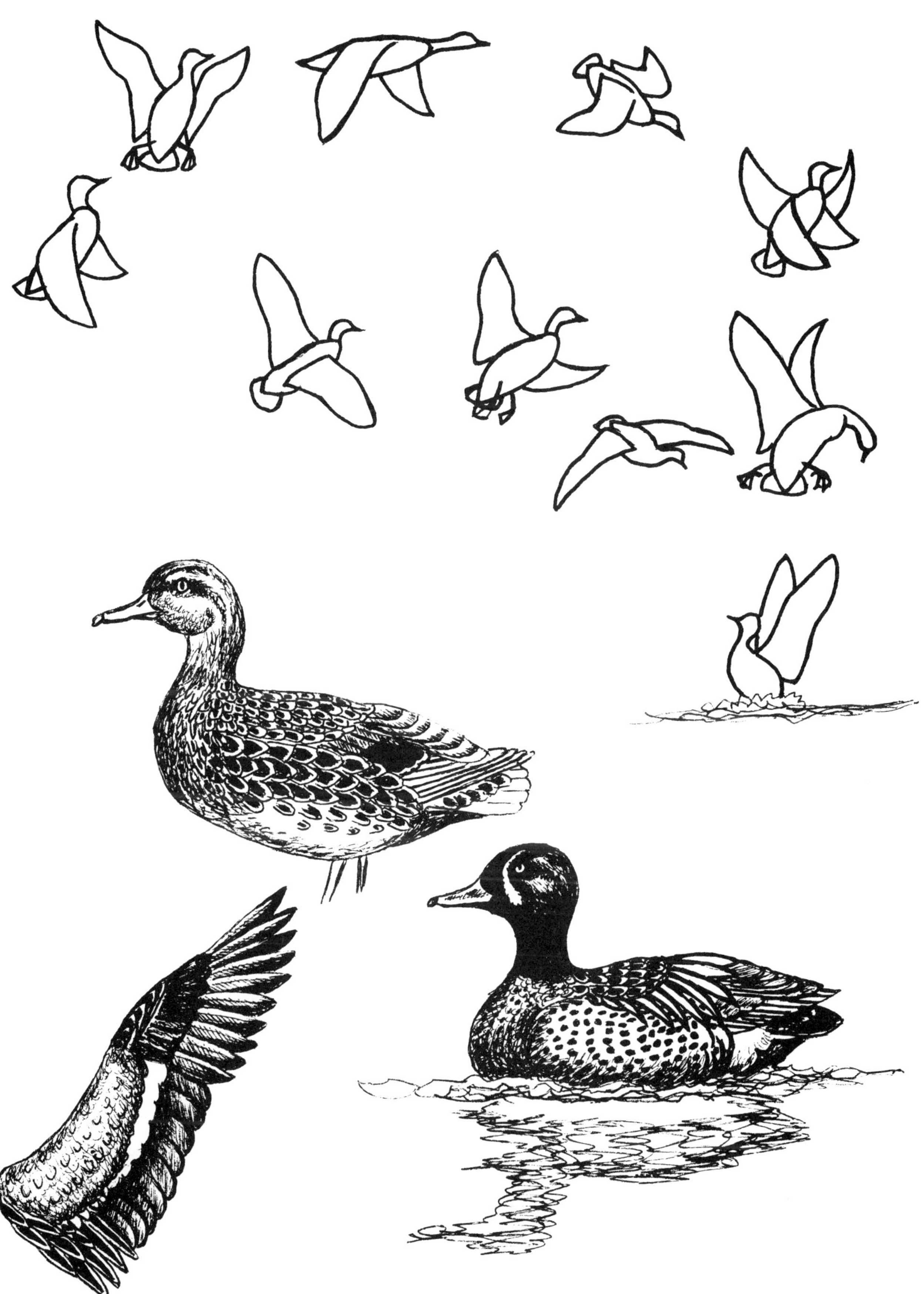

Figure 4.4 To start you off on the next project, that of grouping your flying birds and (in this case) overlapping them, the pencil sketch at the top of the page shows three green-winged teals, two males and a female, winging their way across the sky in grand style. In this case their wing motions are almost the same in order to give the impression of a synchronized flight pattern and also to show the colorful secondary bar markings. Note that the top bird is slightly smaller than the one in the lower left, whose wing overlaps slightly. The female's head is brought in to overlap the far duck, giving the illusion of distance between them and perspective. The picture could include smaller birds in the background to further show depth.

The teal's head pictured in pencil shows how the gradations of color—the chestnut head with its green insert surrounded by a whitish, yellow band—is rendered. Almost too perfect, here it is done in this fashion to show the construction of the head's feather combinations. Loosen up on this one a little, it isn't always so pat. The pen and ink of the male shows just how the detailing can be rendered in this magnificent bird. Note the white half-moon strip just ahead of the wing on the upper breast. This can be seen from quite a distance when the light is right on the bird. The overlapping black-and-white shoulder feathers drape well over the flank feathers. The female doesn't carry the crest or any of the male markings. She is kept drab for protective coloration when sitting on the nest. Note the feather detail I have included for your ease in working. Turn that pen-and-ink duck around to about a three-quarter view and then go to work. You'll have a nice picture.

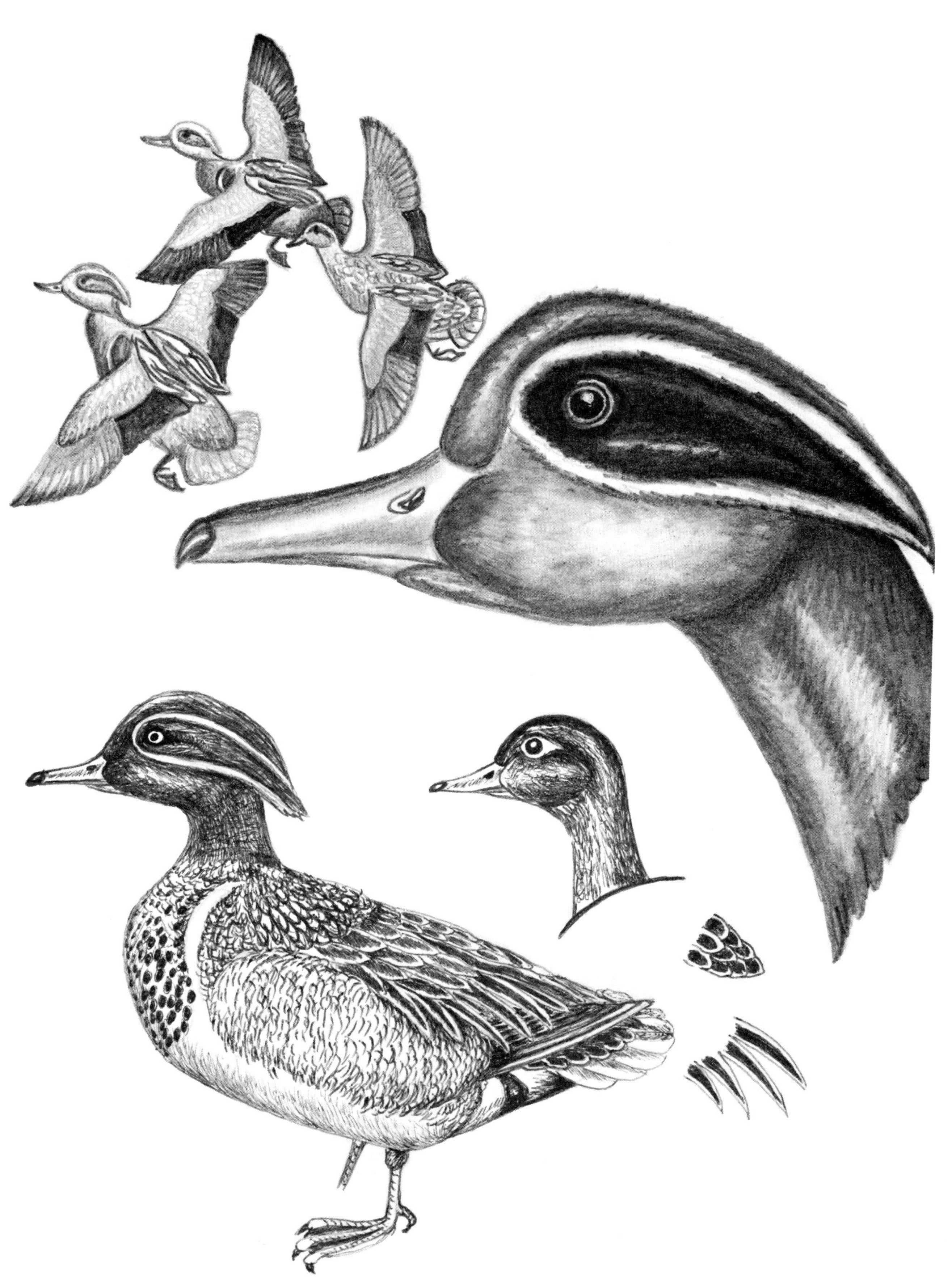

Figure 4.5 You are intentionally left alone on this one, the wood duck. Actually, we did some preliminary work on it in Chapter 1, so I would like you to concentrate on ways to angle the wings when the bird is in this position. Move the bird around into another angle and try and direct the wings so they appear to be in correct position for flight. It is great practice to work this way, checking against your research file of good photographs and pictures done by other artists. Always check the proportions of the wings to the body and the head to the body. Don't make the feet too large or too small.

Working from this bare outline (and referring to your research for feather combinations, how they lie and sometimes fold), you should be able to do a nice pencil sketch, an even better wash, and, if you are painstaking, a fine pen and ink of this magnificent bird. Play around, experiment with wing positions and body angles, and then, whatever your feather training, fill in and finish. Work as large as the example here at first. When you want to go smaller you can group some birds as shown in other drawings in this chapter.

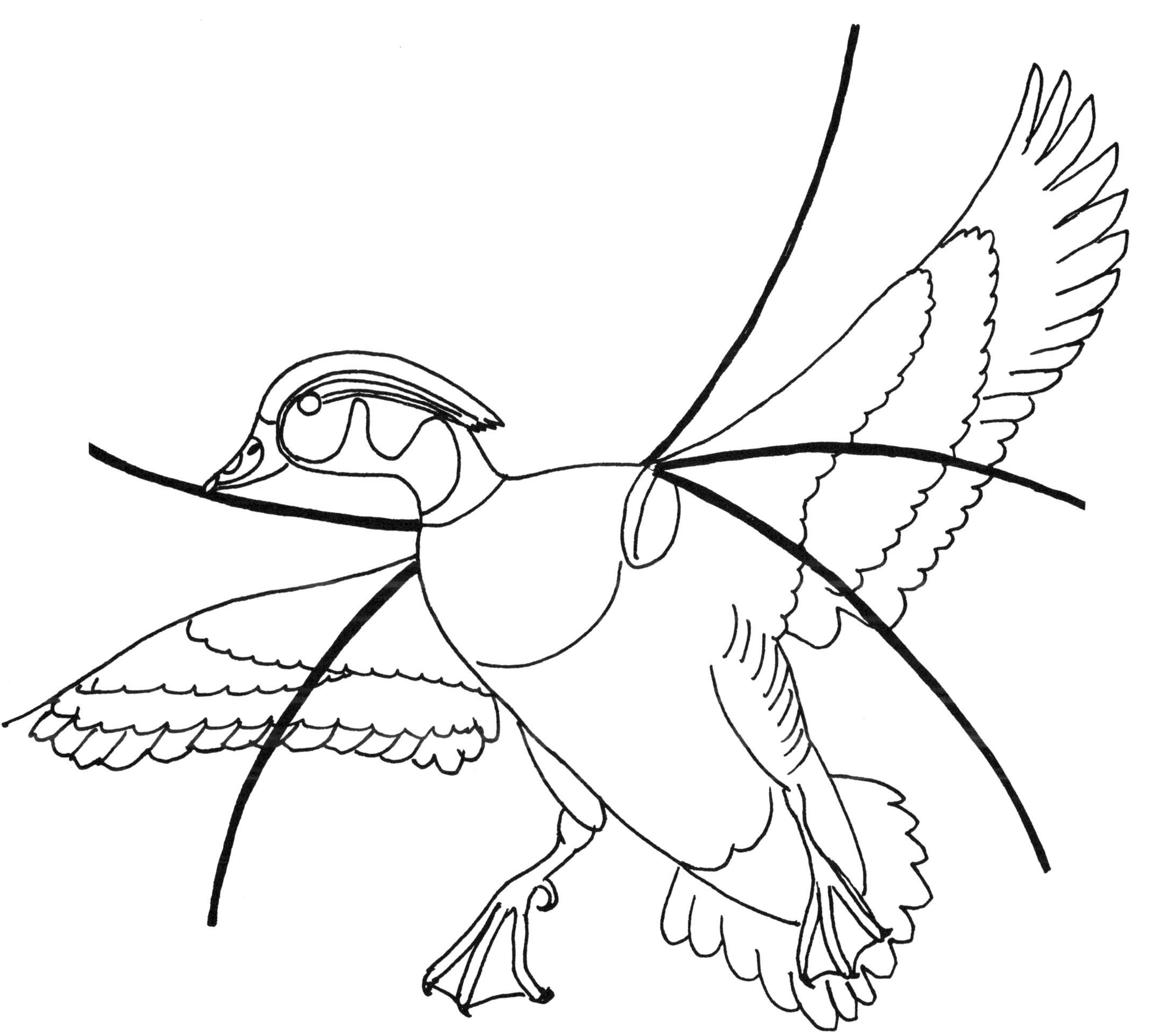

Figure 4.6 Look at this flight of some ten canvasbacks whizzing by in close formation. One of the fastest and most direct of flyers, the canvasback means business when underway; this is a characteristic that can be shown by drawing it in a sleek, clean line, suggesting unlimited speed. Grouped together like this, you can take the same number of birds and come up with a completely different layout. You will note that most of the ducks in this flock are showing their backs. It is interesting to note that ducks flying in a group often wing in unison, carbon-copy lookalikes of each other. This is also quite apparent when ducks or geese are seen flying in a line or in the customary V-formation, so don't be afraid of drawing many of these birds in your layout with the same general wing pattern. Overlap them, playing up the light and dark shading.

The canvasback is a diving duck and, along with many other species, has to skip along the water surface until it gets enough lift under its wing to take off. Therefore, don't draw it rising straight up as you would the mallard. This species has an unusually long beak, sharply pointed forehead, and longish head blending into its fairly thick neck. All diving ducks have shorter wings than the puddle ducks, and their wings are also squatter or broader.

This pen and ink of the canvasback shows the direction of pen marks to indicate feather markings and to show the form of the head and bill. A softer version based on the same lines can be done in wash or even pencil and appear a lot smoother. The pen and ink is here to show how marking should be done in the first stage. Even this drawing could be enhanced with wash. Note the foot and beak detail.

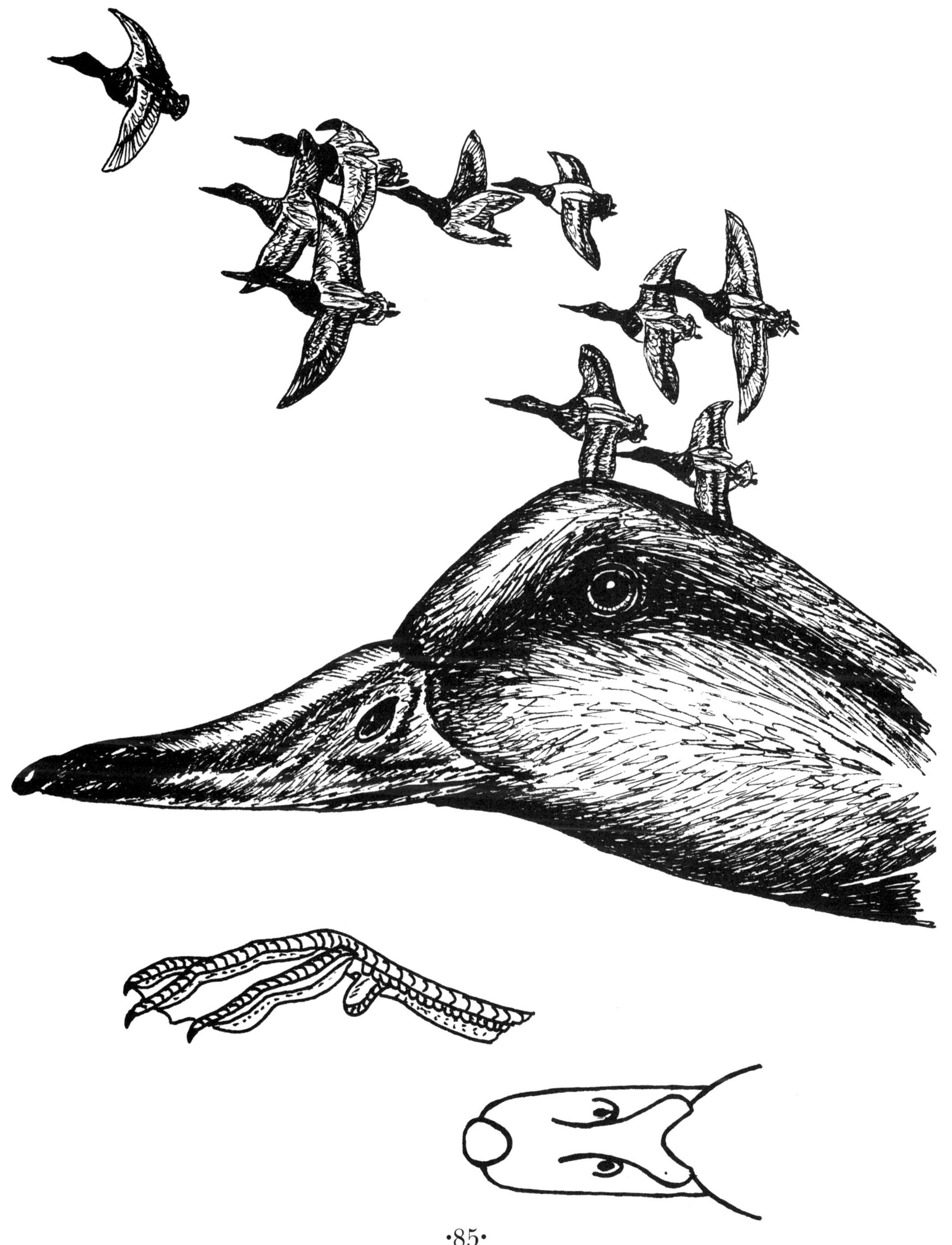

Figure 4.7 These are redhead ducks. The fellow in the middle done in wash, heading almost right toward you, gives the impression of standing in midair as he puts on the brakes by lowering feet, flapping wings, and lowering his tail. This interesting pose, not usually done by the conventional artist, is an effective one, especially when several other birds are included coming in for a dramatic landing right in front of you.

I have left the bird in the lower left up to you to complete, along the lines of the bird shown in the center since they are both wash drawings. Note the beginning of the shading of head and neck and of the rounded chest. Follow through with your pencil or brush, or both, and do as well as I did. Make sure you shade the feathers correctly and artistically—not too well defined, yet not vague either. Be accurate.

The two little ducks in the left corner are merely additional outlines to make use of as they, too, are heading in, about to stall their speed and make their descent.

Note the bill lines of this bird, and study the bird books for the colorations that are unique to this species.

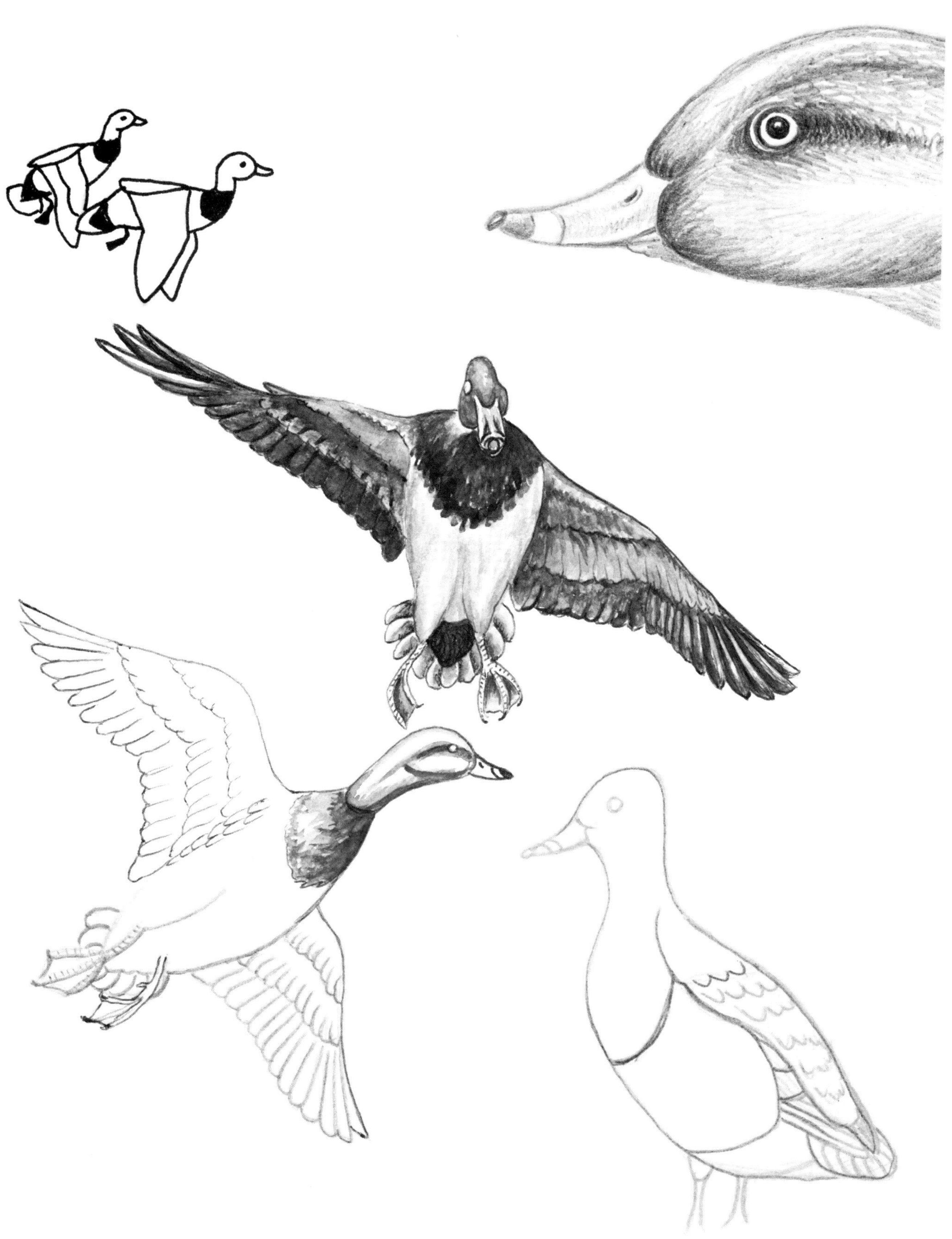

Figure 4.8 A bird as pretty as the teal, the American wigeon is a fast flyer that darts around in the sky and sometimes takes off on strange flight patterns. Here's a good chance to ad lib with the wing directions and the twists of the head and neck. I have not finished the bird but rather have indicated where to go with brush, pencil, and pen. The head and neck are left alone. If you wish to finish them in pen and ink, merely shade in a little, leaving the black spots to stand out—also the white top or "pate" of the head, and the dark-green head insert that is surrounded by a thin black line.

The shoulder of the wing is almost a white color and should appear so in contrast to the rest of the wing. I have shown the wing's flight feathers merely lined in with feather fiber markings, penciled in and washed in, in stages to show how to proceed.

The line of the abdomen is just suggested here and is dark, assuming that you are going to show the underwing as being darker.

The bottom wing is left blank for your experimentation. Note that the feet are relaxed and slightly lowered from the flight position they assume when the bird is fully underway, that is, straight back and under the tail feathers.

With the fill-in and blending experience you have gained so far in this book, it should be an easy task to fill in this bird in whatever medium you choose and end up with a good rendition of this pretty little fellow.

His mate is drab in coloration, though she has definite markings, especially in the flank feathers, that you can pick up from photos or from your favorite bird book.

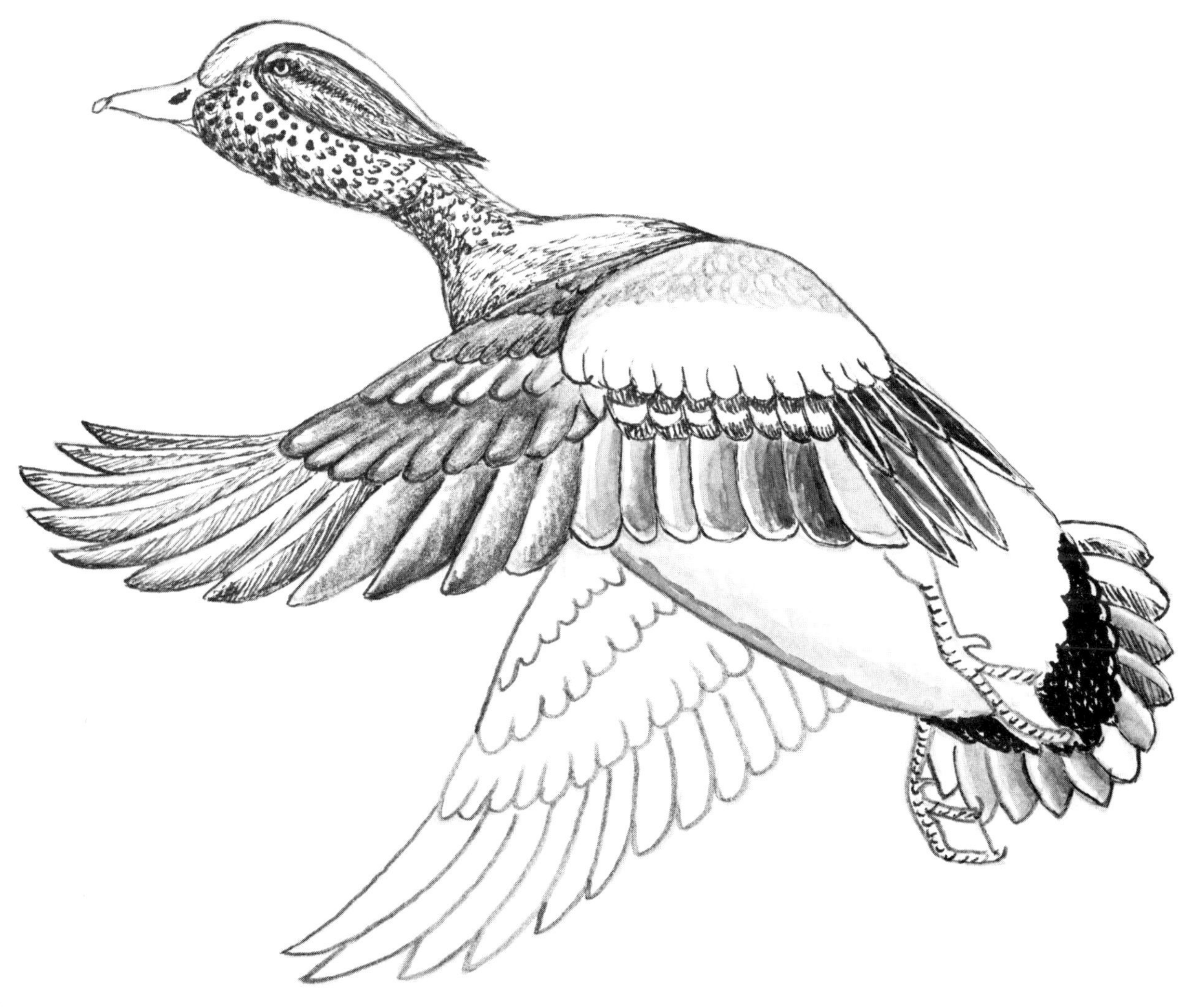

Figure 4.9 The shoveller is the real weirdo of the duck family. No one knows what got into Mother Nature when she fashioned this one. The shoveller's unique with its long, broad, and heavy-looking bill and its special manner of feeding. Don't ask why, just use this bird for an appealing subject, whether it be a closeup study of head and bill or in a candid position to bring out the duck's characteristic shape.

The shoveller's a colorful duck, small in size yet a very active species and quite common. Instantly recognizeable in a flock of ducks on the pond, the shoveller invites notice and comment. Put your comments on paper. Your work will get a smile.

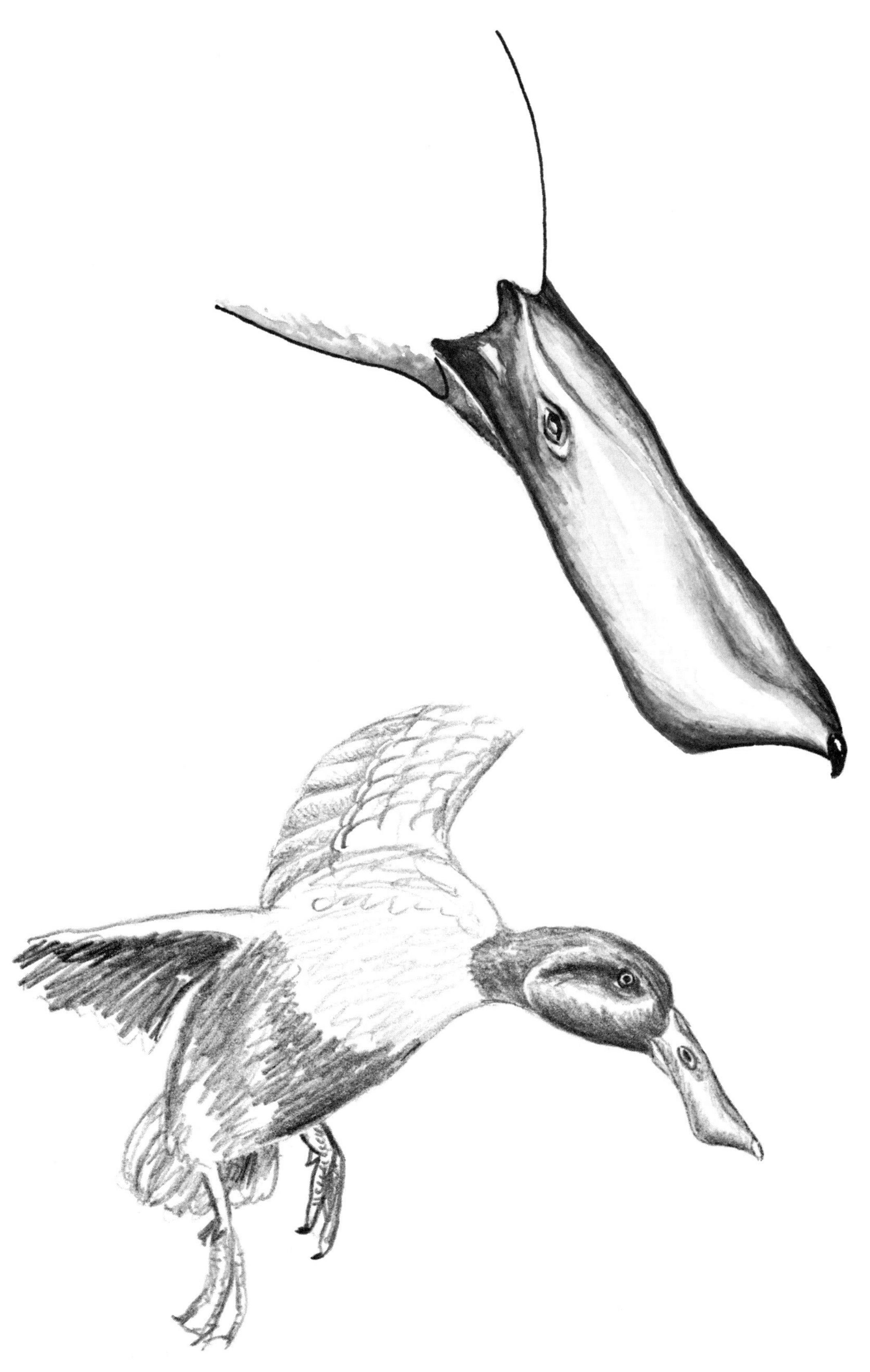

Figure 4.10 Canada geese are just big ducks with long necks and small heads. Note the variety of rendering possibilities in the four flying geese, the first done in pen and ink, the second in pencil, the third in stronger pencil and a little pen to strengthen, and lastly the wash version.

Take your choice, and if you like the wash technique for this bird, take a look at the big goose in the center of the picture. Note that the feathers on the back and sides are all ringed in white, though in actual color they are yellowish against a tan background. This technique is done easily with the outline of the feathers done in a broad pencil and the coloring of the feathers put in around the pencil markings. When the fill-in is complete, all you have to do is erase the pencil and, lo, there is the effect you looked for. The darker wingtip feathers are merely intensified more than the body feathers. The white tail band, a prominent marking on this bird, is left open and accented by the slightly darker tail feathers.

The sketches of the two Canadas coming in for a landing represent a typical sight on prairies and cornfields, or as they are seen from a blind by hunters. They come in fast, tilt sideways like some pilots do to slough the wind out from under their wings for the quick descent, put their feet down and, there, they are in.

Note the distinctive beak outline that is quite different from any of the ducks. It is almost pointed, but broad at the base with the suggestion of the angle of the head.

The brant, a close member of this family, is a stockier bird than the Canada goose with almost the same markings. Since the Canada is quite a hunter's favorite, you will see many good photographs of it in magazines such as *Field & Stream* and *Sports Afield.* The Canada is a majestic bird and one to render in a positive, proud way, whether it be standing guard over its nest, defending itself against an intruder, or soaring high and fast in the traditional V-formation across the wetlands. Capture its freedom, zest, and smooth aerodynamic form and, when you do a closeup, try and give it a little personality.

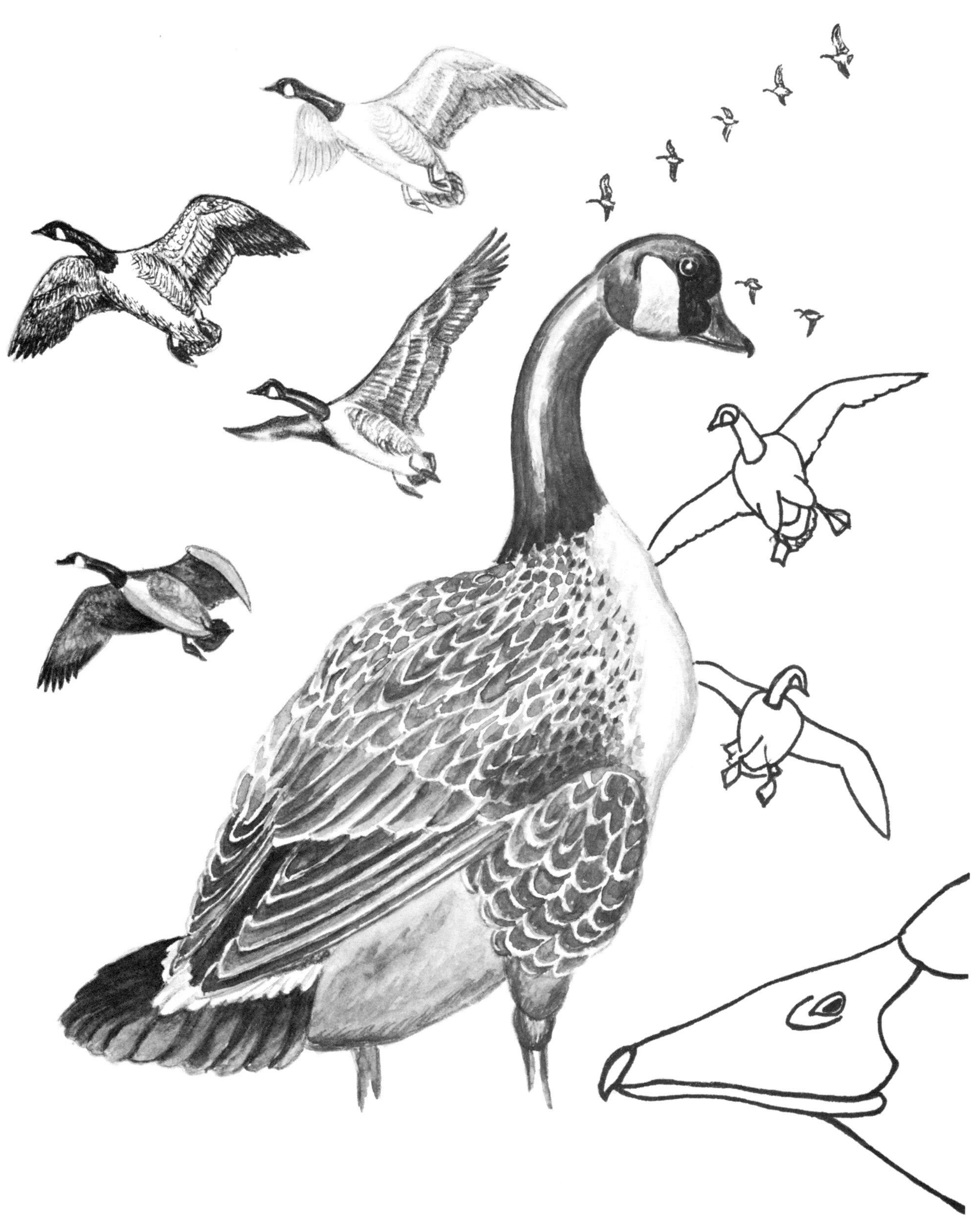

Figure 4.11 Shown here are three of the most popular of the geese, the white-fronted goose, blue goose, and snow goose, drawn in pen and ink to show the differences in markings and characteristics. Note especially the difference in wing values and feather arrangements. Again, here is your opportunity to overlap them in a bunched up aerial flyway and show both backs and fronts as they fly by, or group them in a small cluster beside the water, feeding, resting, even sleeping.

Geese can be fun. And if you allow your creativity to run a little rampant, you can end up with an imaginative picture, not a caricature but a dramatic portrayal of an incident in the life of these unusual birds.

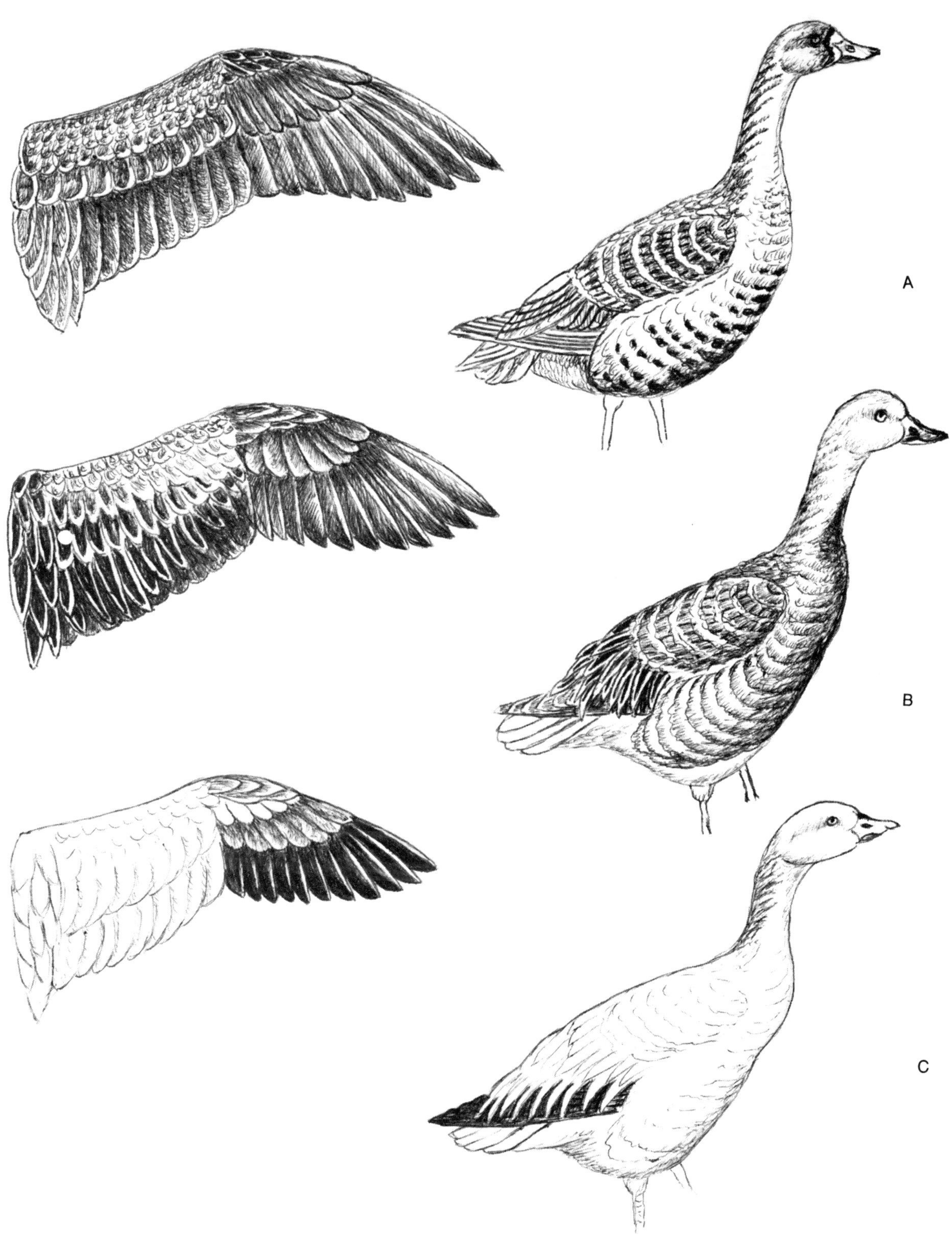
A
B
C

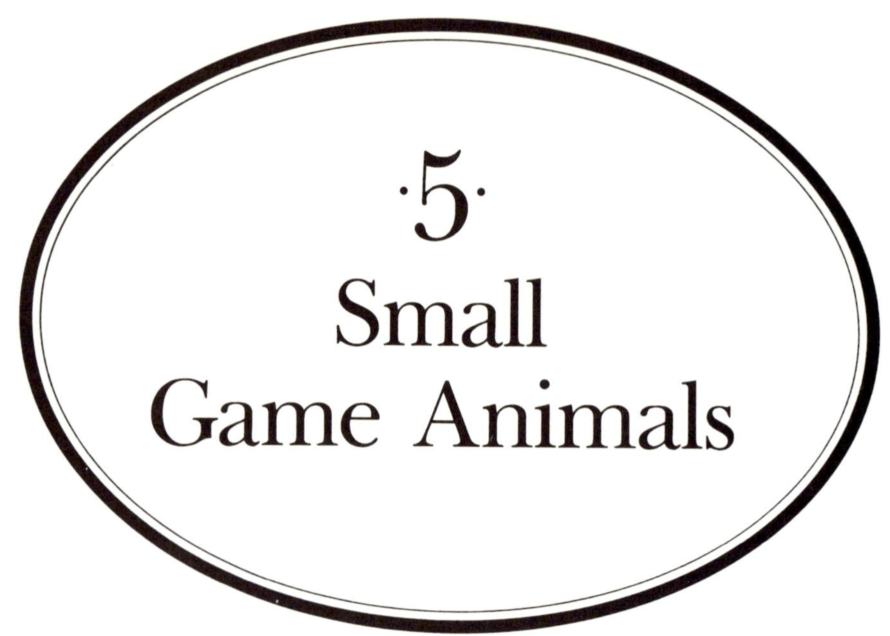

·5· Small Game Animals

The rendering of game animals, small or large, requires more attention to the actual animal form than do birds, generally speaking. The species covered here, a cross section of the smaller animals that inhabit this country, are the best known and loved by naturalists, animal watchers, and hunters.

You will see in the following pages just how to render the various types of fur: the tufts found on the bobcat; the longer hairs of the squirrel's tail; the shiny stickiness of the beaver's pelt. You will also find that you have unlimited freedom of expression as you create a particular motion or act being performed by the animal. Here, eye expression, the tilt of an ear, the twitch of a tail, the relaxed pose or the alarm pose, can all be shown in striking emphasis. Color or the rendering of shades of color is very important to lend authenticity to your drawing. Good photos, good artwork by experts, and preferably some actual observation of these animals is a great help. Few of us have ever seen a fox in the wild, but the thrill of that quick view is etched deeply in our memory.

The many species of small game that inhabit this country and Canada afford much inspiration for hunting and nature study. More hunting licenses are issued for the harvesting of the small game crop, especially rabbits, than all other species of game birds and animals. A great percentage of hunters also prefer to hunt predators, particularly in the time of the year when the formal hunting season is closed. The naturalist is limited to no season, and these animals afford a continual source of interest, whether for the animal watcher or photographer.

Most of the small game animals are found in abundance everywhere, many of them residing in or near the farmer's fields. Many of the more wary species can be seen in remote fields and forests and particularly in national parks and state forest preserves. Some are hunted with the aid of dogs; others are patiently stalked. Several are nocturnal (active only at night) and are either treed, cornered by dogs, or trapped.

The animals covered in this chapter are the most common and easily studied. Many are, like the game birds, to be considered a game crop, to be harvested each fall after the young have grown wise and strong. Many are completely unprotected by law, being either numerous enough not to require controlled hunting or, as in the case of some pests, to be held in control by hunting. Several are fur-bearing animals of value in the market. However, most people today are against the killing of these animals in their wild state merely for the sake of their pelts. (This does not apply to ranch-raised beaver, mink, etc.) The other interest in game animals is, of course, their highly esteemed food quality on the gourmet's table.

Despite the fact that they hunt them, sportsmen have always been the main source of protection for these animals. Through their license fees and club efforts, great strides in wildlife conservation have been made, giving these species protection from overhunting and trapping, better living conditions and habitat, and a general increase in numbers so that all can see, enjoy, photograph, and hunt them. Millions of sportsmen's dollars have been the sole annual support of conservation bureaus in Washington and of game commissions on the state and private preserve level.

The future of game animals and game birds, in fact all wildlife, lies in educating more people to know these creatures of our land. This will create a much wider interest in protecting them and their habitat, for the ecology which supports them also supports man himself. And, the artist is their greatest "salesman."

Raccoon *(Procyon lotor)*

Found from the woods of the northeast down to Florida and west to the dry areas, and across the north country to British Columbia, the raccoon is abundant in the wilderness and also quite numerous in settled regions. Primarily a nocturnal animal, the raccoon is sly and crafty, often raiding garbage cans and refuse dumps.

As a game animal, the raccoon provides fine sport for hunters with dogs, because a smart 'coon can lead hunters into the worst tangles of forests and will elude the smartest dogs. The raccoon is also trapped for its valuable fur. It makes a good pet, either as a temporary visitor or actually in captivity. Full of fun, wearing an unusual mask of black across its face, the raccoon is inquisitive and pesky. It is easily recognized in the flash of the car lights by its mask and the black-and-white ringed tail. Its fur is rather coarse and ranges from brown-black to gray-brown. Though primarily a vegetarian, it will eat almost anything that man leaves behind.

There is little danger of extinction, except by the removal of den trees and the destruction of forests and swamps the raccoon inhabits near new houses and industrial plants. Although an egg robber and considered by some a pest, the raccoon is protected in most states by annual hunting seasons.

Due to a wide distribution and varying conditions, the raccoon ranges in weight from twelve to sixteen pounds and attains a length of from thirty to forty inches. It generally has a ten-inch tail. Found in most of the United States and southern Canada, the only area where it is seldom found is in the high Rocky Mountains. As to habits, it is one of the most adaptable of all animals and can live comfortably but slyly with man. It walks with a shuffling sort of gait but can cover the ground quite rapidly to avoid dogs and other predators, and it is a tree-climbing expert. Raccoons breed during January and February and into March. Gestation is from sixty-three to sixty-four days and as many as five or six kits are born. Father helps with the chores. The normal life span is between seven and ten years. Some consider the meat of the raccoon to be quite good, unless of course the raccoons have been feeding from neighborhood garbage cans.

Underneath the coarse dark fur of the raccoon's body is a thick underfur of reddish brown, with the dark guard hairs tipped with white. The belly and the insides of the legs are pale yellowish or grayish. The muzzle and a band across the forehead are white, causing the black mask and nose pad to stand out in sharp contrast. Raccoons have five long toes on each foot, the forepaws being exceptionally limber—useable like hands to open jars and doors, pry into containers, and tear packages apart.

Red Fox *(Vulpes vulpes)* and Gray Fox *(Urocyon cinereoargenteus)*

The red fox and gray fox live in the more remote spots of almost all of the continental states, Mexico, and Canada. The red fox is better known because it tends to run and show itself more than the gray. The countless fables and stories about the cunning of the fox are true enough, although like any living creature they can be outwitted or even, at times, show some very unintelligent characteristics.

Both foxes are small animals and good targets for wildlife photographers and hunters. The red fox has been the chief actor in the sport of fox hunting and has been the traditional fur piece of fashion.

Both foxes give birth to as many as six or eight little ones. In a couple of months the youngsters are running about hunting for themselves. They eat anything that they can catch, from lizards, toads, and frogs to song, game, and other birds. Rabbits are one of their best staples. Often when the rabbit population becomes too thick, the foxes move in and control their numbers. As such, the fox is a valuable predator and worthy of protection.

They weigh between five and ten pounds and reach a length of three-and-a-half feet. Some gray foxes are larger, particularly in the more northern states. They build their nests in hollow trees and dug outs under rocks deep in the forests.

The fur of the red fox ranges in color from yellow to rust, with white-tipped tail and throat. In winter its coat is long and silky, the color in the more northern regions ranging to black, with some featuring black hairs tipped with white (the silver fox). The upper part of the fox's face is a rusty color with a black nose pad. The back is darkest, with light flanks shading to a white belly. The feet are black. Its tail is generally the same color as the back, lighter on the underside and featuring a large white tip. The tail is very bushy and almost cylindrical in shape. The fox has yellow eyes with elliptical pupils and pointed, erect ears.

The gray fox can be confused with the red fox because it also has a rusty-red color on its flanks, the ears, and the area directly below the ears. Its back and the top of its head, however, are a salt-and-pepper gray. The throat, chest, belly, and the inner sides of the legs are white. Its tail is gray with a conspicuous black band running down the top to the black tip. The gray fox has upright ears and dark eyes.

Both foxes have five toes on each front foot (four main toes and a dewclaw) and four toes on the hind feet.

Coyote *(Canis latrans)* and Timber Wolf *(Canis lycaon)*

The coyote and timber wolf, two doglike hunters of the northlands, have been grouped together because they have somewhat similar habits despite the fact that they live in different parts of the country.

The coyote ranges from Alaska to Central America and throughout the western parts of the United States and Canada. They prey on jack rabbits and other small game and pests and are not averse to gaining a meal of game birds or even songbirds. They are smart and crafty, often avoiding hounds that are specially trained to hunt them. They are also sly and able to live next to man despite the poisons and traps set to kill them. American folklore is filled with the wild tales of clever and fierce coyotes. From three to six pups in a litter is average, though as many as fourteen pups have been found in nests.

The timber wolf ranges from the Rocky Mountains to areas in the Great Lakes states, though it once ranged over the entire continental states. It survives because of its ability to reproduce in large whelps and is as tricky and sly as the coyote.

Both are excellent subjects for wildlife study. For the hunter they offer the challenge of difficult shots at long ranges, but they should be protected. Where they once kept small animals and pests in balance, their elimination has posed problems to conservationists.

Wolves and coyotes have five toes on the forefoot, although the "thumb," which is high on the foot, is merely a dewclaw. (This member is always removed from German shepherd puppies.)

The upper part of the coyote's face, the top of its head, and the outsides of the ears are a sandy reddish-gray sprinkled with black hairs. The inside of the ears and around the mouth and the throat are white, setting off the black nose pad. Their eyes are yellow with round black pupils. In general the body color ranges from dull yellow to gray, being darker on the back and whiter on the belly, with dark hairs on the back creating wavy lines and a dark tip at the end of the tail.

The coloration of the wolf ranges from nearly pure white to coal black, the underparts and the legs being lighter than the rest of the body. Wolf pups are covered with a woolly, soft brown hair, while the adults' fur is thick and long. The forefoot of the coyote is longer and narrower than a dog's, but the wolf's forefeet are extremely large as this animal is built much heavier in the shoulders than in the hindquarters.

Gray Squirrel *(Sciurus carolinensis)*

The gray squirrel of the city parks and suburban countryside is familiar to everyone who lives in the Northeast, Midwest, or South. It is the second largest of the squirrels, the fox squirrel of the southeastern states being a trifle larger. The gray squirrel is colored a smokey gray with a whitish chest and underparts. The tail is long and bushy, with whitish edges.

Like all the squirrel family, the gray is a nut and berry eater, also feeding on grains and seeds. The gray also likes birds' eggs and even eats young birds from the nest. It builds a nest high in the trees and raises a family of two to four, with mother doing all the family chores.

A keen sense of smell helps protect the gray squirrel, but its eyes can spot invaders, too, be they human, bird, or animal. It has fared well amidst the growth of civilization. As the big forests have disappeared, it has taken up residence in more civilized areas where trees and woods are protected. The gray likes to live with man and becomes quite tame except when hunted, when it turns crafty. One of the mainstays of the diet of Indians and settlers, it is still considered top table fare and is one of America's best known and appreciated small animals.

The common gray squirrel weighs about a pound, with a length of about twenty inches, somewhat shorter in the South. Of the total length, about eight inches is composed of the much admired, beautifully plumed tail. Salt-and-pepper gray is a good color description, the underfur being solid gray while the dark black guard hairs end in white tips. The face, muzzle, ears, and upper part of its paws are yellowish-tan, while the throat, underparts, and insides of its legs are a bright white. Squirrels have four toes on their forefeet and five toes on the hind feet. They have slightly pointed ears and long black whiskers and big, bright shiny eyes.

Cottontail Rabbit *(Sylvilagus)*

One of the favorite game animals in America, the cottontail covers the map with its various species. Where it is in scant supply, state conservation departments help by restocking and improving its habitat.

Rabbits are smaller than hares and jackrabbits. The cottontail does not shed its summer brown coat as does its cousin, the varying hare or snowshoe rabbit, but remains the same color all year long. Its ears are smaller in proportion to those of the hares.

Cottontails are essentially field residents, preferring the cover of forest and undergrowth into which they can run from foxes and other predators. Like all rabbits and hares, they are vegetarian.

The expectant mother rabbit makes her nest by scooping a depression in the ground and lining it with dead grass and fur pulled from her belly. As the young are born nearly naked and with their eyes sealed shut, the mother keeps them warm by covering them with a blanket of her pulled-fur mixed with grass. By the end of the first week the babies are fully furred, their eyes are open, and they can wriggle their ears. By three weeks they are weaned and leave the nest to be entirely on their own.

Generally, the body color of the cottontail is brown with a reddish or buff cast, with black-tipped guard hairs. The belly, chin, and insides of the legs are white. The underside of the tail is distinctly white, looking like a cotton ball as the rabbit bounces off to seek cover. They have five toes on each front foot and four toes on the hind feet.

The rabbit's sense of hearing is indispensable for survival, its ears constantly flicking backward and forward to catch the slightest sound. The ears are about three inches in length, lightly furred on the outside and almost bare on the inside. The large eyes protruding from the sides of the head provide a 180-degree range of vision not shared by other mammals. They range in length from fourteen to nineteen inches, standing about seven inches at the shoulder; the hind legs are about twelve inches and powerfully muscled.

Black-Tailed Jackrabbit *(Lepus californicus)* and White-Tailed Jackrabbit *(Lepus townsendii)*

The jackrabbit is the large rabbit species of the western states. It measures between twenty-two and twenty-six inches in length, with ears that are five to six inches long. In the South it becomes almost a silver-grey in winter, but never really changes coloration as does the northern snowshoe.

"Jacks" prefer the open rangeland and even the more habitable parts of the desert. They can run very fast for long distances and leap unbelievably high to avoid their enemies. Greyhounds were used in Europe and America years ago for the sport called *coursing*—no other hunting dogs could keep up with the fast-running jack.

Jackrabbits are quite a pest to western farmers because they can do great damage to crops. But in most instances the farmers leave the harvesting of the jack until hunting season, when they can gather some wonderful meals and put them in the freezer. Although not considered as good to eat as the cottontail, jacks are nonetheless a prime game animal in the West and were one of the mainstays in the diet of the first settlers. There is little danger of losing this species because they have sufficient land in which to roam and are not affected by civilization.

The white-tailed jackrabbit weighs between six and ten pounds and reaches a length of about twenty-six inches. This is the largest of the species, with ears five to six inches long and a tail that is white on top and bottom. In the summer this jackrabbit is a light brownish-gray over the back and sides, lighter on the belly, with black tips on the ears. During the winter, in the northern regions, it turns white all over so that the only features to distinguish it from the Arctic hare are its long ears and extra-long legs.

The black-tailed jackrabbit has black on its back and also sports a black rump. This jack weighs between four and seven pounds and reaches from eighteen to twenty-four inches. Its ears are longer than those of the white-tail, measuring up to seven inches. Its back is brownish-gray with some black lines in it, the underfur being an off-white. The belly and underside of the tail are white. The ears have black tips, being brown on the inside and whitish on the outside.

Both varieties have bright yellow eyes protruding from the sides of the head, with black pupils. The hind legs of all jacks are longer than usual rabbits' and are used for prodigious jumping and sprinting in the face of danger. The hind feet of the white-tailed jack are over six inches long, while those of the black-tail are just over five inches. They have five toes on each forepaw and four toes on each hind foot.

Their sense of smell seems to be developed to a higher degree than the cottontails, since the desert country swarms with more kinds of danger that the jackrabbit must detect.

Young jackrabbits are born fully furred with their eyes wide open, weighing from two to six ounces. At birth their ears are short but grow rapidly. Shortly after birth, the mother scatters her young to lessen the danger of a predator wiping out the entire family. In a week the young jackrabbits are able to eat vegetation, have finished nursing, and are on their own.

Varying Hare (Showshoe Rabbit) *(Lepus americanus)*

The snowshoe rabbit is really a hare, although it is a member of the same family as the jackrabbit. Because hunters who seek it out in the wintry fields insist on the name "showshoe rabbit," the term *rabbit* has stuck despite scientists' objections.

The varying hare changes its coloration during late summer and early fall, molting from the usual brown to a snowy white for protection from predators during the long winters. This change occurs regardless of whether there is any snow on the ground.

Of medium build, the snowshoe is sometimes a little larger than the cottontail but is smaller than the big western jack. Found in the northern sector of the country from coast to coast, this species thrives on mountaintops and in remote areas as well as in swamps, forests, and brush. Seemingly indifferent to man, it often lives close to farms and settlements. In certain areas of the east where it has been disturbed and hunted hard, the snowshoe has taken to the high hills, thick brush, and laurel groves. Predators have also been a factor in keeping it away from the lowlands. Snowshoes feel safer when there are places to hide at the slightest sign of danger.

Weighing between three and four-and-a-half pounds, they measure about twenty-one inches in length, standing eight to nine inches at the shoulder. In summer they are brown, sometimes grayish, with a dark line running along the spine to a dark rump and tail. The throat is reddish-brown, with the chin, belly, and underside of the tail being white. Their feet are large and hairy, enabling them to run across deep snow that would bog down other animals. There are five toes on the forefeet and four on the hind feet.

The young are born fully furred with their eyes wide open. Within hours they are hopping around, and within a week they are eating vegetation and beginning to wean themselves.

American Beaver *(Castor canadensis)*

Most valued for its pelt, the American beaver has been bred in captivity from specimens captured in the wild. The beaver is not popular with the woodsman, and is hunted for its pelt and killed because of the damage it does to trees. Comparatively easy prey for the big predators, the beaver has a hard life in the ever-shrinking wilderness. Conservation measures are enforced for the beaver's protection despite the forestry industry's dislike for it. Actual restocking of the beaver has been accomplished in areas where its effects upon forests are limited.

Found in the northeast clear across northern America to Alaska, the beaver is a regular inhabitant of swamps and mountain woodlands. It dams up small streams, makes a pond, and builds a stick nest with grass and mud in the center or along the edge where predators cannot enter. When alarmed while swimming, a beaver will slap its tail on the water with a resounding *thwack,* so that all other beavers get the message, and then dive for the protection of its den. Beavers have teeth strong enough to cut into a good-sized tree.

About the size and shape of a woodchuck, the beaver's body is approximately two feet long. The tail is flat and leathery, about a foot long, while its feet are semiwebbed. The beaver has a black nose; short, stiff whiskers; and small ears rounded like a bear's, lying close to the head. The short, dense fur is a uniform dark color. (See Figure 5.7*c*.)

Opossum *(Didelphis marsupialis)*

Another of the more nocturnal species of animals, the opossum inhabits most of the country except the dry deserts. Although hardly a sporting challenge, opossums are hunted as avidly as the raccoon and considered good food by some. Opossums are easily caught in traps, treed by dogs, or merely shot by a hunter who may spy one lumbering clumsily along a path or hanging from the branch of a tree.

The fur is thick with guard hairs that are dark with silver tips, giving the opossum a salt-and-pepper coloration. The underfur, however, is a cottony white. Against the darker body, the opossum has a white face, pink nose, black eyes, and black ears that often feature white rims.

The opossum is the only mammal in North America that has a prehensile tail that can be used for grasping, and in fact opossums hang by their tails while they are sleeping. The long, ratlike tail is nearly devoid of hair. There are five toes on each foot. The legs and feet are black while the toes are white. The opossum's hind foot, with its opposable thumb, looks remarkably like a human hand. All the toes on the feet have claws except this thumb. (See Figure 5.7*b*.)

When the young are born they are tiny and hairless and not fully developed. Their hind feet are mere stubs, but the forefeet are developed, including toenails, which they must use to pull themselves from the birth canal into the mother's pouch, where they must immediately fasten themselves to a teat. There are usually thirteen teats inside the pouch. If there are more babies than teats, any baby that doesn't find one at the start perishes and is expelled. The surviving babies remain fastened to the teat for four to five weeks in the sheltering warmth of the mother's pouch.

At two months the young opossums have grown to about the size of mice. As they venture out of the pouch they crawl around on the mother, riding around by clinging to her fur. By three months they are ready to go out on their own.

Although opossums like birds' eggs, they are not considered as dangerous a pest as the red squirrel or even the raccoon or fox. Their diet is mostly of greens and swamplife, and in cold weather mice, shrews, and moles. They will sometimes raid a chicken coop and will even eat reptiles, frogs, and toads.

Everyone has heard of the opossum's ability to play dead. Some but not all opossums do this. When frightened by your approach an opossum is likely to collapse on its side, the mouth will fall open, and it will become completely limp. If you pick the opossum up and shake it, it'll flap around like a rag doll. You can even carry it home in this state without tying it up. But once you leave its presence the opossum will come out of this comatose state and vanish. An amusing animal, sometimes kept as a pet in the country, its predator is the fox. Needless killing of the opossum is a great waste of wildlife.

Porcupine *(Erethizon dorsatum)*

Contrary to popular belief, porcupines cannot "throw" their quills or shoot them out from the body. When threatened, a porcupine lowers its head, turns its back with all its quills erected, and lashes out with the thickly quilled tail. If the attacker tries to circle the porcupine, it keeps swiveling around to keep the armed tail at the ready. The dog or other would-be attacker that gets close enough to bite will get a face and mouthful of barbed quills that can be fatal.

The porcupine has a chunky body about thirty-four inches in length. The tail is six to twelve inches, with the quills about three inches long each. The back is highly arched, and the legs are short and bowed with four toes on the front feet and five on the hind, all equipped with strong, sharp, curved claws.

There are no quills on the underside of the porcupine's body, while the shortest quills are on the cheeks of the face. When the porcupine is relaxed, the sheet of muscles just under the skin is also relaxed and the quills lie flat. The porcupine has conscious control over those muscles and, when disturbed, contracts them, erecting the quills. In the winter it has a dense coat of soft wool between the quills, which falls out in the summer revealing bare, pink skin between the quills. The guard hairs between the quills are black or brown tipped with white in the eastern porcupine. Western porcupines have yellow guard hairs. (See Figure 5.7*a*.)

Porcupines live only in the heavily forested areas of the north country, from coast to coast. They prefer spruce, fir, and pine to all other trees, eating the bark and tender young shoots. As they do a great deal of damage to the trees, the pulp and lumber companies kill them to some extent, but by and large the porcupine is not often molested.

The female builds a nest in a rocky den, discarded chuck hole, burrow, or hollow log. Usually only one baby porcupine is born. Its guard hair is very dark and the quills are already formed, although these are not dangerous to the mother as the baby is born inside a placental sac and the quills are short.

Within a half hour after birth, the baby's quills harden and it knows how to slap its tail at anything that would be dangerous, and within hours the baby is nursing and can climb. In less than a month the baby, weaned, has learned to chew bark and is strictly on its own.

Porcupines eat bark primarily in the winter, but in the spring and summer they like to feed on water plants and raid cultivated fields for alfalfa, clover, carrots, potatoes, lettuce, melons, apples, and such. They love salt, and anything left outdoors that has been touched by a man's sweaty hands, such as axe handles, gloves, saddles, and canoe paddles are sure to be ruined by them.

Bobcat *(Lynx rufus)* and Canada Lynx *(Lynx canadensis)*

These two feline marauders are found from coast to coast in the northern regions and found through the Rocky Mountains and eastern mountains as far south as Mexico and Florida.

The bobcat can weigh as much as thirty pounds but averages about fifteen. The lynx will weigh about ten to fifteen pounds heavier than the bobcat.

Their habits and feeding are similar. Rabbits and hares form the bulk of their diet, but they eat anything that they can catch, including fish, toads, and even grasshoppers. Both have been hunted for their predation on game, and have been trapped for their furs.

Two to four kittens are born in the early spring in a den the mother has prepared in a fissure of rock, a hollow log, or a hollow under interlacing tree roots. They are born with spotted coats and with eyes sealed shut. As soon as they can manage them, the mother brings the kittens small birds or pieces of game to eat. Bobcat kits will stay with their mother until fall, when they will be about half-grown. In the winter they scatter to go about on their own. The lynx kits stay with their mother all winter, hunting in a family group to learn all the tricks of stalking their prey. When the kits are a year old they separate.

The most prominent features of these cats are the spots, tufted ears, big feet, and short tail. Both have large face ruffs, making the face appear to be very broad. In the case of the lynx, the ruff is so large that the points almost meet beneath the chin.

The coat of the bobcat varies in color with its location. Cats of the northern forests are darker, generally a reddish-brown with bars or spots of a darker color. The southwestern desert cats are a lighter color, yellowish or gray, with darker spots or bars. They have a reddish-pink nose, with white around the eyes and under the chin. The throat and belly and underside of the tail are also white, the tail being barred with black and having a black spot above the tip. This short, four- to seven-inch tail has end hairs, however, that are white. (See Figure 5.8, bottom.)

The basic color of the lynx's coat is a soft smoky gray with sometimes tan mixed in. Its exceptionally large face ruff is white with black bars. It also has white around the eyes, inside the ears, and around the muzzle. The insides of the legs are off-white. The tail is only four inches long, more heavily furred than the bobcat's, and features a solid black tip. (See Figure 5.8, top.)

Both cats have long legs in proportion to their bodies, the lynx's even more so than the bobcat's. Both have large, furry feet with five toes on the forefeet and four on the hind. The eyes are yellow, and—like a domestic cat's—the pupils shrink to vertical slits in bright light.

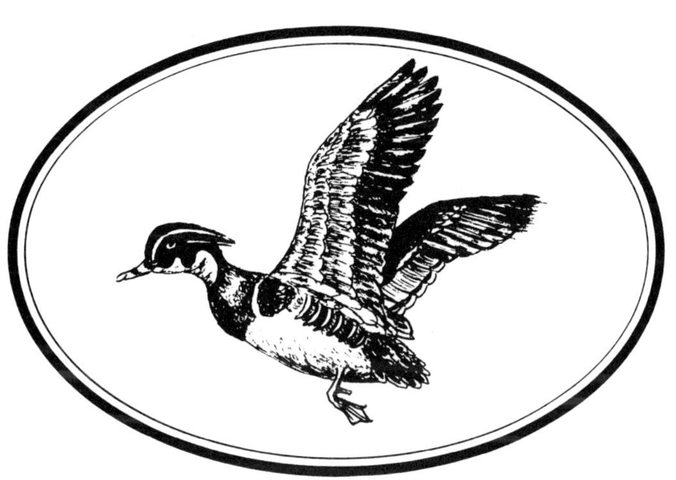

Figure 5.1 Some of the small game animals have interesting and sometimes unusual characteristics that can be caught by your pencil. The raccoon has humorous possibilities as opposed to the wolf or bear with their ferocity. Try and catch the mood and traditional qualities of the animal rather than producing a rendering that says only , "This is a raccoon."

The masked face and the ringed tail are the raccoon's best features to work on, plus the way it uses its little front paws. In studying the animal you will come up with poses that can make a very informative as well as impressive picture.

The pencil rough at the top of the page is a start for a head portrait, or you can fill it out with body and tail if you like. Start with sketches like this one and the one of the small head at the bottom of the page. The full-body picture is done in pen and ink, showing how the long but twisty fur can be done in its true form, not smooth like a dog's fur. Note the stages of rendering the tail. Start light in pencil, go over it in light pen, and then gradually strengthen. The large head portrait at the bottom of the page is done in pencil to show that even the soft medium is good for this subject. It is only half completed to show how you intensify once the hair direction and texture are sketched in first.

The raccoon's a night creature, so don't put him in bright daylight.

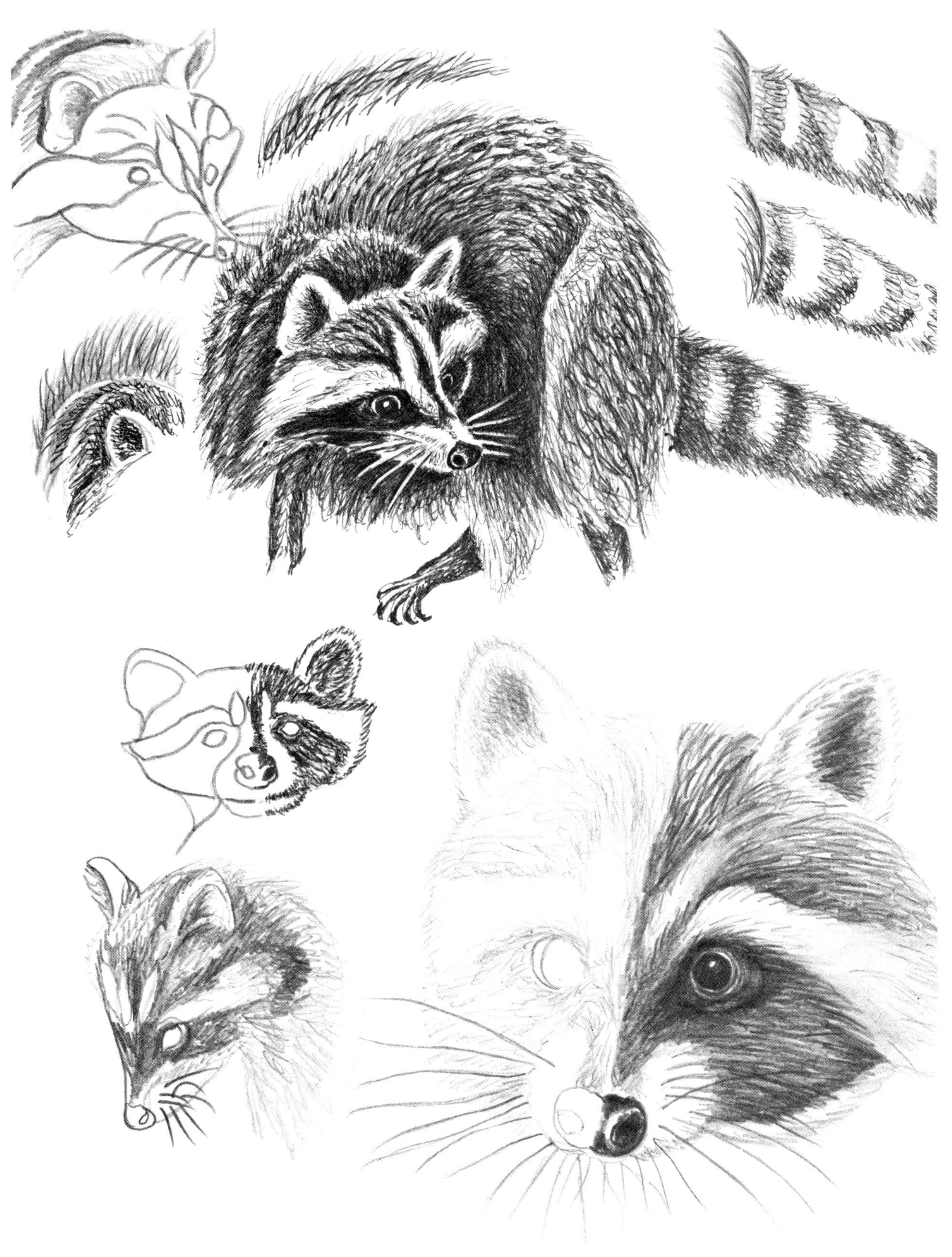

Figure 5.2 These two so-called "varmints," the red and the gray fox, are traditional sporting art subjects, especially the red. You can render them in typical poses working from good research and place them in appropriate backgrounds. Although they might superficially suggest dogs, they are vastly different than dogs of similar size and form. Try and capture the shy and sometimes sly look, the nervousness and high tension they present. Captured in pen and ink as done here, a pair snuggled together in the den, they can also be shown in action trying to capture a bird, or merely standing there looking at you.

Try to avoid caricature, but at the same retain accuracy of form and personality to set the mood of the picture. Do one of him sneaking along an old stone wall. The fox sees *you* but wants to avoid being seen.

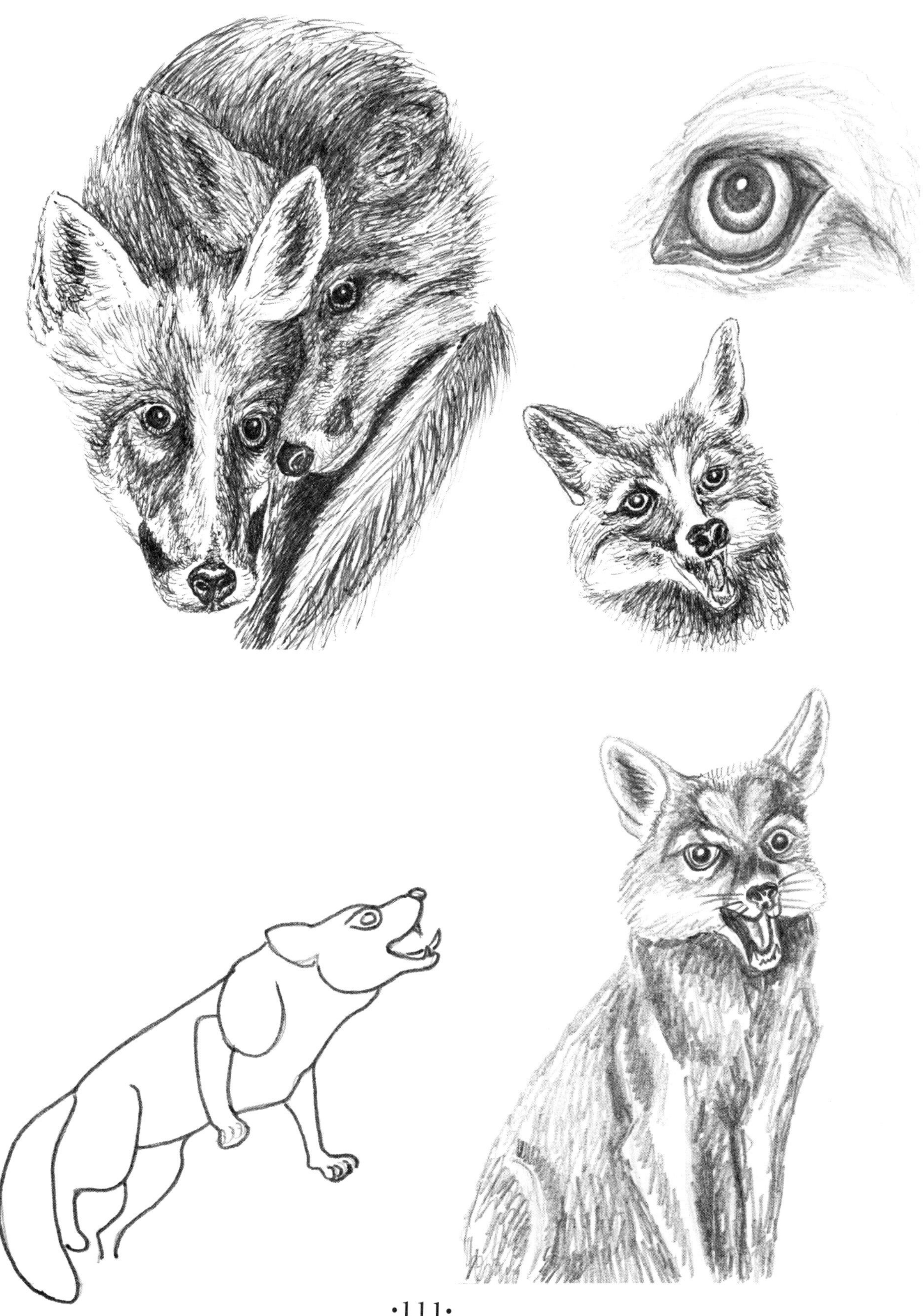

Figure 5.3 There are subtle differences between the wolf and the coyote, and I suggest extensive research on both if you are going to do them in any degree of accuracy. I have only suggested a few poses here and worked in pencil exclusively, to show how the folds of fur can be handled in your rendering.

The most exciting way to portray these animals is in some kind of action, such as stalking their prey, actually catching a rabbit or a bird in a wild jump, or even fighting each other. Other suggestions are den studies as they play and wash their little ones. All of this of course requires excellent research, which can be found if you look patiently through magazines.

In the actual rendering, begin with the all important anatomical outline and make sure of the body proportions, the positions of the legs, and the general physical makeup of the animal. The rendering of the fur follows the natural lines of the animal and can be indicated at first as you begin to fill in; these lines will guide you as you complete the picture.

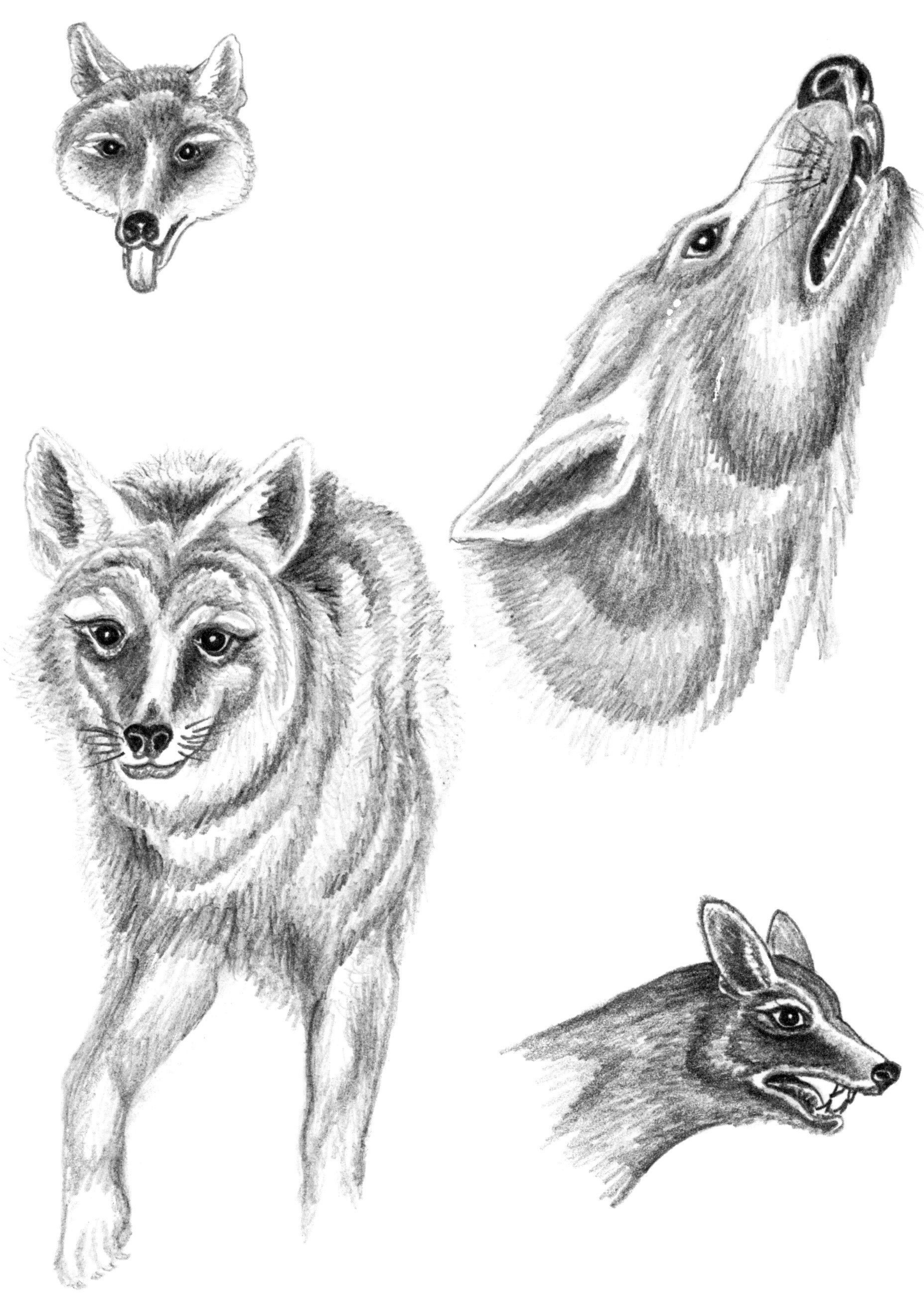

Figure 5.4 On one hand animals are far simpler to render than birds and ducks, since they do not require the details of overlapping feathers to contend with. But fur, on the other hand, must be made to appear as close as possible to the real thing. The fur of the raccoon and the wolf are far different and, as you can see, the squirrel's fur is vastly different from the other animals.

The squirrel done here in pencil is drawn with very short pencil strokes; this indicates the short and sometimes tufted fur that covers the body in loose rolls and the curves needed to suggest light and shadow areas. It is a very subtle fur to texture, even in pencil.

Try it first in pencil and then, using the same form, go over the pencil with pen, lightly at first, trying to duplicate the textures. You will need a really good photograph to work from. Note the length of the tail hairs.

The separate head portrait is a bit more complete than the head on the full-body picture, to show that "going a little further" deepens your picture and enhances the subject's personality.

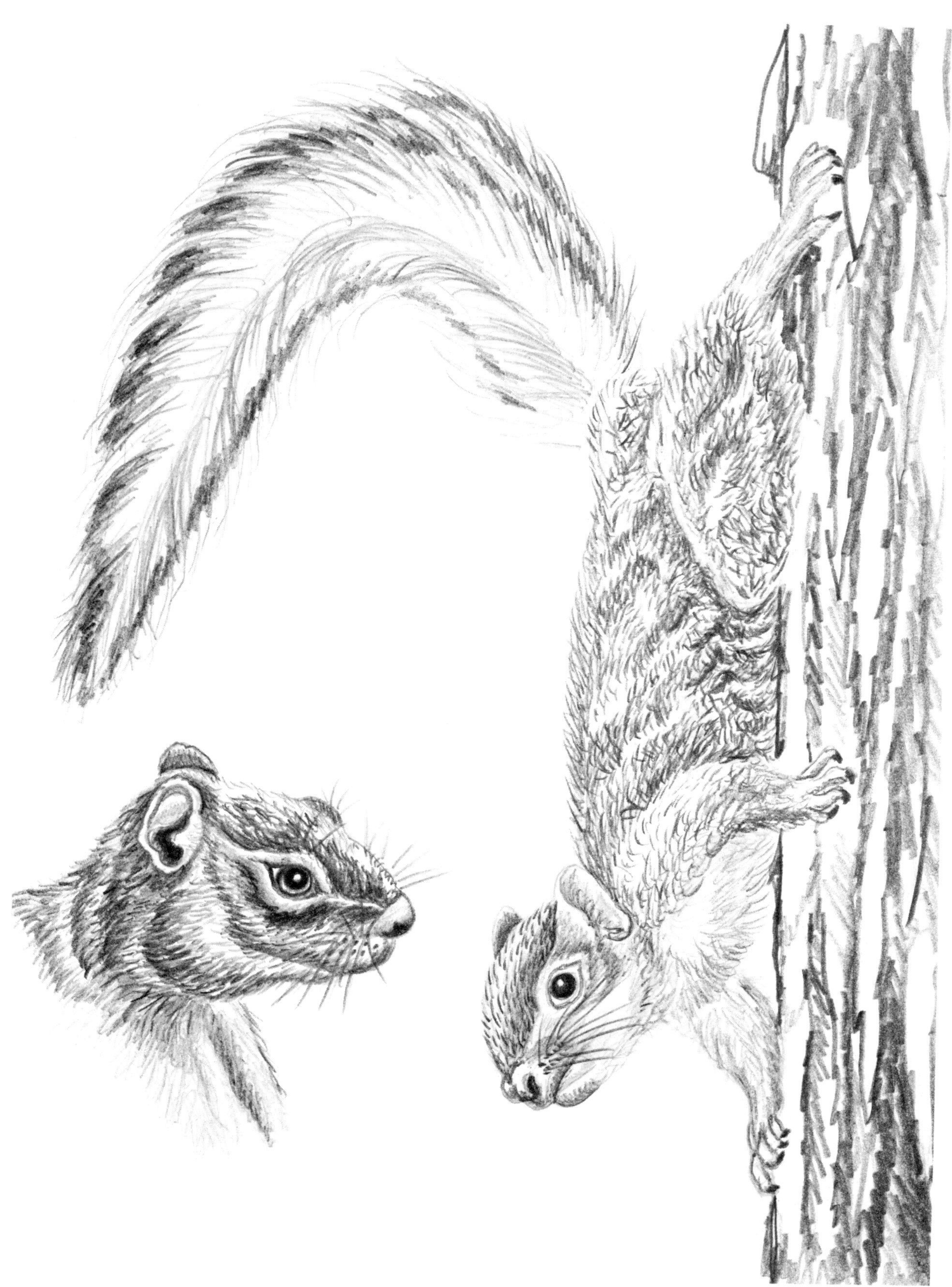

Figure 5.5 The rabbit can present a problem since there have been so many interpretations of this animal in caricature and cartoon. Actually, these cartoons can help you to visualize some very interesting poses to be used on this very ordinary animal shape. There is not that much to work with in form here; but with a sense of humor and well-conceived premise for your choice of angle or pose, a very good rendition can come about.

You can be creative with this subject and still not produce a caricature. I have done one in pen and ink here, and you will note the texture of the fur as it drapes the body in slight rolls. I have also indicated slight shaded areas to bring out the form, especially of the hind legs and upper shoulder. You can angle those ears to your heart's content and turn that cute little head any way you like. Make a lot of thumbnail sketches before you settle on one to complete. It's fun to work with rabbits. The penciled head, only partially completed, gives you a start to show how you begin the basic body outline.

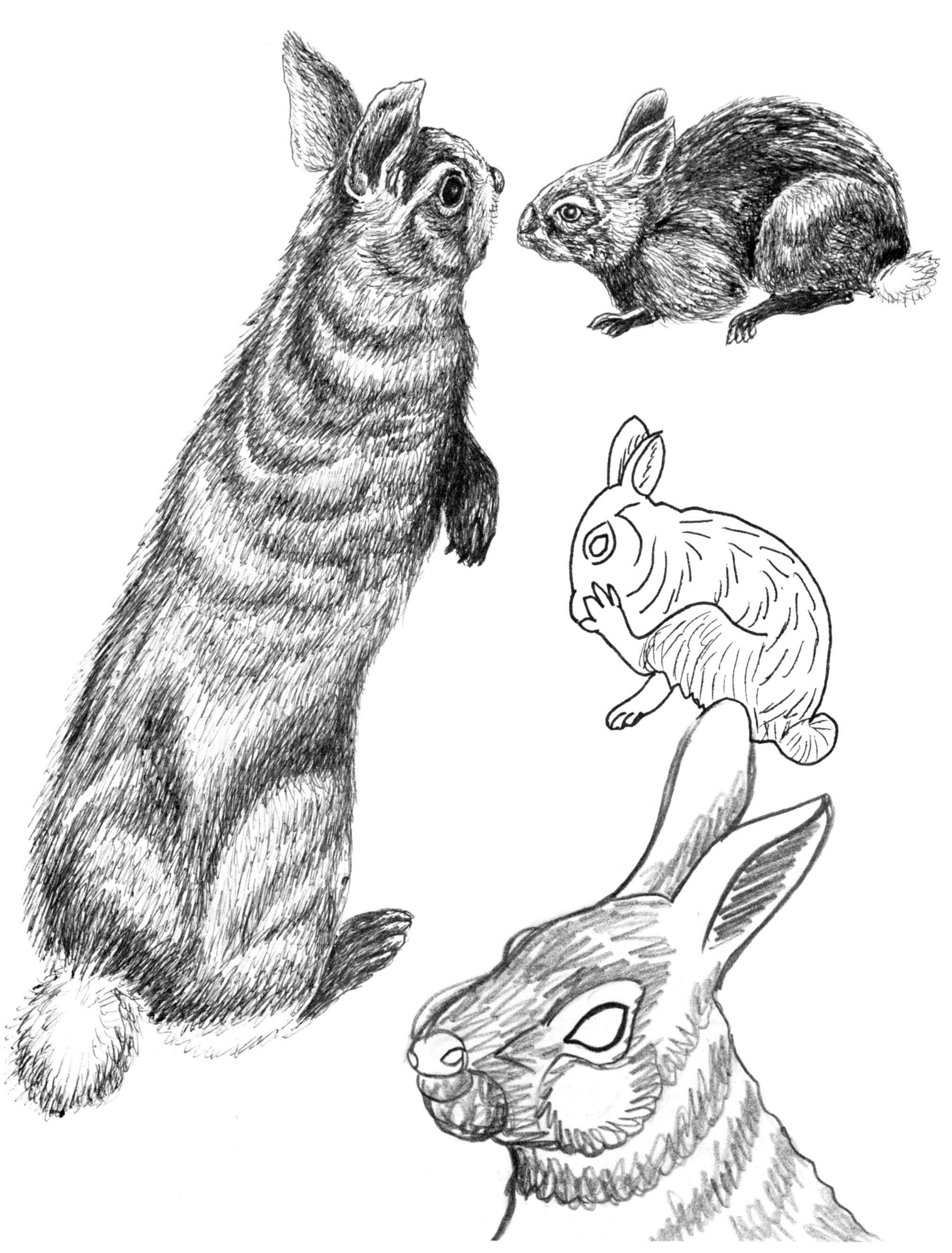

Figure 5.6 The jackrabbit is a larger animal than the conventional rabbit, with longer legs and ears, a fact of construction you can use to advantage as you have it bounding over the grass, leaping up into the air, or simply running along a wood road. The fur texture is nearly the same as the rabbit, though a bit longer.

The snowshoe hare is shown in summer garb and white winter fur, the only species that changes color during the year. Note the very soft pencil on the white version, showing that you can actually represent white in a soft way. Against a darker background it would of course stand out, but if you pose the snowshoe in bright, blinding snow, it will appear ghostlike, the characteristic view many hunters see.

Get some good research on these two. You can have much creative fun with them.

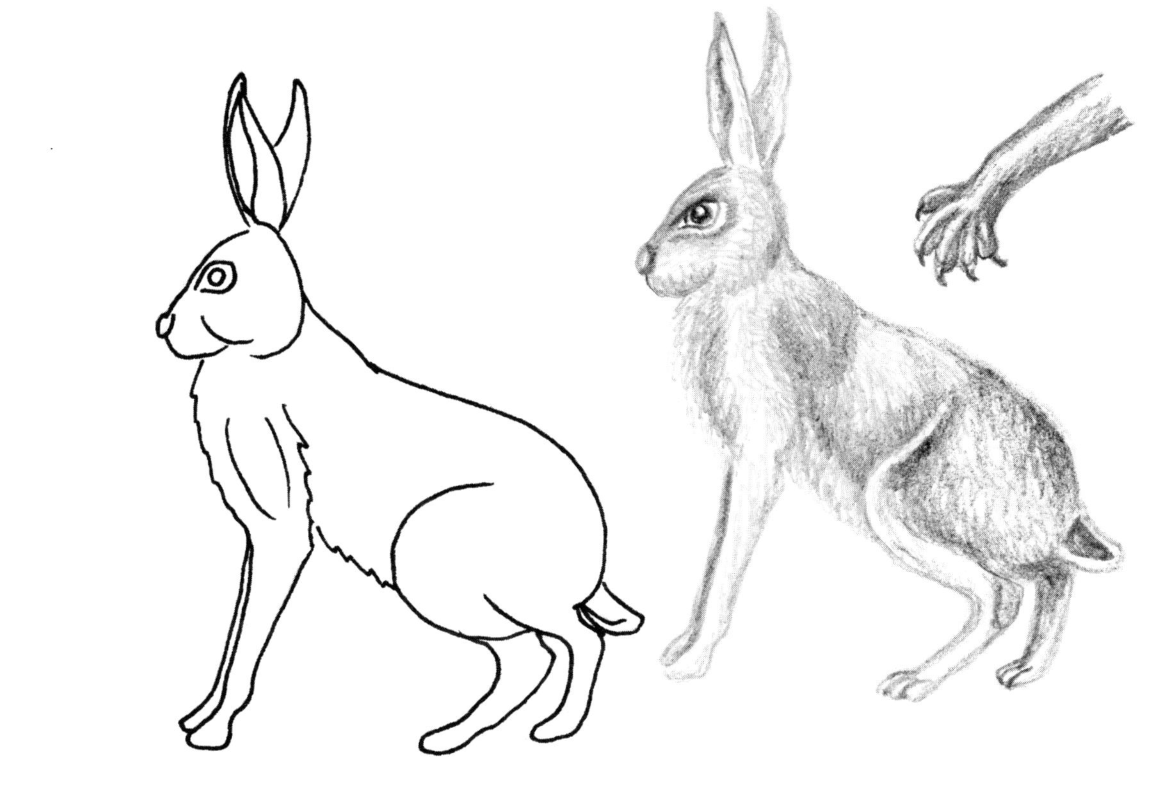

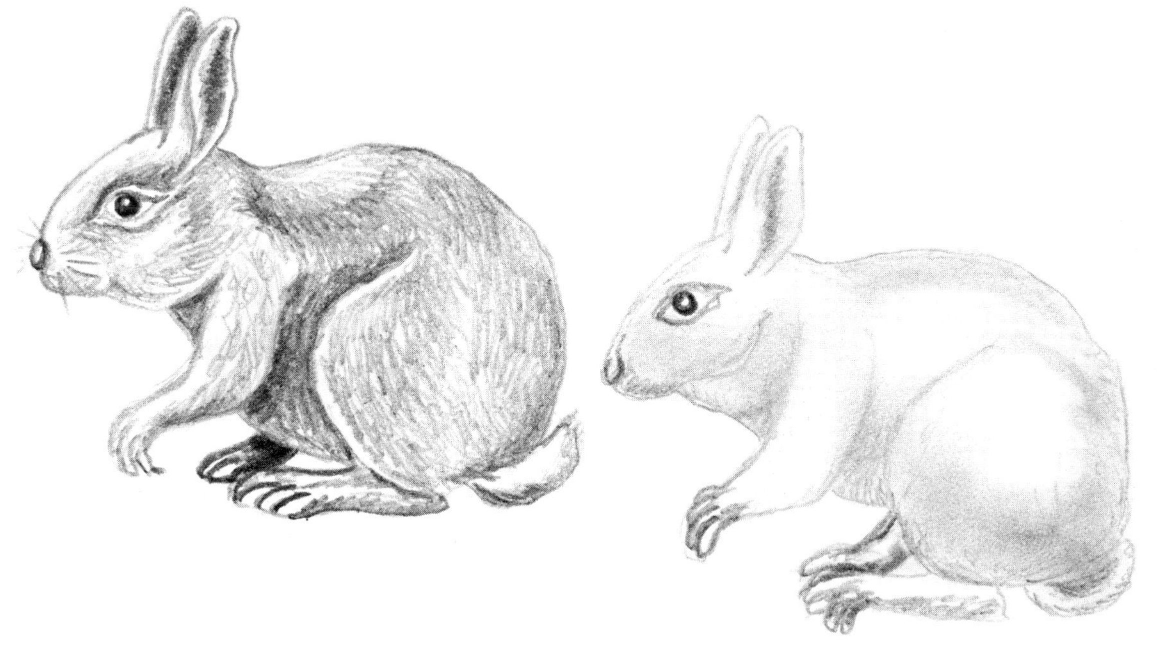

Figure 5.7 The porcupine, opossum, and beaver have forms that are not especially sensational to work with. The porcupine, particularly, is just one big ball with quills pointing outward from the body when alerted, the pose that most artists try to show as its most exciting characteristic. Have the porcupine climbing a tree or, if you can find some good research, put it into a family setting.

Same with the opossum. They carry their little ones clinging to their backs and, given a good photograph, you can make a pleasing picture of this, much more interesting than mine in which the animal is simply lying down.

The beaver with its slick fur is a pretty sight poised atop its dam of sticks and branches. Again, you will need some good research here. And don't minimize the tail, the beaver's most unusual feature.

Try all three media—pencil, pen and ink, and wash—on these animals just for your own practice. Try for lifelike poses, and pay attention to rendering the specific fur textures demanded to make them authentic.

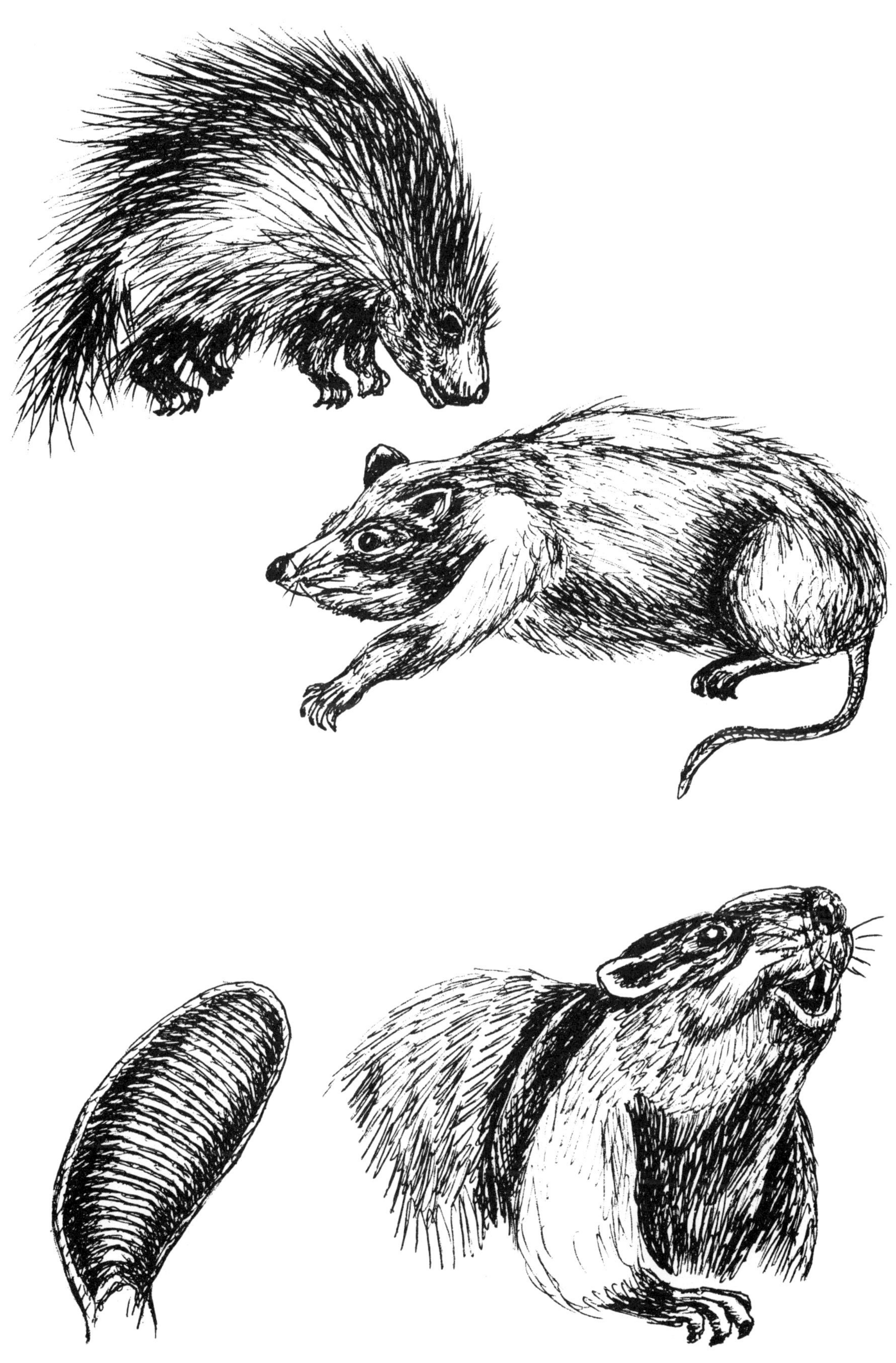

Figure 5.8 Now, with the lynx or the bobcat, you have a chance to portray drama. You have an animal that is dramatic even when simply standing still just looking at you—a truly wild creature, one of the fiercest predators in the books. Portray the lynx or bobcat that way, either chasing something, in the act of capturing it, or at bay high in a tree looking down at you in angry defiance.

Cats, always a feature of our heritage, have been done over and over by all manner of artists and illustrators. But don't let that discourage you. Rather, it should encourage you to outdo them, or at least come up with something different and exciting.

Good research is needed for the anatomical form. From there it is a matter of interpretation and experimenting with many thumbnail sketches before you settle in to complete a given picture. There are special body markings, particularly on or near the head and face, to work with, and the texture of the fur is important here. Some of the head fur is long, some of it short, appearing in tufts. The body fur is generally short and tufty, so indicate this by shaping the fur to point out from the body rather than along the flank direction. If you can find a good closeup photo of a head, you can actually copy the most prominent lines and work out the shadings as I have here—a simple pencil sketch of a cat's head, its mouth open ready to strike out from the paper.

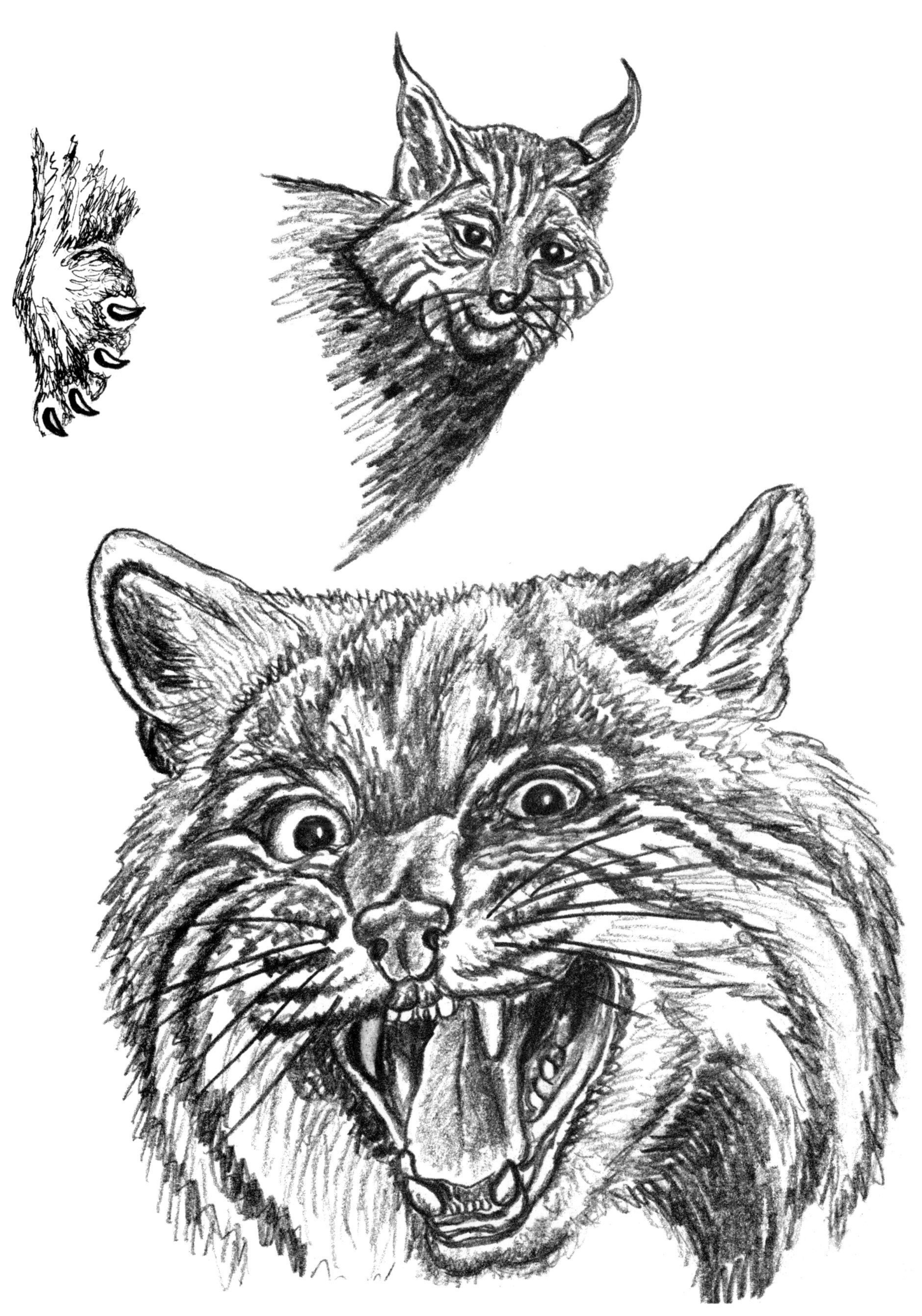

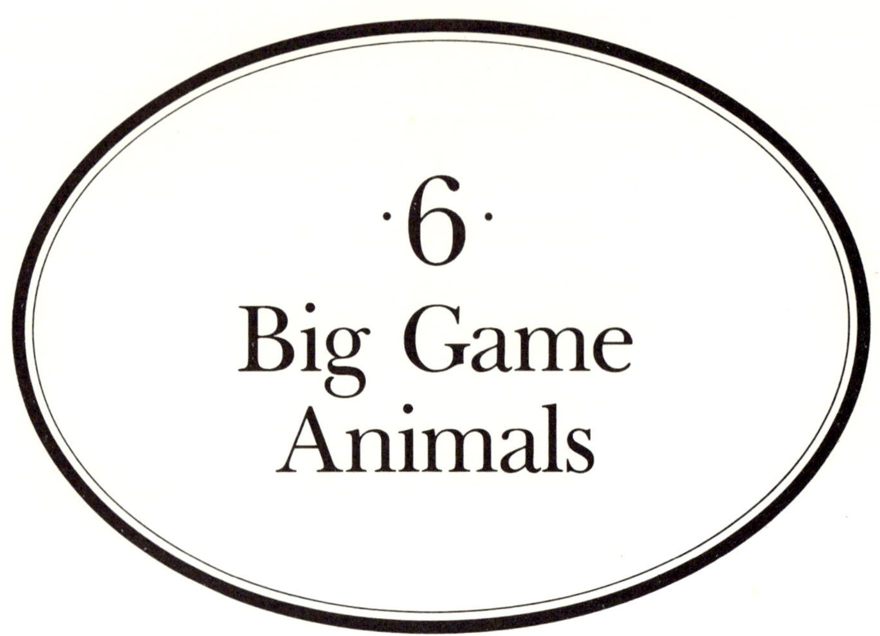

·6· Big Game Animals

Now comes your opportunity to really show the dramatic form and action of the prime subjects in our animal kingdom: the big game animals—majestic in form and strength, whether leaping, striding, or crouching.

But, like the horse, big game animals are not the easiest to render unless you have very good research to work with. The antlered species, for example, offer innumerable possibilities for dramatic flair and the showing of muscle strength. But their complex though smooth-flowing anatomy contains subtleties of form that require faithful rendition in order to bring this out. Shown in their most interesting poses in their own environmental settings of wilderness or the rugged outdoors, they become a dramatic addition to any den wall.

Whitetail Deer (*Odocoileus virginianus*)

The whitetail is probably the most widely distributed and widely admired of the deer family in North America. It is estimated that the present population is about 5 million, a considerable increase since the coming of Europeans to the shores of this continent. This is due in part to the changing of the forests and open spaces of the land and the resultant increase in areas suitable for this species.

Ranging from northern Canada and down into Mexico, sometimes overlapping with the western mule deer, this animal was the mainstay of the family dinner table during pioneer days. Indians fought over hunting grounds that contained large herds of whitetails. Today conservation agencies and private interests conserve the deer populations by regulated hunting seasons and adequate game laws, not only to protect them against overhunting, but against underhunting as well. If the deer numbers become too large for a given territory, they are subject to devastating winter kill and loss through disease and accidents when they stray down from the hills to the highways and farmlands.

Whitetails are greyish-brown, sometimes with a decided reddish or rust cast. The tubular construction of the hair enables the animal to keep warm during the winter and also helps the deer stay afloat when swimming. Their winter hair is also longer and somewhat kinky, filled with many air pockets to increase its insulation properties.

The deer's face is brown, with white circles around the eyes and white bands just behind its jet-black nose. The insides of the ears, underside of the chin, and a large bib on the throat are pure white. The coat is darkest on the spine, shading lighter until it meets the white stomach. The upper portions of the legs and the top side of the tail are brown, the tail bearing a black stripe down the middle. The underside of the tail—or "flag" as it is called by hunters—is large and triangular and sparkling white. Often the most a hunter sees of his deer is the white tail bouncing up and down as the deer bounds its way to freedom.

Whitetails weigh from eighty to more than three hundred pounds. The smaller species are found in the South and in areas where minerals do not allow the animal to become large. The average height is from thirty-six to forty inches at the shoulder, with especially big bucks being forty-two inches high. The elevated head crowned with a full rack of antlers will fool the eye, causing the deer to seem much taller than it really is. The biggest deer in the east are found in Maine, northern New England, and the maritime provinces of Canada.

Deer are primarily forest animals. They prefer, however, broken forests that have been burned or lumbered over; they must have the tender young shoots of trees and bushes, and the nuts and berries not found in thick timber forests. In the east, they are found in and near abandoned farms and old orchards where they can feed on the residue crops and apples. They also like to eat farmers' vegetables, particularly cabbage, lettuce, and the like.

Fawns generally are born in ones and twos—in areas of good food a doe may produce as many as three—and most are born in late May or early June. As soon as they can walk the doe leads them away from the birth place in order to hide them from the scents left by giving birth. In their rusty coats with yellowish-white spots, fawns are almost impossible to see and almost odorless. In about three or four weeks the little ones are strong enough to follow the doe around as she feeds. They then begin to imitate her and gradually begin to need less and less of her milk.

The antlered buck is not seen during this period since all bucks shed their antlers in December and January and new ones do not begin to grow until April. Even then they are no more than bumps. During the summer, however, the antlers grow rapidly, and by September they are full size and beginning to shed their "velvet." Bucks live separately from does and their offspring except during the breeding season and part of the winter. Neither do bucks lead herds: Even when part of a herd, bucks do not take over but are led by an old doe. Young bucks leave their mothers the first autumn, but the young does stay with their mothers throughout the winter.

During the nonhunting season deer generally become very tame and even bold, but with the first fall colorings on the trees and that first burst of cold northern wind, they automatically become touchy—aware of the hunter lurking about with his gun. Very wily animals, particularly when living near man, with foliage gone, they sense danger very quickly and keep sharp eyes for the advance of man through the woods.

Deer are great creatures of habit in the wild state, following the same routine, the same trails, day after day. They may alter their routine only because of weather conditions and the availability of food. They generally start to feed at dusk, making their way to water at some nearby swamp, brook, river, or lake. The middle of the night is spent resting, chewing their cud in a field or brushland, and at about dawn they begin to feed again. Before full light they have retired for the day, spending it in heavy cover in thick woods or high on the mountain tops. Their travel pattern is usually a well-trodden trail made over generations from one area to another. When a road construction crew cuts a road through or across such an established deer trail, a "deer crossing" sign must be put up to warn motorists. It takes the deer some years to change their pattern away from such danger. In order to successfully hunt deer with a camera or gun, it is necessary to know their travel and living patterns. Once these facts are known, it is a relatively simple matter to intercept these animals.

Mule Deer (*Odocoileus hemionus*)

The mule deer, the western deer of North America, is much larger and heavier than the whitetail. "Mulies," as called by hunters, weigh well over the 300-pound mark and carry much broader and higher antlers than those found on the whitetail.

They grow to almost seventy-eight inches in length with a shoulder height of forty-two inches. They have a stocky body and stout legs. Their color is reddish-brown in summer and a somber grey-brown in winter. Rather than the large "flag" tail of the whitetail, the mule deer's tail is round with white hairs on the top down to a black tip that is two inches long.

The mule deer's face is more striking than the whitetail's. The nose and a band around the muzzle are black while most of the face, including the area around the eyes, is white. The cheeks are gray, and a cap of jet black extends down between the eyes. The ears are white on the inside and rimmed with black. The name "mule deer" comes from their ears, which are exceptionally large, eight to nine inches long from the opening, and about six inches wide. The throat has two white patches, one above the other, divided by a bar of dark color. The belly, insides of the legs, and the rump area are white.

The antlers are large and heavy. Each antler branches into two main forks, and each fork in turn branches into two more. There is also a single tine near the base of each antler, but these are much smaller than those on the whitetail.

Mule deer prefer the high country of the West, selecting thick forests where they can hide from man and predators, but ones which contain open areas where they can feed on the young growth of trees and bushes. Berries and nuts and farmers' vegetables are part of their diet. Generally they summer in the valleys. They winter in the highlands and mountains, ranging from British Columbia down through the western states, sticking pretty well to the Rocky Mountains.

Feeding and watering habits are similar to the whitetail; and mule deer can eat almost any vegetation they encounter. As they live in a more inaccessible area, mule deer have not been subjected to as much hunting pressure and are somewhat less wary than the whitetail. Where hunting is banned and predators eliminated, deer herds grow; and as their numbers increase so do their food requirements, and forage plants begin to dwindle. Countless mule deer have been wasted each year through starvation, and what once were lush ranges have been destroyed through overgrazing by excess deer. Game managers have had to educate the general public to the facts and workings of game management, so that deer herds can be brought into balance with their habitat.

The family life of mule deer is essentially the same as the whitetail's: the bucks prefer to remain bachelors most of the year, joining the does during breeding season. Bucks often fight for supremacy and breeding privileges just like the whitetail bucks, and when a battle is in progress the "racking" of the antlers can be heard for quite a distance. Occasionally the bucks' antlers become locked; if they cannot separate, they will both starve to death. Most mule deer fawns are born in late June and July and have typical spotted, camouflaged coats. By September they have shed their spotted coats and are weaned. Most mule deer youngsters follow their mother until she gives birth again, being driven away by the doe just before this event.

Moose (*Alces alces*)

The bull moose is the easiest of the deer family to identify as it is the biggest, growing to a length of 10 feet or more, with a shoulder height of 6 to 7½ feet, and weighing upwards of 1300 pounds. The moose has long legs, with powerful forequarters that taper back to much smaller hind parts, ending in a stubby 3-inch tail.

A moose's head bears a long overhanging snout that is wide and floppy, and under the chin hangs a flap of skin and fur called a bell or pendant, the purpose of which is unknown. The ears are larger than those of a mule, and a mane of long hair reaches from the ears down to its shoulders and under the legs. The color of the coat ranges through all shades of dark brown and russet, the predominant color being black. The nostrils, eye circles, inner parts of the ear, and the lower portions of the legs are grayish white.

The crown of tremendous, palmated antlers are what give the bull moose its impressive appearance. These antlers can often measure six feet across at the widest point and weigh up to ninety pounds.

The male has a nasty disposition and will fight a tough battle, particularly during the rutting season. Its only thought is to find and breed a mate, and anything that comes between a bull and the goal is subject to instant attack. Many people have been forced to spend hours in trees while an angry bull paws the earth below and batters nearby bushes with its antlers. Rutting bulls have been known to attack cars, bulldozers, and even trains. In a confrontation, bulls of equal size come together head on with a terrific crash. As with some other species, if their antlers lock they are both likely to die. From September to the end of October the bulls seek out cows to mate with. Generally bulls do not build up harems; if a bull finds a receptive cow, he may stay with her for a week or more before looking for another.

Calves are born in ones and twos in May and June. The newborn moose calf weighs between twenty and twenty-five pounds and has a light, reddish-brown coat that is not spotted. Since a cow is very protective of her calf, any other creature in the vicinity had better be cautious. A cow that believes her calf to be threatened is a fury to be avoided at all costs. The bull moose, too, sometimes takes on the duties of protective parent. He will often help a cow defend her calf against attack, and if a human comes upon the family group suddenly, the bull will be the first to grunt disapproval and threaten attack. Even during the summer moose are animals to be avoided except for a quick look or a fast snap of the camera shutter.

The moose's range is from Alaska, down the northern Rocky Mountain states, and across to the maritime provinces of Canada and up into Labrador and Newfoundland. The largest specimens are to be found on the Kenai peninsula in Alaska; Siberia and other subarctic European countries still have small amounts of them. In the intermountain West, Wyoming has permitted limited moose hunting in recent years, and there are conservation movements going on to widen the distribution of moose. Moose used to be found in the northern New England states, and Maine is trying to encourage a comeback in the more northern counties owned by the lumber interests. The national parks of the West support small bands of moose, and limited permit hunting is allowed in certain years when the animals become too abundant.

Although moose are forest animals, they sometimes prefer the barren wilderness of low growth where they can see an invader for many miles before it sees them. Their diet is found mostly in streams and particularly in ponds, where they feed on water grasses and lily pads. They can often be seen during the summer months half-submerged in water, feeding on the water weeds at their feet. Out of the water, moose prefer to browse upon brushy twigs. Alder, mountain ash, maple, honeysuckle, chokecherry, dwarf birch, cottonwood, cranberry, and elder are among the foods most admired by moose.

Elk (*Cervus canadensis*)

The elk, or *wapiti,* is the largest antlered member of the deer family after the moose. (In Europe the animal we know as the moose is called an elk, and the animal resembling our elk is known there as the red stag.)

Elk weigh from 800 to over 1000 pounds, and a large bull will stand 5 feet high at the shoulder and can be 8 to 10 feet in length. Elk are colored a brownish-gray with very dark legs and a belly that is almost black. The head and neck is covered with long, chestnut-brown hair, while the rump area and short tail are a whitish-yellow. In the spring elks molt into a summer coat that is somewhat reddish.

The bull elk carries the most impressive antlers in North America. Much more widespread than deer antlers, they sweep back and outward from the brow, branching into many magnificent points. The brow tines project much longer than those of the whitetail and mule deer. A set of antlers of a mature bull elk can measure five feet across from tip to tip and over five feet long, measuring the outside curve along one beam. It is a wonder this animal can make its way through the trees! Unlike other deer the elk's antlers begin their growth as early as the first of March, and they have achieved maximum growth by late July.

By September they are in their rutting season: The bulls separate to seek out the herds of cows. Each bull elk strives to gather a harem of as many cows as he can locate and keep away from other bulls. Some will manage to gather as many as twenty to thirty cows, and most of the bull's time is spent keeping his cows from being lured away and making charges at other bulls that may try to infiltrate the herd. Occasionally two bulls will compete fiercely for control of a herd, and the sight of two elk battling with locked horns is an extraordinary experience. During the rutting season the bugling of elk can be heard for miles.

Calves generally are born one at a time in the latter part of May or early in June. The newborn elk calf has a dark russet coat liberally spotted with white along the back and sides. By the time it is a week old and can run moderately fast, the mother takes it to join other cows with their calves. This provides group protection, as danger to one calf will alert all the mothers. By the time they are a month old the calves will be feeding on grasses, although they will continue to nurse from their mothers as long as permitted. By September the youngsters have shed their spotted coats and look like scaled-down models of the adults.

Thanks to much conservation effort and hard work by private citizens, the elk's future seems secure although limited to restricted territories. Most of the elk were exterminated in the east back in the 1800s and it was only the creation of Yellowstone Park that saved the elk in the west. The park provided breeding stock that was shipped out to repopulate the rest of the country. In this protected environment the elk herds increased to devastating proportions and did so much damage to the range that now only 5000 elk can be supported there. One of the basic tenets of wildlife management is that a given number of acres can support only so many units of various animals. Then either the range must be increased to support the increase in wildlife, or surplus animals must be eliminated to maintain a balance. Elk are now restricted to the Rocky Mountains from British Columbia to northern Arizona and New Mexico, and along the Pacific Coast from Vancouver to San Francisco Bay. There are also some elk in the Black Hills of South Dakota, in northern Arkansas and western Texas, as well as up in Manitoba and Saskatchewan. Some effort is being made to reintroduce elk to some parts of the east, and given the proper habitat and protection, with systematic harvesting according to the particular requirements of each area, it may someday be possible for man to again enjoy this grand and majestic animal east of the Mississippi River.

Black Bear (*Euarctos americanus*)

The black bear is the most common and the smallest of all the bear species on this continent. It ranges from Labrador and northeastern Canada to the southern mountains of the Southeast, and is abundant in the intermountain West and into Canada and even into southern Alaska. Quite an attraction in the national parks and state forests, the black bear is among the most popular and heavily hunted big game animals in America.

Blacks weigh from 200 to 400 pounds, and 500-pound specimens are not unusual, the size varying with the available food and natural conditions for growth. The black's smaller size and color make it easy to distinguish from the other native species when found with them.

When seen in profile, the black bear's face is quite flat. Black bears come in every shade of brown, and some are even rather blonde. The hair around the muzzle and around the small eyes is lighter in the dark-colored bears. Most also have a patch of white on the chest. They have well-rounded ears and five toes on each foot, each toe being armed with a curved claw that does not retract. The front claws are more than an inch long, enabling this bear to climb trees. The black bears do not have the prominent hump on the shoulders that characterize grizzlies and brown bears.

Bears have only one mating season in the year, during June and July, and the cubs come two or three and occasionally four at a time in late January or early February. Born covered with fine hair, their eyes are sealed shut. Cubs weigh about eight ounces at birth; at forty days, when they open their eyes, they weigh about four pounds. The mother bear is the sole provider and protector of the cubs and is instantly capable of defending her cubs from any intrusion or threat.

This is one big game animal that has learned to live with man despite his invasion of the wilderness. In fact, like the deer, the black bear has actually increased where man has opened the forests and otherwise changed the ecology of the land. Their ears are their best sensor of danger, the nose second, and their eyes third. They see poorly except at close distances; but if the hunter makes any false noise or brings along a smell alien to the woods, the bear will have him quickly spotted.

Although the phrase "clumsy as a bear" might apply to this animal when seen in a zoo, one has to see it spring through the woods and disappear before one's eyes to appreciate its ease of travel and lightning speed.

Although cubs in national and state parks may seem playful, the bear is not to be fooled with in the wild state, particularly a mature bear, and more especially a female with her cub. They are very powerful beasts and too often are underestimated by man. Many deaths and bad wounds have been received by people who lacked respect for this seemingly cute and clownlike animal.

The bear's fur makes a good coat, or at least a prized rug for the den. The head is sometimes mounted as a trophy. In the early days of this country, rendered bear fat was used for cooking, frying, baking, as medicine, in the tanning of leather, and for many other purposes.

Often the black bear's curiosity results in its undoing. Bears are fascinated by the operations of man and are prone to investigate anything that excites their curiosity. This gets them into trouble. They also are not averse to coming to town occasionally to see what all the bright lights are about. They are not dumb animals, as some accuse them of being. Certainly, any animal can be caught napping, or one can come upon them in the wilds quite by accident. But by and large the black bear has learned the ways of man, and its craftiness has kept its numbers relatively high. Not being a true hibernator, the black bear can be instantly active if disturbed in its winter den, something to remember when approaching a likely cave.

Grizzly Bear (*Ursus arctos*)

Man and bear have been enemies since the dawn of time; primitive humans drew pictures in their caves that included the bear. Never has the bruin been considered a helpful, friendly sort of beast, but rather one to be feared. The sportsman also fears the bear, despite being armed with fire power. Bears, particularly grizzly bears, have been the subject of many thrilling tales of outdoor adventure.

Although the grizzly is not as large as the Alaska brown bear, it is nonetheless ornery and hard to handle at close range. It can tear trees out by the roots and raise havoc in a farmyard or camp. It can maul a man to death in a few seconds, and one swipe of its powerful paws can knock a man to the ground. With forepaws bearing nearly four-inch claws, the grizzly can dig squirrels out of their underground burrows with very little effort.

Scientists don't all agree about the species names of the various bears that inhabit Alaska and northern Canada. The grizzly once was named *Ursus horribilis* because of its ferocity, but in more recent years biologists have abandoned the attempt to classify the brown and the grizzly as separate species: Now both bear the Latin name *Ursus arctos*.

One identifying characteristic of the grizzly is its massive shoulder hump. In contrast to the black bear, the grizzly's profile is concave between the forehead and the nose. A grizzly can weigh up to 800 pounds, stand 3½ feet high at the humped shoulder, and grow to about 7 feet long; but its tail is only 2 or 3 inches long. Its ears are large and well rounded, but its eyes are small and piglike. The jaw muscles are powerful, giving the grizzly tremendous crushing power. The coat is dense and long. Most grizzlies have dark brown hair with white-tipped guard hairs, but their color can vary to yellowish-brown and even blonde.

With the exception of the polar bear, the grizzly is the most carnivorous of the bear family, eating elk, moose, deer, and other game animals. In the springtime when the bear comes out of hibernation, it gorges on the new grass shoots, roots, and tubers, and the eggs and young of birds, mice, snakes, and frogs.

Grizzlies pair up during the mating season in late May and most of June, but while they may show affection during the courtship, their tempers have hair triggers and they will tolerate no other animal except a bear of the opposite sex.

The cubs are born mostly in twos and threes in January—covered with short gray hair, and with their eyes tightly closed—and are about eight or nine inches long, weighing about a pound and a half. In late April the mother and her cubs leave the den and she begins to educate her children in finding edible foods. In the summer the cubs begin to eat meat, such as squirrels or mice, and by late fall they are usually weaned. The cubs spend their first winter in the den with their mother.

Grizzlies are now found in Alaska eastward almost as far as Hudson's Bay and southward through the Rocky Mountains to northern New Mexico. In the days of the early settlers, grizzlies were seen to attack and kill adult bison on the Great Plains. A grizzly could smash a charging bison's head or break its neck with one blow.

Alaskan Brown Bear (*Ursus arctos*)

The Alaskan brown bear is the largest carnivorous land animal in the world today. Sometimes the polar bear reaches the same size, but the brown is heavier and stockier. A full-grown male can measure almost five feet at the shoulder and reach a length of eight or nine feet. Most big males weigh between 800 and 1200 pounds, with the females somewhat smaller.

The brown has the same dish face and humped shoulder as the grizzly, and its hair is long and thick and comes in varying shades of brown. The color of the coat can vary from blonde through russet to a dark brown that is almost black. Like most bears, the brown has a keen sense of smell but rather poor eyesight, although it can detect movement. The brown bear's legs are short and stout, different from the polar bear or even the small black bear. Despite this, the brown can cover long distances with great speed.

Brown bears range over a comparatively small area in coastal Alaska, from the tip of the Alaskan peninsula south along the coast to the northern reaches of British Columbia. They feed primarily on salmon, rodents, carrion, and tons of berries as well as other plants.

The breeding season lasts about a month from the middle of June through the first part of July. Sometimes a male brown bear will share his mate with another brown of the same size and disposition, but usually a big male will drive away all other contenders. One to four cubs are born in January or February, covered with short brown hair and with their eyes still unopened. In May the cubs are large enough to leave the den with their mother and to learn the techniques for finding food. The greatest threat to young cubs is a large, old male. Adult males will kill a young cub just as they would any small animal. The mother bears know this, and if any male comes near a mother bear's cub she will roar, bare her teeth, and charge. A prudent male usually retreats. The female brown bear keeps her cubs with her until they are almost two years old, and sometimes until they are almost three. Then they must leave, for now she will have new cubs to care for.

In the early 1900s the brown bear was mercilessly hunted by salmon fishermen and sportsmen. Though bear meat is not the greatest on the table, it did provide a staple food for the pioneers and prospectors of the Northwest. In recent years strict conservation measures have assured the continuance of this tremendous beast, one of the last of the big animals to inhabit this continent.

Polar Bear (*Ursus maritimus*)

This is the most popular bear of the zoos, for few people other than Arctic explorers, prospectors, and big-game hunters even see this bear in its natural environment. The Eskimos call it *nanook,* and it is a relative of the bears that once lived in the Northern Hemisphere during the first of the several Ice Ages that marked the Pleistocene era. One of the largest predators on the earth today, the polar bear has few of the characteristics of the brown and grizzly bears that live nearby on the dry land.

Reaching about the same dimensions as the brown bear, although slightly longer, the polar bear can weigh as much as 1700 or 1800 pounds. Its fur is long, thick, and silvery white. (The long strands are used in many of the streamer-fly patterns used in fresh and saltwater fishing.)

The neck is long and the head small and tapering, giving the polar bear a more streamlined shape than the other bears, a great help in swimming. It has long legs and large feet with very sharp claws, but shorter than the brown and grizzly. The eyes, nose, lips, and toenails are the only parts of the bear that are black. The ears are small and placed low on the head.

With its white coat the polar bear is nearly invisible against the snow while stalking prey. Any dark object represents food to the keen-sighted polar bear, and it is usually hungry. It can spot a man or a seal at a considerable distance. (Unlike many other bears, the polar bear has excellent eyesight but poor hearing.) Its sense of smell is also highly developed, and polar bears have been known to travel twenty miles tracking down the source of an appetizing odor.

Breeding season is in the midsummer, with the cubs being born in late December and January. Cubs come in twos and sometimes threes and are born with a dense but fine coat of white hair, with their eyes tightly closed. They live in an ice den, warmed by mother's fur, as she does not leave them until their fur has grown enough to protect them against the cold. Polar bear cubs stay with their mother for almost two years, by which time they are nearly as large as she is. Not until mother is about to give birth to another family are they sent out on their own.

Most bears hibernate during the winter, but the polar bear stays awake and is very lively all year long. They are found in the Arctic coastal regions from the Seward peninsula of Alaska across to Labrador and south along the shore of Hudson's Bay to James Bay.

Mountain Goat (*Oreamnos americanus*)

The mountain goat is the comedian of the mountains—the young goats particularly, who spend much of their time in play dashing helter-skelter over rocks and cliff sides.

Dressed in a shaggy yellowish-white coat of long fur with 9- to 12-inch sharp-pointed horns, its hooves, nose, eyes, and horns are jet black. Mountain goats are about 5 to 6 feet long, stand about 36 to 40 inches at the shoulder, and weigh up to 300 pounds. Both sexes wear beards composed of long hairs coming from below the jaw. Even when they shed during the summer they retain the beards. (See Figure 6.8, bottom.)

Mountain goats never hurry; an adult goat will often stand perfectly still in one spot for hours. They pick their way over almost perpendicular cliffs, choosing each step with great care. They seem to defy gravity as they ascend rock faces that have no visible ledges.

Though called a goat, this animal is really a type of mountain-dwelling antelope and is closely related to the chamois of the European Alps. Four western states have considerable populations of these animals, which number only about 15,000 in all. In our mountainous West, civilization has had little effect upon these animals who live far from roads and other improvements made by man. If civilization does not take over the forbidding mountain passes, canyons, and rugged cliffs, the mountain goat's homeland will remain secure.

Breeding takes place in November and December, with occasional bluffing and posturing between competing males. From the middle of May to the middle of June the young kids are born, usually one at a time, weighing between seven and eight pounds and standing about thirteen inches high at the shoulder. Within hours they are able to follow the mother over the rough terrain. After about three or four days of solitary life in such a protected area, the mother takes her kid to join similar family groups. Within a week the kids are nibbling the plants they see their mothers eat and, in six to eight weeks, are weaned.

Hard, cold winters seldom force the goat to go down from the high peaks unless food becomes scarce. In summer they have been seen feeding in company with domesticated sheep, and even caribou in the remote mountain meadows.

Mountain goats are found along the steep slopes of the western mountains from Idaho and Washington to southern Alaska and central Yukon. Some were introduced into the Black Hills of South Dakota.

In the summer when the goats shed, the Indians of British Columbia gather the clumps of white hair found clinging to bushes and spin them into strands, which they use for knitting and weaving clothing that is very warm.

Bighorn Sheep (*Ovis canadensis*)

Though certainly not the most beautiful trophy, the mountain sheep is probably one of the most coveted by big-game hunters. The sheep is technically a member of the family *Bovidae,* which includes the ox, most cattle, bison, antelope, and domesticated sheep and goats.

At a time before the invasion of the white man, the wild sheep's homelands ranged from Alaska southward far into the mountains of Mexico, but they were gradually driven from their ranges almost to the point of extinction. Were it not for the extensive law enforcement and conservation methods employed by far-sighted individuals, the sheep might not be with us at all today. In some parts of the West the species is making a slight comeback, but it is still in danger. Despite their sharp eyes and unbelievable ability to hear danger, plus the ability to climb impossible terrain, hunters and predators have cut down their numbers alarmingly.

Although chunky and heavily muscled, they have beautifully proportioned bodies set on strong, sturdy legs. A heavy neck supports the head and the massive horns. Mountain sheep generally reach between 5 and 6 feet in length, stand under 4 feet at the shoulder, and weigh from approximately 185 pounds to 300 or more.

Mountain sheep have hair rather than wool. The bighorn's coat varies from pale buff to dark brown, depending on whether it lives in a desert area or the northern mountains. They have a white muzzle, a large white rump patch, a light underbelly, a white patch around the eye, a short black tail, and white edging running down the backs of the legs. The eyes are a yellow-amber with black horizontal pupils.

The ram's horns are huge and can weigh as much as twenty pounds (Figure 6.7, top). Usually dark brown, they make more than a full circle in the adult ram, and to prevent his side vision from being obscured the ram must rub the tips of his horns against rocks to blunt and shorten them. The ewes have delicate-looking, slender horns that curve into no more than half a circle.

There are several sheep in the bighorn family residing in America—the Rocky Mountain bighorn, the desert bighorn, the Stone sheep, and the Dall sheep. Many of these overlap each other, and it generally takes a biologist to accurately tell one from the other. The Dall and the Stone have thinner horns than the bighorn, which flare outward at the tips and do not obstruct the vision, and they are generally a light yellow in color.

Bighorns are famous for their keen eyesight and especially for their jumping and climbing abilities. They can spot a man or a predator five miles away and be out of the territory long before danger threatens. They can run down steep slopes covered with loose rock at full speed and never stumble. They can ascend rock "chimneys" by leaping from one face to the other, landing on tiny ledges no more than four inches square, and thus up to the top. In the middle of the day they generally lie down on some rocky ledge or exposed area where they can see for miles in all directions, where they enjoy the sun's warmth.

Rams and ewes travel in separate groups until the breeding season, which starts in October. Then the rams begin to show antagonism toward each other and to battle for dominance over certain chosen ewes by making head-on charges at each other. The noise from the impact of their horns can be heard for a great distance. In late May and early June the lambs are born, usually no more than one at a time. The little lambs are about ten inches high at the shoulder, weigh about eight or nine pounds, and are covered with a dark gray fuzz. Within a few hours the lamb is able to stand up and nurse, and by the end of the first week it is nibbling bits of grass. At that time the mother leads it to join the main flock.

Pronghorn (Antilocapra americana)

The Pleistocene period bequeathed North America with a lone species of native animal that we have incorrectly called an "antelope." It happens, in fact, to be neither a goat nor an antelope—not even an antelope-goat. It is a pure American species, one of its kind, with no relatives in any part of the world.

The pronghorn is a favored species with hunters, as well as nature lovers who roam the plains and arid lands of the West just for a quick glimpse of this animal. It is an easy animal to identify since none of the big game animals are found in company with it. The fully developed horns of an adult male measure from twelve to twenty inches in length with one prong jutting forward and the main tine curving sharply backwards. Pronghorn shed their horns each year and grow new ones through spring.

Compared to deer the pronghorn is small, weighing about 100 to 140 pounds, reaching a length of 4.5 feet, and standing less than 4 feet high at the shoulder. A rich, reddish-tan on the upper half of the body and the outsides of the legs, they have white underparts and a large white rump patch. The throat is white, crossed with two wide, dark brown bands, so that a pronghorn appears to be wearing two white bibs. The horns are jet black.

The pronghorn's eyes protrude from its skull, providing it with such a wide angle of vision that it can see backward as well as forward. Vision is so sharp that a pronghorn can spot a small object in motion four miles away. One of the fastest animals in the world, they have been clocked at seventy miles per hour and can maintain speeds of forty and fifty miles per hour for long periods.

Pronghorns breed in September and October, the males gathering up harems of up to fifteen does, with rival males fighting fierce and bloody battles. In May and June the young ones arrive, generally as twins. The kids weigh between four and five pounds at birth and are a pale, solid-dun color with no spots or other markings. By the end of their first week they are able to run fast enough to keep up with the mother, at which time the family joins the main band.

Pronghorn are found mostly in California, Colorado, Montana, North Dakota, South Dakota, and Wyoming. Reasonable numbers are found in Idaho, Nebraska, Nevada, New Mexico, Oregon, Texas, and Utah. Conservation efforts and law enforcements are strict, a reason why the pronghorn is making a comeback, particularly in areas where they were driven off by the grazing of cattle and the changing of the land by sheep herders and early settlers. Efforts are also being made to increase their range. Kansas has been importing pronghorns from Wyoming; and even in Florida, forty pronghorns were imported from Colorado and released on Florida's Kissimmee prairie.

Mountain Lion (*Felis concolor*)

The biggest native cat found in North America is the mountain lion. Also known as the cougar, puma, panther, painter, catamount, and American lion—as well as numerous Indian and Spanish names—it once ranged over the entire map. Now, due to the advance of civilization and the unwise elimination of this cat, its range is limited to high mountain areas of the western states, Mexico, and Canada.

Mountain lions vary in size from 6 to 9 feet and weigh sometimes more than 200 pounds; they measure about 26 to 31 inches at the shoulder. They can be seen today in national parks and wilderness areas, although they are not easy to come upon even when they know they are protected.

Being big animals, they are attracted to large prey such as cattle, sheep, and other farmyard livestock, as well as game as big as deer. For many years several states paid generous bounties for their hides because of their inroads on cattle.

The body color is uniform, with russet to almost gray fur that is about an inch long all over the body. Color may vary seasonally. (Sometimes what are called "black panthers" are seen in Florida, but these are not a separate species.) The face is dark around the eyes and upper muzzle, and the front of the mouth, belly, and lower flanks are an off-white. Mountain lion eyes are usually yellow with black pupils that contract to vertical slits in bright light. The animal has well-rounded ears and conspicuous white whiskers, and the tip of the nose above the white mouth is as pink as a rubber eraser. The head is generally rounded and appears small in proportion to the size of the body. There are five toes on the fore feet and four on the hind, with retractable claws. The tail is close to three feet long and has a dark tip; when stalking its prey, the cat lashes its tail back and forth. The mountain lion is extremely strong and lithe, making very long leaps, and able to gain terrific speed for short spurts to catch its prey.

There is no set period for breeding. Several males may wage fierce battles over a female, and the victor will stay with the female for about two weeks. In about ninety-six days the kittens are born two to four at a time. Kittens come with spotted coats at birth, a ringed tail, and with their eyes tightly closed. In about two weeks the eyes open, and in about a month they are feeding on bits and pieces of meat brought by the mother. When they are two months old, the kittens weigh about ten pounds and begin to follow the mother around. At six months they weigh about thirty-five pounds and are beginning to hunt their own food. The mother keeps the young ones with her for at least a year and sometimes longer.

Although persecuted by relentless hunting practices since the days of the Indians, today it is gradually being recognized that the mountain lion deserves credit for helping to maintain the balance of nature: In taking out the old and crippled animals and by killing sick specimens, the mountain lion is contributing to the general health of the prey species.

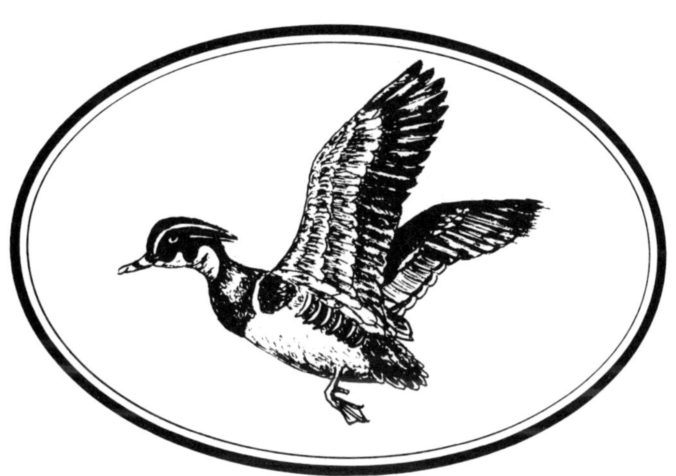

Figure 6.1 Now we come to rendering the big game species, quite a challenge since their bodies are much more flexible and have forms that require exact construction and detailing of motion. The first requirement is good research and, in the case of deer, there are literally hundreds of pictures of them published in the sporting magazines every year. Many of these photos show little of the actual anatomy, but they are good enough for you to follow in making impressionistic sketches or even detailed studies.

Shown in Figure 6.1 are several action poses done directly from photographs and then altered slightly, very slightly, to bring a bit more feeling of life to them. Make several copies of good photos on worksheets, and when you find one that appeals to you but seems a bit stiff, since the action has been "frozen" by a camera, play around with it until the lines of the legs, the angle of the head and antlers, the general appearance, is pleasing to you. There is no artistic law against copying. The best of us have copied Audubon and others and, rest assured, if some day you become famous, others will copy you! But copy for the sake of authenticity and correctness from what the camera has given you.

The next figure goes into more detail on structure and rendering of the deer.

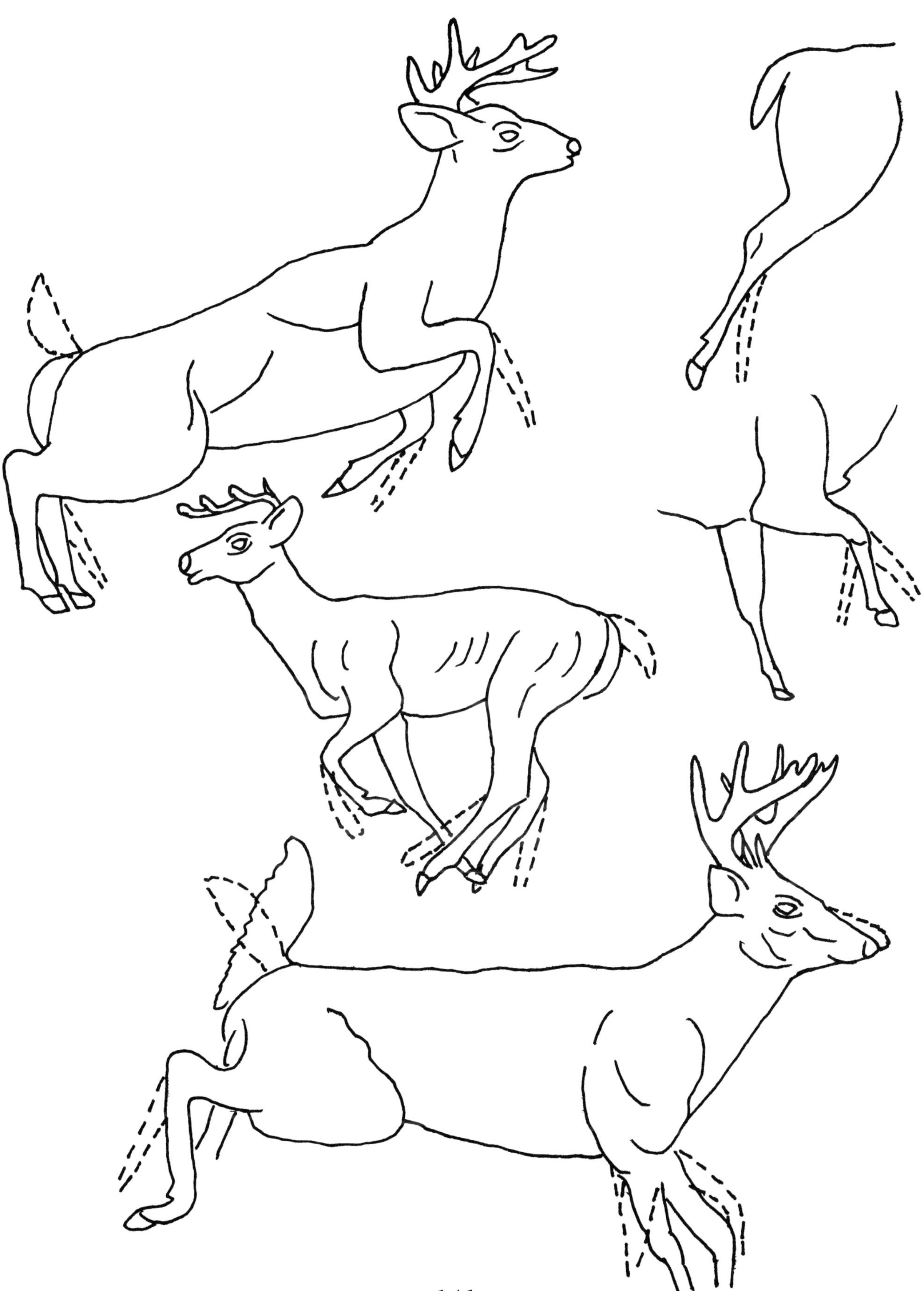

Figure 6.2 Once you have settled on the action pose you want, the next step is in the rendering of the finished picture, a far simpler operation than you had to perform with the game birds, yet one which requires that you adhere to the animal's structure.

The mule deer's head with its prominent black cap is different from the whitetail, as your good research will show, and the antlers are vastly different from those of the whitetail, even though both are "deer."

The partially finished whitetail head and antlers should be compared with the broad and long antlers of the mule deer. All deer and many of the big game species have almost circular white rings of fur around their eyes that show up prominently when they are seen even from a distance. Note the black tail of the mule deer as opposed to the flashy white tail of the whitetail deer, and note that the hairs are much longer in the whitetail.

If you want to create your own "Bambi," get some good photos of a young specimen and create a really appealing little fawn, helpless as it sits in the grass before you. If you want to do a family grouping, don't make the mistake of showing the male with complete antlers. When the young one is born and growing up, the antlers of the buck are long gone.

The pen-and-ink detail on the spotted fawn can work beautifully, as I have shown in the partial illustration. You can really work in the textures here and come up with a very pleasing picture.

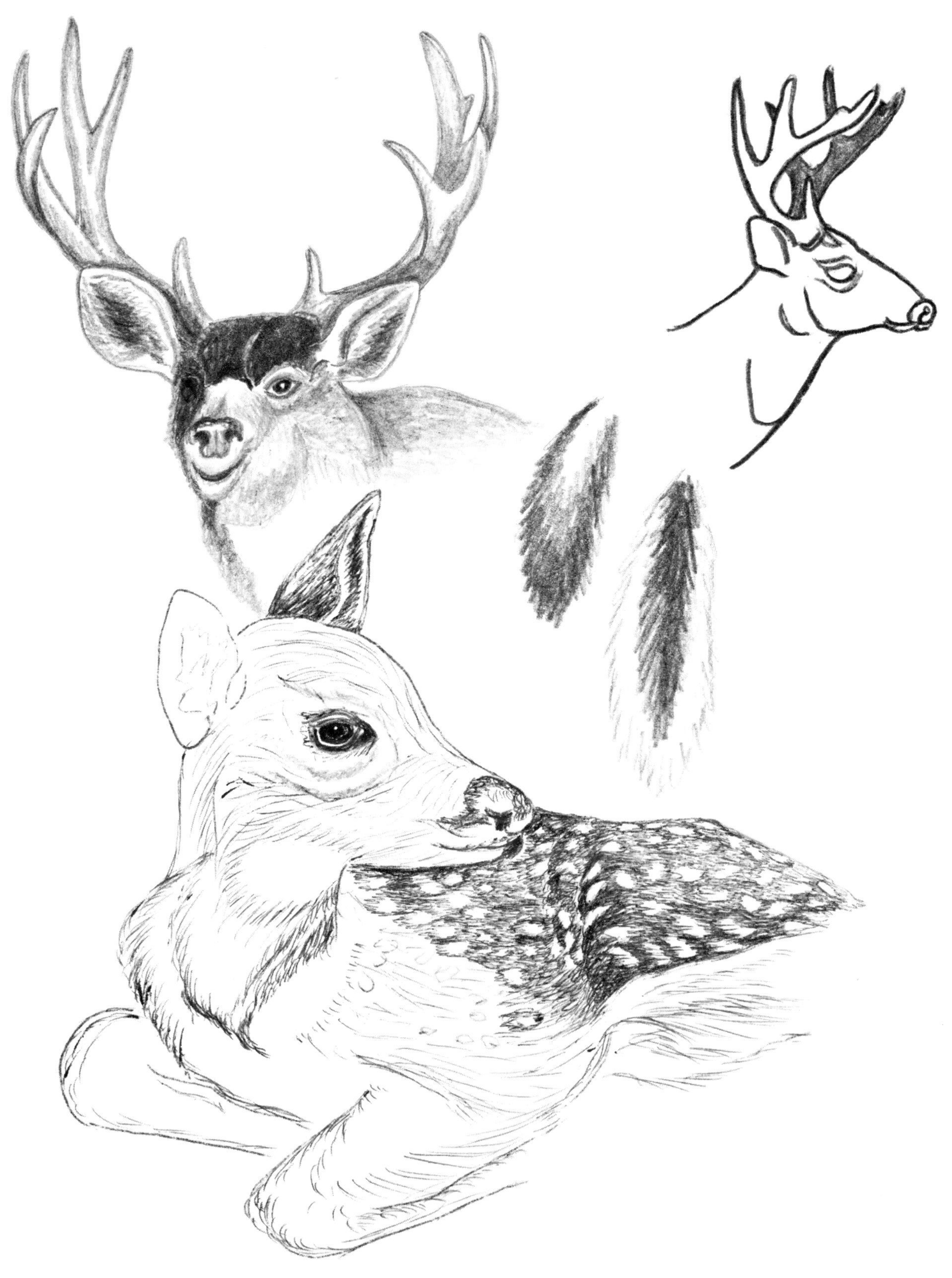

Figure 6.3 What the deer in action offers is magnified by the drama of the mere presence of the moose, whether standing still in the forest or along a lake shore feeding on lily pads.

No matter how you show the moose, given anatomical accuracy, your picture can't help but be a good one. Those magnificent antlers of the male and that long snout—what a combination! Use it to its full extent and show him off for what he is, a great big monster of a bull, just ready to tangle with anyone who gets too close. What a trophy the moose makes, looking at you in finished form from your paper, whether in pencil, pen, or brush. Make several thumbnail sketches from your magazine research, and feel free to turn him around so that the antlers are not shown in a confusion of points.

The upper pencil version is worked from an actual photocopy and merely filled in lightly. The spread antler on its partial skull gives you the general outline of the antlers, and the two lower pictures show the bull facing away from you and with an alternate turning of the head, to show that even this much change can make a better and more interesting picture. Note the shaggy fur on the back of the moose and the typical hanging "bell" of fur. Bring out the feeling of wildness in the background and wildness in your subject.

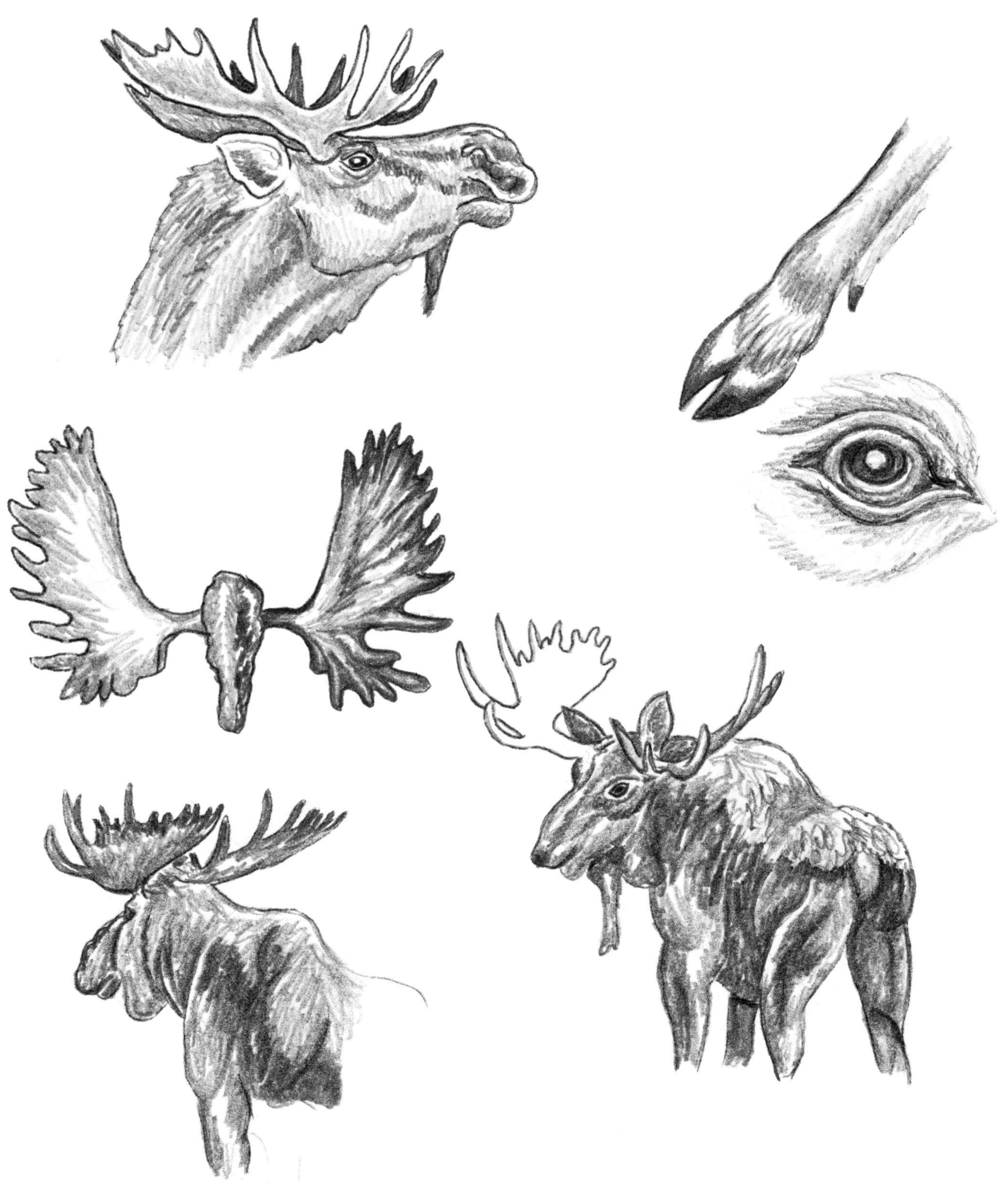

Figure 6.4 The elk is another big game animal that benefits from good research—shown here with a detailed copy of a photograph to give authenticity to the drawing. Note I have outlined the antlers in a dark line in preparation for setting the elk against a light background. Working quickly in pencil, I have indicated the various character lines of the head, particularly the snout and mouth/nose area and sharp, pointed ear. The pen outline of the laid-back antlers with chin held high represents a typical position that the animal assumes when underway through the forest and can be confusing to draw and to view. So keep it simple, minimizing the backside antler and allowing the nearside antler to stand out against them. The cow is outlined in case you want to try an antlerless pose.

This is a wilderness giant to be portrayed in a nervous, strong, or even fighting mood. Avoid the side view with standing animals when possible. Make your subject do something, or about to do something, to add zest and interest to your picture. Don't merely place it there woodenly with the label, "Elk."

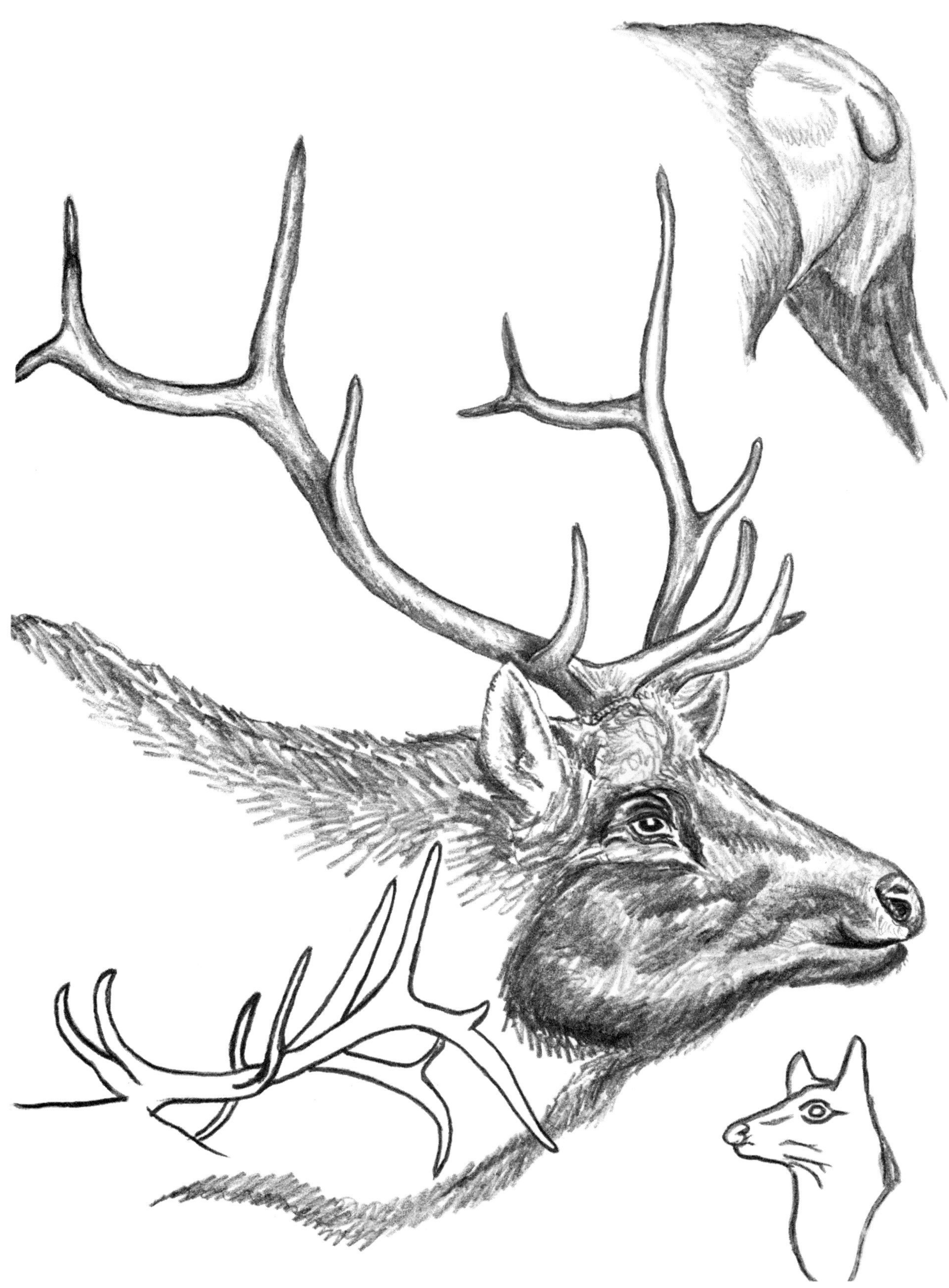

Figure 6.5 With the bears we have one of the most familiar groups of animals seen in the zoo and pictured in children's movies—the biggest, furriest, fiercest, most powerful animals in North America. Show all of these qualities in your work. This is another chance to include drama. If not overdone, it can add immeasurably to the quality of your creative talents.

You can come quite close to caricature when drawing bears simply because they give the impression quite often of being "silly" or acting in a funny way, even though they are not intentionally hamming it up. Watch bears on TV and in the movies, and collect studies of them from photos in the sporting magazines. Quite often they are featured as magazine covers, usually with their mouth open showing their ferocious teeth. Although there are strict differences in the species that can only be seen and studied from good research, their forms are essentially the same. The black bear is smaller and black, the grizzly and brown bears are big and much heavier, with long fur that tends to gather in bunches. Shown here are sketches to get you started, three simple and fast renderings in pencil.

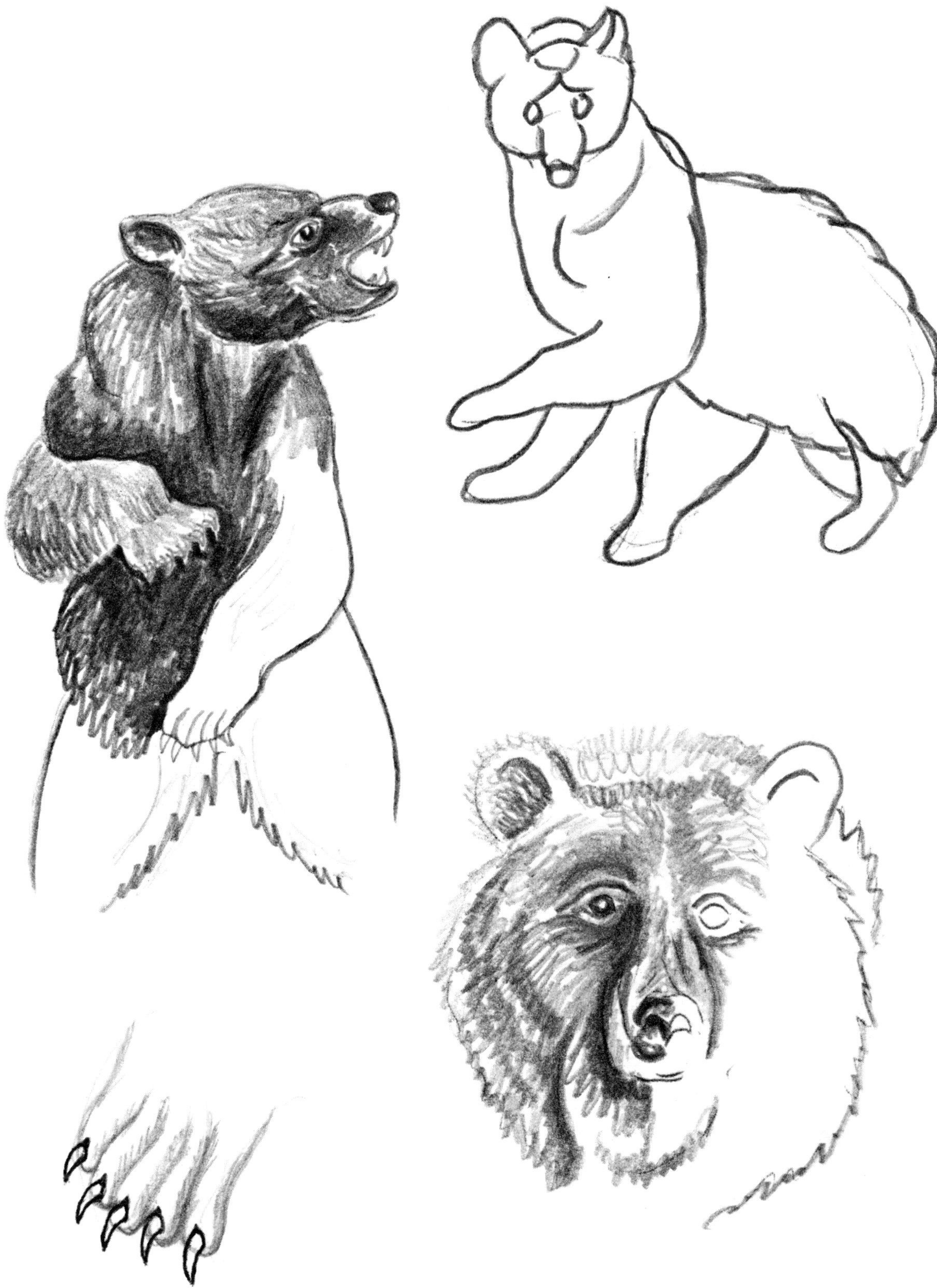

Figure 6.6 Using a good photo to work from, you can draw your own closeup view of this brown bear. Note the very definite clusters of hair and fur and the directions that have to be indicated, including some of the hair that is pointing straight out toward you, not lying flat. This study shows the extremes of fur textures of a typical bear. Note that I have indicated the direction by the groupings of fur as it circles around in the folds of the neck or drapes softly down the side of the face. The hairs on the top of the head are neatly combed but show the construction of the head and particularly the muscles around the eyes. Note the shorter hairs on the muzzle and chin. The nose texture is done in short dots and points to denote the actual nose flesh. The piglike eyes poke out from their lids as the big one peers out across the Arctic scene, looking for danger, a possible mate, or for something good to eat.

This study started with a basic anatomical form, was then zoned into sections with light indications of the direction of fur growth in each zone, and then simply filled in, to be intensified in the final rendering. Try this one for practice, and work it up slowly until you reach the peak of the needed contrasts. Don't go too far or too dark. Learn to stop when it is finished and avoid overdoing it.

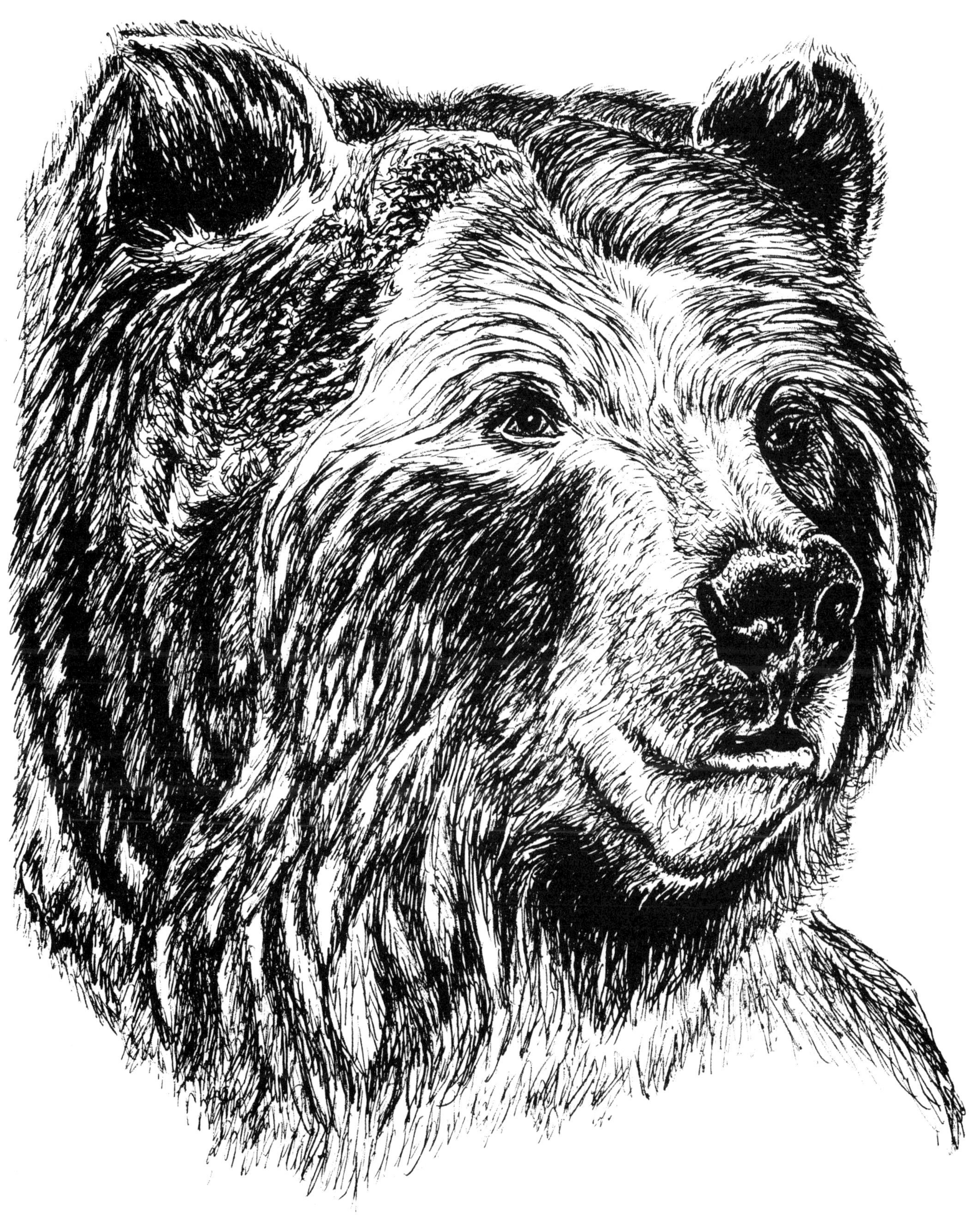

Figure 6.7 Two interesting characters of the western high-mountain country can make magnificent pictures when you have good research to work from. I have done them both in pen and ink to show just how to perform the needed detail, especially in the case of the ram's horns and the picky texture of its fur, plus the longer hairs along neck and back.

The goat can be individualized a bit more, since this animal suggests greater "personality" due to its propensity to assume funny and unexpected attitudes.

Play around with these animals. Put them in appropriate backgrounds, like mountain scenery acquired from nature, sporting, or travel magazines. Work large, and don't be afraid to do a closeup of the head and horns, similar to the one I did on the brown bear. These handsome animals will look nice on the den wall.

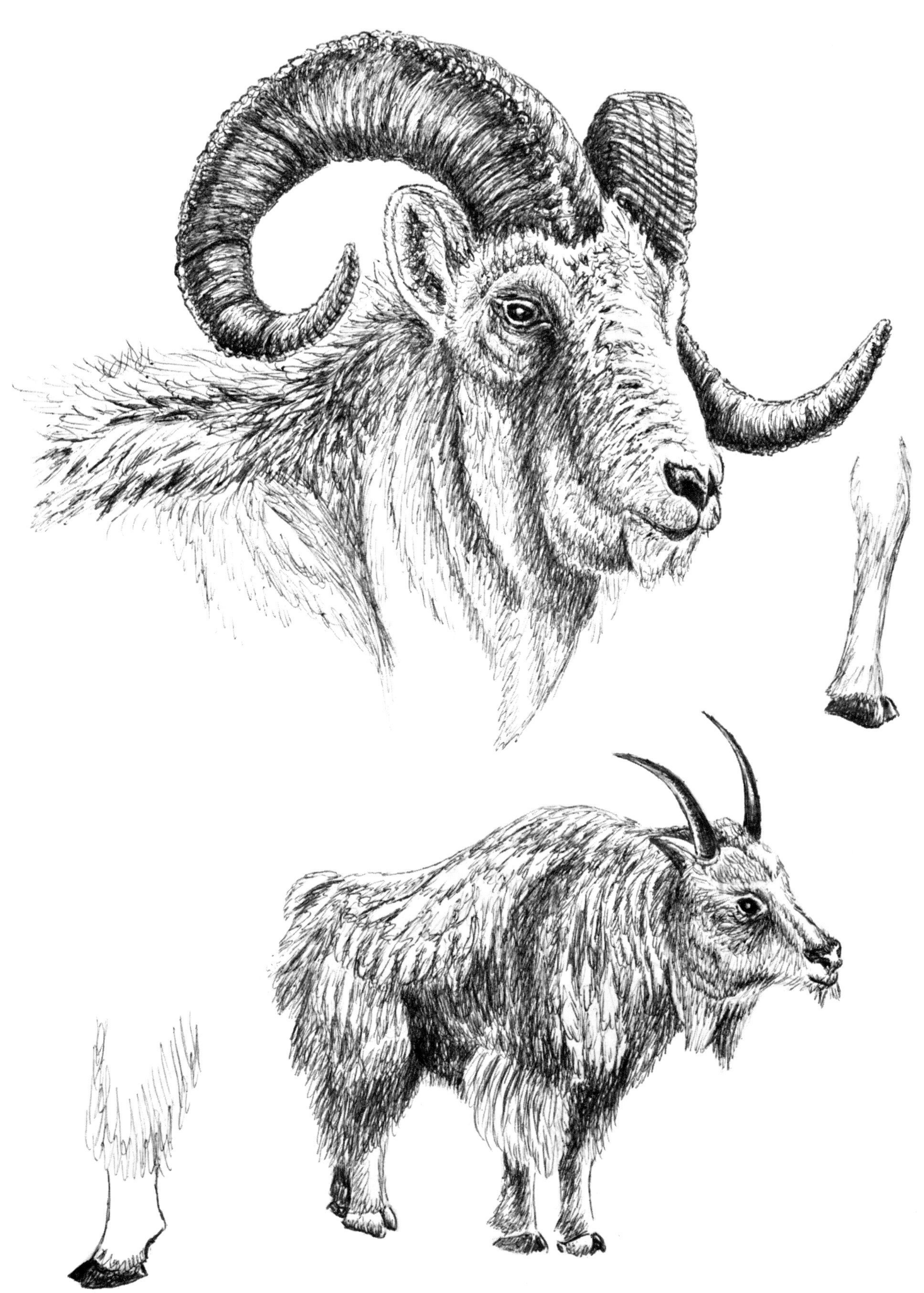

Figure 6.8 The antelope, creature of the wide open spaces—being exposed in the open, he's always alert and can bound away at the slightest hint of danger. Picture the antelope as nervous as you can make it, or speeding away as fast as its legs can function, or do a closeup. This one is inspiring.

Note the upper illustration, which is merely a copy of a photograph, lightly filled in and showing the first step in rendering. Note the leg lines that have to be shaped and the almost awkward stretch of the neck and the angle of the horns. This is a typical posture of this animal as it moves along out in the open.

The big drawing is an attempt to show light against dark in the forming of the horns. If you choose a dark background, edge the horns in white, forming the semicircular form with a dark shadow near the center line to show the contour. If you choose to project the horn into a light background, you can sharpen the outer edges of the horn and build the rounded form to a highlight near the center line. I have merely indicated the head lines so you can begin to fill in the rest for yourself. Good research will show you how to do the nose and mouth. Note the difference in the antlers—they are not always perfect sets. This antelope had one of its horn tips broken off, perhaps in a mating fight.

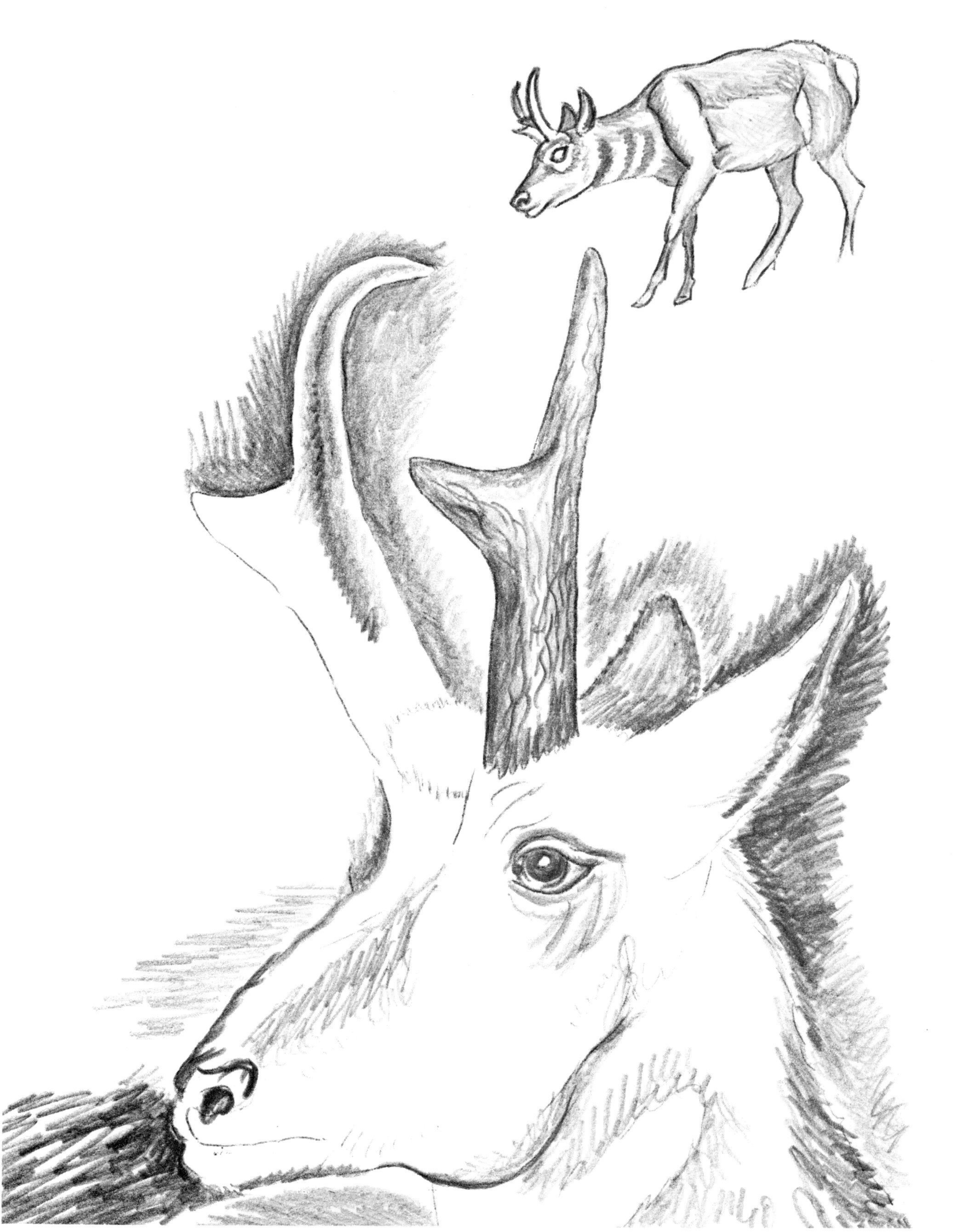

Figure 6.9 Our biggest cat, the mountain lion, suggests built-in drama in every inch of its powerful body. Work from good research and bring out all the feline qualities of this magnificent animal. The bare outline of the head was taken from a photo I've left for you to finish, as I have finished the somber face done in pencil. Note the tufty fur quality. I have slightly overdone the layers of fur on the head, which should be softened a bit; they are there for study. The action outline of the stalking cat is another suggestion to work with. Note also the detail of the eye.

I leave you now to your own creativity. Having gone through several of the big game animals already, try to capture the mood and manner of this subject, paying particular attention to the structure of the muscles and draping the fur over them in an authentic way.

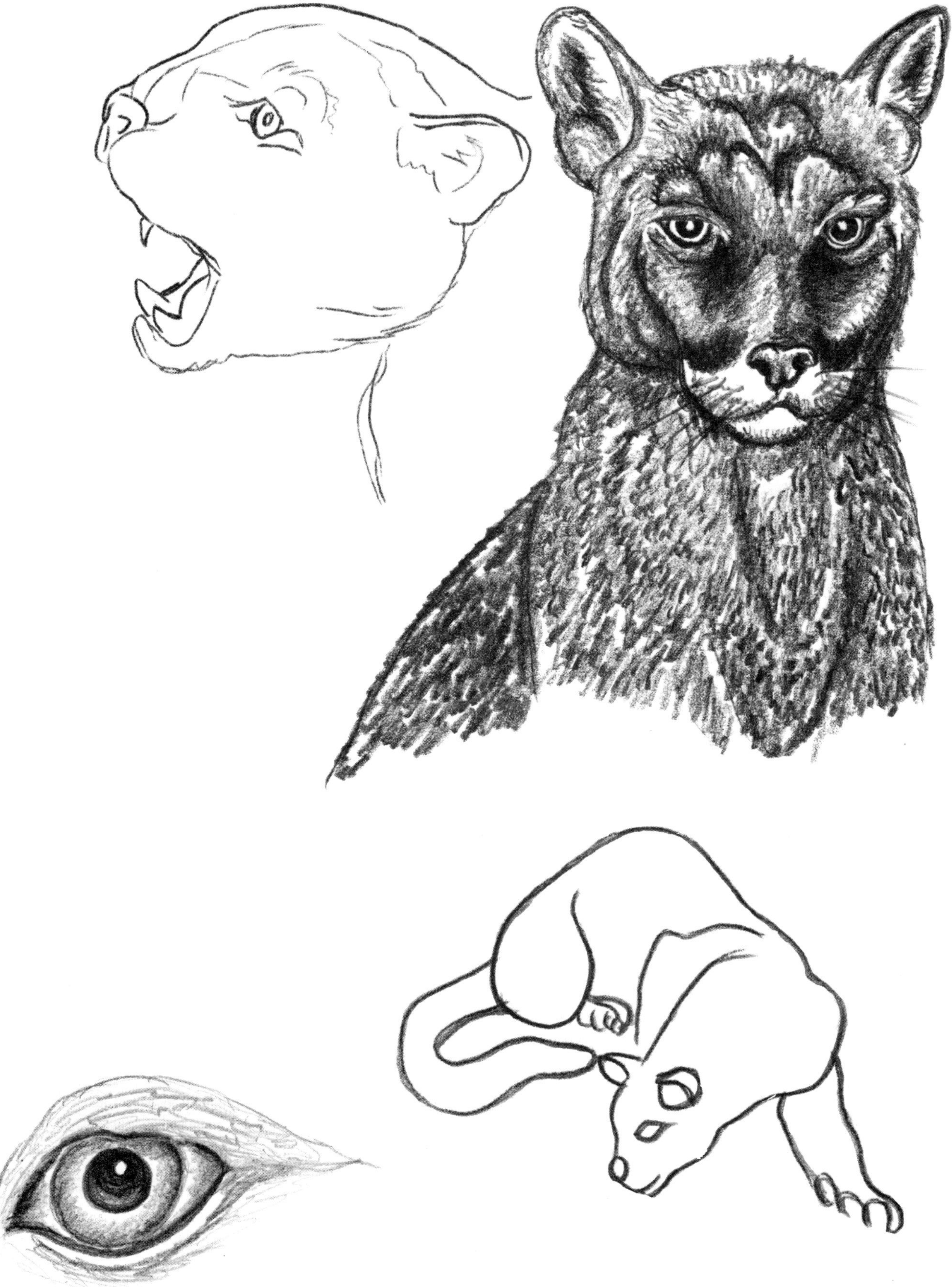

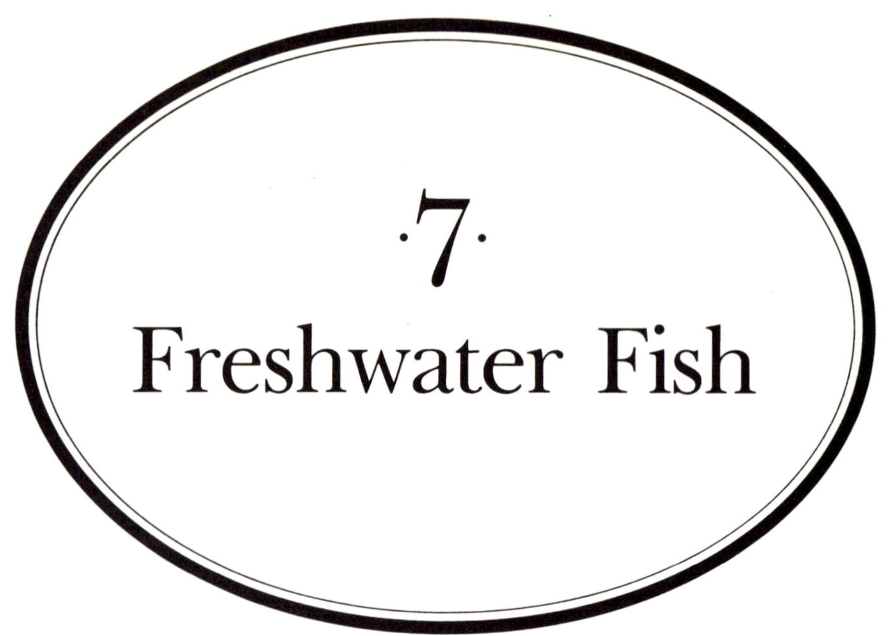

·7· Freshwater Fish

How do you place on paper a rainbow of colors and reflections—a shining trout jumping out of the water—and do it realistically? It happens in an instant: Stopping that motion and making it realistic is quite a challenge. But be assured that no one has ever seen it in clear detail, so you are free to go your own way. Here's your chance to really go creative.

North America, and particularly the United States, is blessed with a generous list of freshwater fish. The earliest settlers on Cape Cod enjoyed sea-run brook trout for their first Thanksgiving. Many species quickly became basic table fare for the new settlers, and continued so as they went west all the way to the Pacific Coast. They learned from the Indians the ways of catching and cooking these fish.

Later, when the country attracted the barons of Europe, these gentry brought with them a well-established form of sport known as angling. These were followers of a sport made immortal by Izaak Walton and other pioneers of this recreation. "Gentlemen of the rod" they were called. They were expert in angling, particularly fly fishing, as practiced on the chalk streams of England. The art of angling gradually developed in the new world into an avid interest and, in more recent times, has become a way of life for millions of men and women with leisure time at their disposal. Sport fishing in particular is a major recreation. More books have been written about fishing, particularly fly fishing, than all other sports combined.

Aside from angling, there are a number of interesting ways to observe various species of fish. One way of course is by simple observation from the shore. Bass and sunfish nest along the shore, and their nests can be readily seen from the banks or rushes of a lake. A quiet approach to within hand distance of the nest can be made and pictures can be taken.

Other species of fish can be observed during their spawning runs in the high and remote tributaries of streams frequented by these fish. A rigorous hike to a high mountain tributary in the spring or fall will likely produce a show well worth photographing. Later, after the eggs have hatched, the little fingerlings can then be observed.

Other opportunities are at state and commercial fish hatcheries where fingerlings are on display, or the docks where anglers come in with their catches, providing opportunities to photograph and study the specimens.

Rainbow Trout *(Salmo gairdneri)*

The rainbow trout was at one time native to the Pacific Coast from southern California to Alaska, but since its discovery as an excellent game fish it has been introduced into many waters around the world. Good rainbow fishing can be had in Ceylon and in South America, notably in Argentina, Chile, and Peru. Transplants are thriving also in New Zealand and Australia. Germany, France, and Japan also have their rainbows, which originated on our Pacific Coast. Many of our better eastern trout streams now boast "native" populations of rainbows, and wild rivers all the way south to Georgia and Arkansas can claim terrific catches of oversize rainbows that are natural spawn.

The rainbow should be considered the same fish as the steelhead trout, except that it does not have access to saltwater if stocked in landlocked rivers or lakes. But if there is a reservoir or lake at the bottom of the stream into which it is stocked, it will migrate down to the lake, spend the better part of the year there, and then ascend each year to spawn in a tributary sometimes far away from the main lake.

Like the steelhead, the rainbow trout feeds on crustaceans, worms, smaller fish, and especially aquatic and land-bred insects. It is fair game for all types of angling methods. Its coloration is olive-blue-green on the back, a gold and mother-of-pearl blend on the body side, with a yellowish-gold belly. In some waters the fish are almost black or blue-green-black, with very prominent black marks. There is a distinct, very brilliant red stripe down the center of each side, intensifying at the gill covers and bleeding out to the top and bottom of the fish, making it a fireball of color. (See Figure 7.2*a*.)

Rainbows reach a weight of forty pounds in deep, cold lakes, but the average size is from two to ten pounds. They vary in shape to some degree: Some found in lakes will be plump with very large and fierce looking heads, while others will be slim with very small heads.

Many of the waters below man-made impoundments have become excellent waters for rainbows since the water coming from the portals remains cold enough for all-year residence. New England, New York, Pennsylvania, Michigan, and all far-western states have excellent lakes and streams with goodly supplies of rainbows.

Brook Trout *(Salvelinus fontinalis)*

The true native trout of the Northeast, the eastern brook trout—or "squaretail," as it is known—is a species apart from the technical trout or salars. It, like the lake trout and the Dolly Varden, is a char, not a salmon. This is the fish that was reportedly the first to be sampled on the Pilgrims' Thanksgiving table—trout that came from the ponds and creeks of Cape Cod, where the brook trout is a sea-run fish. The range of the species at that time was from Cape Cod north into Labrador, west into Ontario, and south into Virginia. Since then extensive plantings have been made in all parts of the country, including the Rocky Mountain states, where the "squaretail" has fared even better than in its native waters due to superior food conditions, water levels, and temperatures.

Generally the brook trout ranges in length from about ten to fifteen inches and weighs from one-half to two or possibly three pounds. The "brookie" rivals the golden in beauty and is immediately recognized by the vermiculation marks on the back in a dark-green shade contrasted against an olive or sometimes orange cast. These marks resemble those of the Boston mackerel. The trout's blue-purple burnished sides are pockmarked with yellowish, blurry dots and, between them, sky-blue dots with brilliant pink centers. As if not enough, the brookie also wears bright orange fins with a black and white bar, a marking also found on the broad tail. (See Figure 7.2*b*.)

The brook trout likes cold water, secluded brooks, and deep lakes. It is seldom found on broad, open stretches of rivers or streams where the rainbow and brown reside. It spawns in the fall along with the brown trout, as opposed to the spring spawning habits of the rainbow clan. Many states stock the brook trout for early spring fishing, stocking the browns and rainbows later.

Brown Trout *(Salmo trutta,* or *Salmo fario)*

Known in European waters as the Von Behr trout, *salmo trutta* is both a sea-run and a landlocked trout similar in habits of migration to the rainbow trout. It was imported into the United States in 1880 from German stock and planted in a few streams in the northeast. Since that day, the brown trout has spread to the point where it can be truly called a "native" American, since it has adapted to its environment and breeds strongly and well and grows to prodigious size wherever good clear, cool water abounds.

Brown trouts average five pounds, but record fish go as high as twenty or thirty. Essentially yellow and brown, they also show greenish tinges with prominent black spots surrounded by white rings. There are several reddish spots along the sides. (See Figure 7.2*c*.)

The brown trout can sustain its lifecycle in much warmer water and more open stream conditions than the brook trout, is a much more adaptable fish than the rainbow, and is found in waters where smallmouth bass would not thrive.

Golden Trout *(Salmo aguabonita)*

Unquestionably the golden trout is the most beautiful of all trout, yes, even surpassing the brilliant and very special eastern brook trout. Born in the volcanic streams originating in the high peaks of California's Sierra Mountains, notably the Soda Creek and Volcano Creek area and the South Fork of the Kern River near the Sequoia giants, this trout is limited in its range to the 10,000 foot level. It reverts to the rainbow markings and habits when removed from its very small regional home high above the clouds. (See Figure 7.2*d*.)

Fortunately, early conservation efforts were put into effect by sportsmen and conservationists until the California Fish Commission restricted the catch and also restricted the development of its waters. Since then a few adequate hatcheries have been able to maintain and extend this particular strain of rainbow variation and keep it pure. Goldens have been exported to the nearby states of Idaho, Wyoming, and Colorado; there, these trouts have been bred in special high-altitude hatcheries where similar qualities and streambed conditions help the fish to retain their unusual markings and color. Since there is little minnow life and still less aquatic insect life in their native water, goldens rely almost wholly on a species of freshwater shrimp found only in their locale.

The golden is more red-orange than gold. The back is generally an olive with a slight golden-orange cast. The brilliant blue parr marks, or large splotches spaced in a line along the side (known as the lateral line), are sometimes sky blue against a brownish-orange stripe. The lower sides are yellowish, with a sometimes pink or orange mother-of-pearl coloration. The bottom edge of the belly is solid reddish-orange and sometimes the color of fresh blood. There are a few black spots near the tail and along the top of the back, though few in number. Some specimens include these spots on the gill covers and on the back of the head. The fins are spotted similarly to the landlocked rainbow.

Cook's Lake, Wyoming, produced a golden trout weighing eleven pounds in 1948, but generally goldens weigh a pound or less.

Atlantic Salmon *(Salmo salar)*

The one main difference in the habits of the Atlantic salmon, as compared with the Pacific, is that the Atlantic salmon is programmed for several migrations upstream to spawn. Tagged salmon have been observed to make as many as six or seven trips. The Pacific salmon has only one chance to perpetuate its species. Atlantic salmon have been transplanted to the Pacific in order to bolster the fisheries there, but they have not survived. In fact, several salmon released in Pacific waters were found a year later in their natural stream in New Brunswick, having made the long and hazardous trip across the Arctic water wastes back to their homeland! It is this kind of stubborn and testy power that the angler enjoys when he hooks a big one.

Atlantics range in size from six to nine pounds in the grilse stage, that is, the first-year run salmon. The adult salmon ranges up to thirty and sometimes fifty pounds, although the usual weight is about twenty to twenty-five pounds.

Salmon are known to jump clear out of the water and are rivaled only by the southern tarpon in this talent. A most inspiring spectacle can be witnessed when salmon assault the falls in a river. Intent on the move upstream, they will jump and jump repeatedly, testing the strength of the water flow, and finally, in one stupendous burst of energy, sail high over the foam and rocks and with a flip of the powerful tail propel themselves into the pocket water at the head of the run. There they will rest in a pool, to later continue their run toward the spawning grounds in a shallow tributary, far in the wilderness.

As with the Pacific salmon, there are periodic runs during the year depending on the conditions, latitude, and water temperature. Generally, three basic runs constitute the schedule: spring, summer, and early fall. Early May in northern Maine constitutes the first run, and the last ascension in New Brunswick on the famous Miramichi River can be as late as the last week in October. Spawning takes place in the fall when the water temperature drops to about fifty degrees. The young fish return to the ocean in about their second or third spring.

The Atlantic salmon color is blue-green on the back with silvery sides generously spotted with black pepper marks. It darkens considerably after being in fresh water.

Great Northern Pike *(Esox lucius)*

Smaller brother of the muskie, the northern pike is as capable a fighter and as good a table delicacy. Its range is similar to that of the muskie, except that it is found in the waters farther north into Alaska and into the mid- and central-western states and the southern tier of the central states.

It has distinctive whitish or yellowish markings that fully distinguish it from the muskie or the chain pickerel, though it is almost identical in shape and fierceness to the muskie. (See Figure 7.4*a*.)

The northern pike, like the muskie, is very cannibalistic, feeding on its own kind and, in fact, on anything that moves in its vicinity, making it a good quarry for the sportsman.

The largest pike of authenticated record was taken in New York's Sacandaga Reservoir in 1940 and weighed over forty-six pounds. Habits and spawning activity are similar to the bass and other pikes. Northern pike are found in northern rivers and sometimes even in creeks but reach their greatest size in the largest and deepest lakes far into the northern reaches of Canada and into Alaska, where they are an important food for the Indians and Eskimos there.

Chain Pickerel (*Esox niger*)

Smallest of the pike family, the chain pickerel is well named because of the chainlike markings of a dark green or bronze, contrasted against a greenish-yellow and sometimes light-bronze background. It has the same type of sharp nose and strong head, with the protruding eyes similar to the pike and muskie. The dorsal fin is located well down on the back near the tail.

In range the pickerel inhabits the same waters as the bass and pike, and likewise its habits are similar to the spring spawning of those fish, liking lakes, rivers, and even small brooks in its range. It feeds on all manner of aquatic insects and fish life, including the fingerlings of its own species. The chain pickerel averages about fifteen to eighteen inches in length, with a nine-pounder taken as a record from Medford Lakes in New Jersey in 1957. Its smaller relative, the barred pickerel, is classed as a panfish, reaching a size of about a foot in length *(Esox americanus).* (See Figure 7.4*b*.)

Mud Pickerel (*Esox vermiculatus*)

The mud pickerel, called the grass pike of the Middle West, and the barred pickerel (*Esox americanus*)—ranging the Atlantic states—are subspecies of the chain pickerel, with similar habits and size.

Smallmouth Bass (*Micropterus dolomieui*)

Smallmouth bass are found native in waters that also contain trout, especially lake and brown. Many rivers that enter into reservoirs and impoundments have native supplies of smallmouths. Many of the better trout streams contain large populations of these bass in the lower and slower sections.

The smallmouth, also known as the bronzeback, is of brown-bronze-green coloration with fainter splotchy marks along the lateral line that usually take the shape of vertical bars. Three lines of dark color span out and back from the eye, covering the gills.

Like the largemouth, the smallmouth nests in the sandy shores of a lake or apart from the strong river currents. The nest is a hollowed-out, bowl-shaped ring about two feet across, where the eggs are laid and cared for until the little fish have grown big enough to forage for themselves.

The nesting is done in the late spring, depending on the climate and water temperature and conditions.

Smallmouths do not grow to as big a size as the largemouth, the biggest taken so far being more than eleven pounds, which was caught in the Dale Hollow Lake in Kentucky in 1955. The smallmouth has been extended in range, and in some waters it is supplanting the largemouth where the water temperature is comfortable. They prefer a sixty-degree temperature for their best activity periods. (See Figure 7.4*c*.)

Largemouth Bass (*Micropterus salmoides*)

Largemouths like the weedy shallows of lakes and are also fond of grassy ledges and pond-lily flats and snags. In rivers they seek out the shallower sections astride the main currents where the passing insects flow during the hatches. Bass frequent the shorelines at night after the water cools. They are most comfortable and feed voraciously when the water temperature is around seventy degrees.

The Florida variety produces the largest sizes, often exceeding the ten-pound mark. Recently they have been stocked in California lakes, namely in San Diego county where they are reported to reach a weight of fifty pounds.

The largemouth is generally a bottle-green color, which sometimes approaches a bronze-green hue. The body is splotched with darker green or brown irregular markings along the lateral line. Three dark bars decorate the large gill covers. (See Figure 7.4*d*.)

This species can be distinguished from its close cousin, the smallmouth, by the size of the mouth. If the upper-lip bar extends to behind the eye of the fish, it is a largemouth. If the bar is shorter than the eye, it is a smallmouth.

Yellow Perch (*Perca flavescens*)

This is a typical fish of the central and eastern states, though it has been introduced into the Pacific states and as far north as British Columbia, where it thrives. It abounds in the Great Lakes and in rivers, ponds, and lakes from northeastern Canada to as far south as the Carolinas.

One of the prettiest of the panfish, the back is olive-green and the sides golden-yellow, with blackish triangular bars extending from the back down almost to the belly line. Its fins are sometimes salmon color or bright orange.

This species is not wanted in trout waters, especially ponds where trout are attempting to gain a foothold. Like all rough fish, the perch is voracious in its feeding habits and takes on the softer and weaker trout, especially the small ones—but they vie for their life in waters that contain bass and the pikes. In fact, the yellow perch of small size is good bait for big bass and pikes, especially the walleye. The perch's food consists of insects and anything small that moves. A school fish, they spawn in droves in the early spring when the water conditions and temperature warrant. They average in size to between eight and twelve inches.

White Perch (*Roccus americanus*)

The white perch is a fish very similar to the white bass, and in fact is called the white bass in some localities. Another Latin name, *Morone americana,* confuses its identification, biologically speaking, but the fish is the same. A dweller in both fresh and saltwater, the white perch migrates to salt or fresh water for spawning. If the fish inhabits a large lake it will also migrate into a stream to spawn. The white perch is one of a large family of *Serranidae,* the sea basses. The well-known striped bass is a close relative, also an anadromous fish.

The white perch has been stocked heavily in lakes where trout used to be plentiful, serving as a food fish for big game species and also as a popular panfish. Being a school fish like the white bass, it can be taken in large counts when a school is located. It is primarily an eastern species, weighing up to a pound, but specimens of two pounds have been taken. This is a bright little fish: golden and silvery with horizontal black markings along its sides. (See Figure 7.5*a.*)

Crappie (Black: *Pomoxis nigro-maculatus,* and White: *Pomoxis annularis*)

Shaped like many of the sunfish family, this fish has a plump, almost oval body, spiney dorsal fin, large, flappy fins, and spectacular coloration. There is little difference between the two species other than range and gradation of color. (The black is simply blacker than the white!) The overall coloration is a clear, silvery-green with darker green and black splotchy markings on the scales. (See Figure 7.5*b.*)

Called by any other name—bachelor, campbellite, tinmouth, sac-a-lait, goggle-eye, speckled perch—it is plentiful in ponds, lakes, and slower marshy water. It has been planted and grows well in California lakes.

It averages in size upwards from one pound, with South Carolina producing the record fish at five pounds, taken in the Santee-Cooper Lake in 1960.

Bluegill (*Leponis pallidus*)

One of a large family of the most colorful fish of the northern hemisphere, the bluegill is a favorite of both anglers and aquarists. It has a variety of local names such as blue bream, blue sunfish, copper-nosed sunfish, and dollardee. Its original range was from the Great Lakes to the Mississippi Valley, from western New York and Pennsylvania and Iowa to Missouri, and from Minnesota to Florida and the Rio Grande country. It has been introduced into many waters since and has thrived especially in waters too warm for bass and trout. Farm ponds and recreational lakes are where it is appreciated, especially by the younger fishermen.

It is the largest of the sunfish family, reaching a maximum weight of about two pounds, usually averaging about a half-pound. It is basically a dark greenish-blue and sometimes has purple head markings: blueish on the back and gold and olive on the belly, with brown-black vertical bars on the sides.

Like all sunfish, bluegill are late-spring spawners and build their nests on the sandy shoreline in the shape of a bowl. They defend their nests against all comers, including the angler's flies. (See Figure 7.5*c*.)

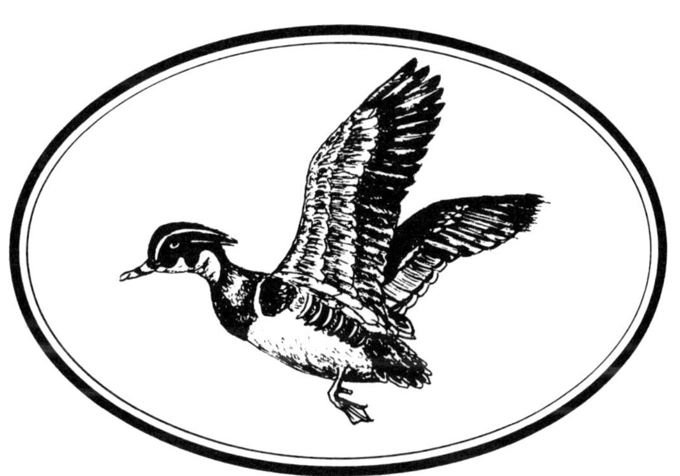

Figure 7.1 Drawing and painting game fish is fun, since you can contort your fish in a number of ways as shown here in these line layouts. Even these can be added to by merely moving them around. *b,* for example, can be flipped in several ways, and so can *d.* Move this page around and see what I mean.

The most important factor of course is proper line and proportion and strict adherenece to species detail—for example, the shape and arrangement of the fins. Trout are quite different from pike, bass are quite different from sailfish. Even bass have very definite structural detail to watch for. The smallmouth bass has its eye placed behind the mandible, while the largemouth's eye is placed ahead of where the mandible ends. Note this in Figure 7.5.

In shaping your rough line drawing for any fish, play around with wide sweeps of your pencil, finding an appealing line you wish to be dominant in the picture and determining just how big or small the fish will be in relation to the size of your work. Do you want a species in closeup? If so, be prepared to delve into a lot of detail work. If the image will be fairly small, however, such detail is not necessary.

Fish can be drawn in an underwater setting, and *a* would be a simple side-view outline for such a picture. A lazily feeding trout like *f* would give the figure a little more life, but still suggesting very easy motion underwater. Although the other views can be used underwater, they are also designed for leaping pictures, as the trout tries for a flying insect or is hooked by an angler's line.

The outline of the fish's anatomy—proportions, fin sizes, shapes—all must be accurate. This is not hard if you have done your research homework. The fishing and hunting magazines offer all kinds of photos to use as suggestions and quite often they are in color, which will be of great help when you work in other than black and white or wash.

Background, especially the splash the fish makes when it comes out of the water or rushes across the surface, is covered later. But for now play around with layout sketches, and when you find one that suits a specific fish you like, go to work on it.

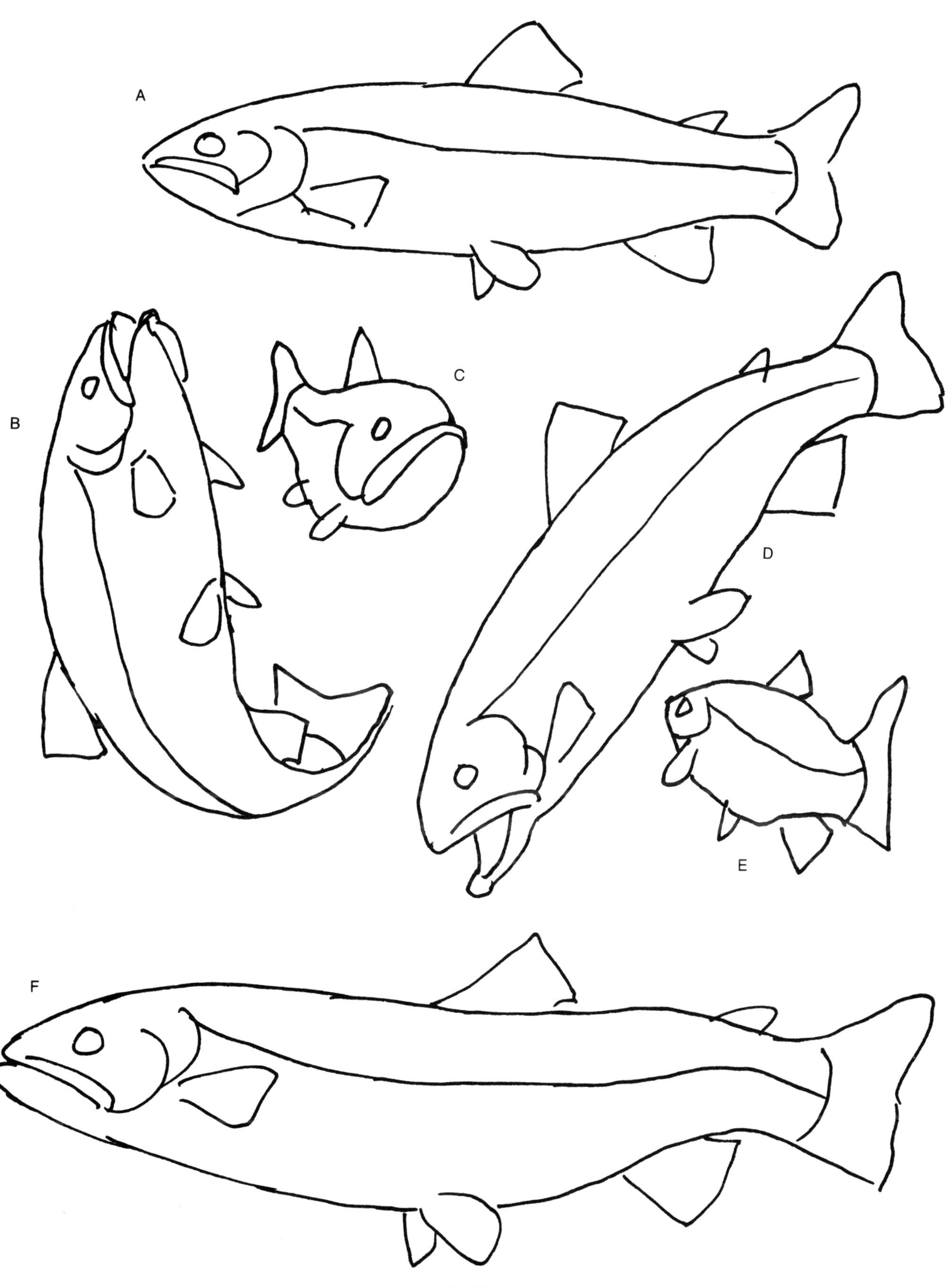
A
B
C
D
E
F

Figure 7.2 Here we have the brook trout, brown trout, rainbow trout, and golden trout. This page of pen and inks shows not only the poses decided upon for a simple side view of each, but also the very distinct markings on each of the favorite trout species.

(a) The rainbow is spotted almost all over except the belly, but the spots are small compared to those on the brown trout, *c*.

(b) The brook trout has a monopoly on vermiculations along the top and upper side, and the open, almost white spots along the side. Note the black line in the tail and other fins, a line not found on the other trout.

(c) Here is the brown trout, larger-spotted compared to the rainbow.

(d) This is the famed golden trout of the high Sierras, a small, reddish species of the rainbow trout. Note the white tips on the fins with the slight bar mark and the centerline dark spots in a row.

Although these shapes are common, there is of course some variance in a fish's form depending on the kind of water and other conditions in which it lives. Some fish are fat, some thin, some with big heads, others with small heads. So you have some latitude here.

Note I have indicated by little arrows the areas where I have begun to shade the fish utilizing the characteristic markings found on them. The brook trout is shaded black against its dark dorsal fin, but below that shading is a bright area which should extend the length of the fish for the suggestion of reflection. Note that the middle of the body is shaded deeply to taper off to a lighter shade on the bottom as the fish's body reflects the light from below.

The rainbow is shaded darker on the bottom to contrast with a suggested lighter background. Just below the rainbow are two sketches to show light against dark and dark against light. You should plan ahead, deciding in advance which contrast you want before you begin shading in your fish's body. I have also indicated how to fill in around the spots and to indicate scale markings when needed.

Visit the aquarium nearest you and watch these trout and other fish, paying particular attention to their actions, their basic colorations, and the play of light that makes them such an artist's challenge.

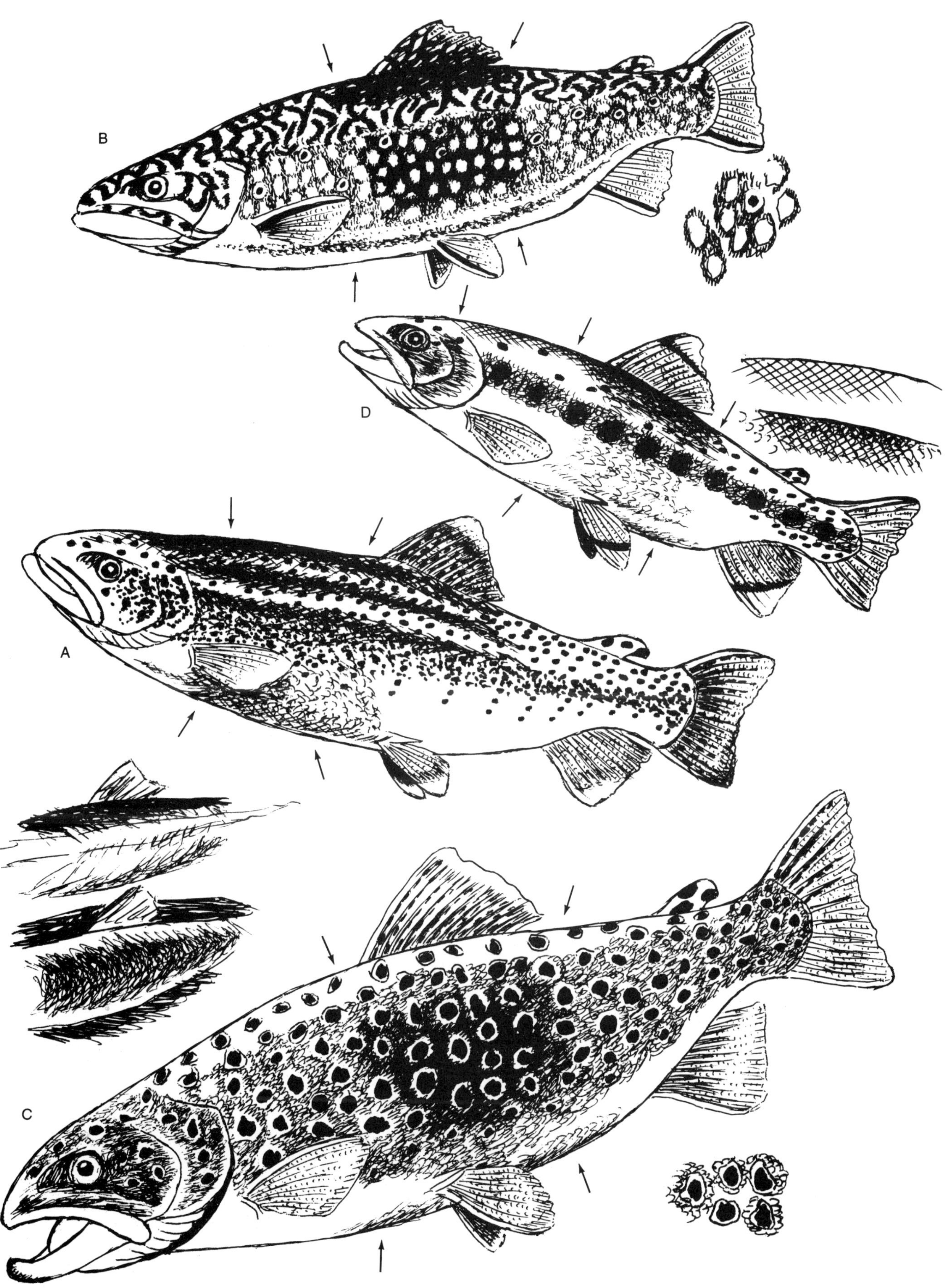
B
D
A
C

Figure 7.3 The king of fishes, the Atlantic salmon, *Salmon salar,* the leaper. Shown here is the female who looks very much like a big rainbow trout and, below her, the buck salmon with his jaws grown out for the scooping up of gravel to make the nest for their eggs. He's a mean looking critter here, with much character.

Again, I have not finished the female, suggesting just how to continue indicating the scales and markings. You can keep her light or make her dark, depending on the background plans for your picture.

Twist the salmon just as you would the trout or other fish to make an interesting and action-packed picture. Salmon attempting to jump high waterfalls are often photographed and show the extremes the fish must go through to ascend a river. Do a waterfall picture with a couple of jumpers in it, and include some of the foliage and rocks in the picture. If you do a closeup of the old buck salmon, place him in a setting of colorful underwater stones, a suggestion of stream weeds and green algae, or perhaps an old snag.

Note the detail in the eye. This is similar to all trout and bass eyes, so follow it. I have purposely overdone the sculpting and shading of the big salmon's gills to show how to intensify and to suggest some reflection at the same time.

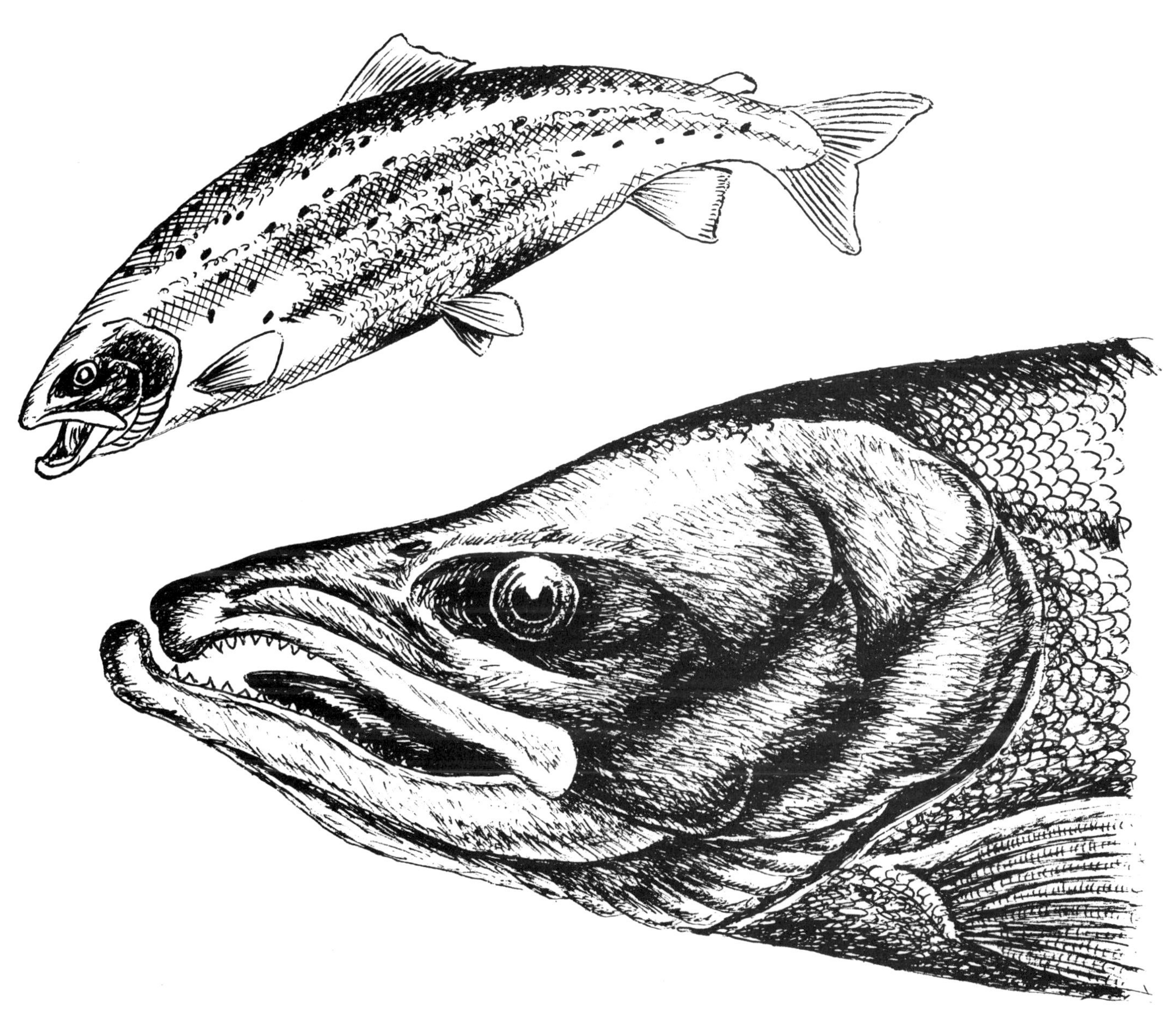

Figure 7.4 Here we have the pike, pickerel, smallmouth bass, and largemouth bass. In this case I have almost finished them for you, at least to the point of the final, very subtle touches.

Note the vast difference in the markings and the fact that the scales of these fish stand out much more than those on the trout. I show here how to start and finish your scale markings, beginning with the cross-hatch and then going over it with "33s"—an easy motion for the hand. Intensify by merely fillng in, but do leave a lot of open spots for the suggestion of reflection. The actual spots that are dark are done as indicated in an extreme closeup; otherwise they are merely indicated by blotching them in.

These are all very common and popular fish, and I suggest you look at the ones you catch yourself with the eye of an artist. You'll discover beauty here, not just a "mere fish." Look, all you have to do to change the coloring is to move the fish in your hands ever so slightly. Available light is also a big factor. A fish caught at twilight glows with a kind of gold that is precious; the blue of the midday sky will show beautifully. Note where you want this to happen.

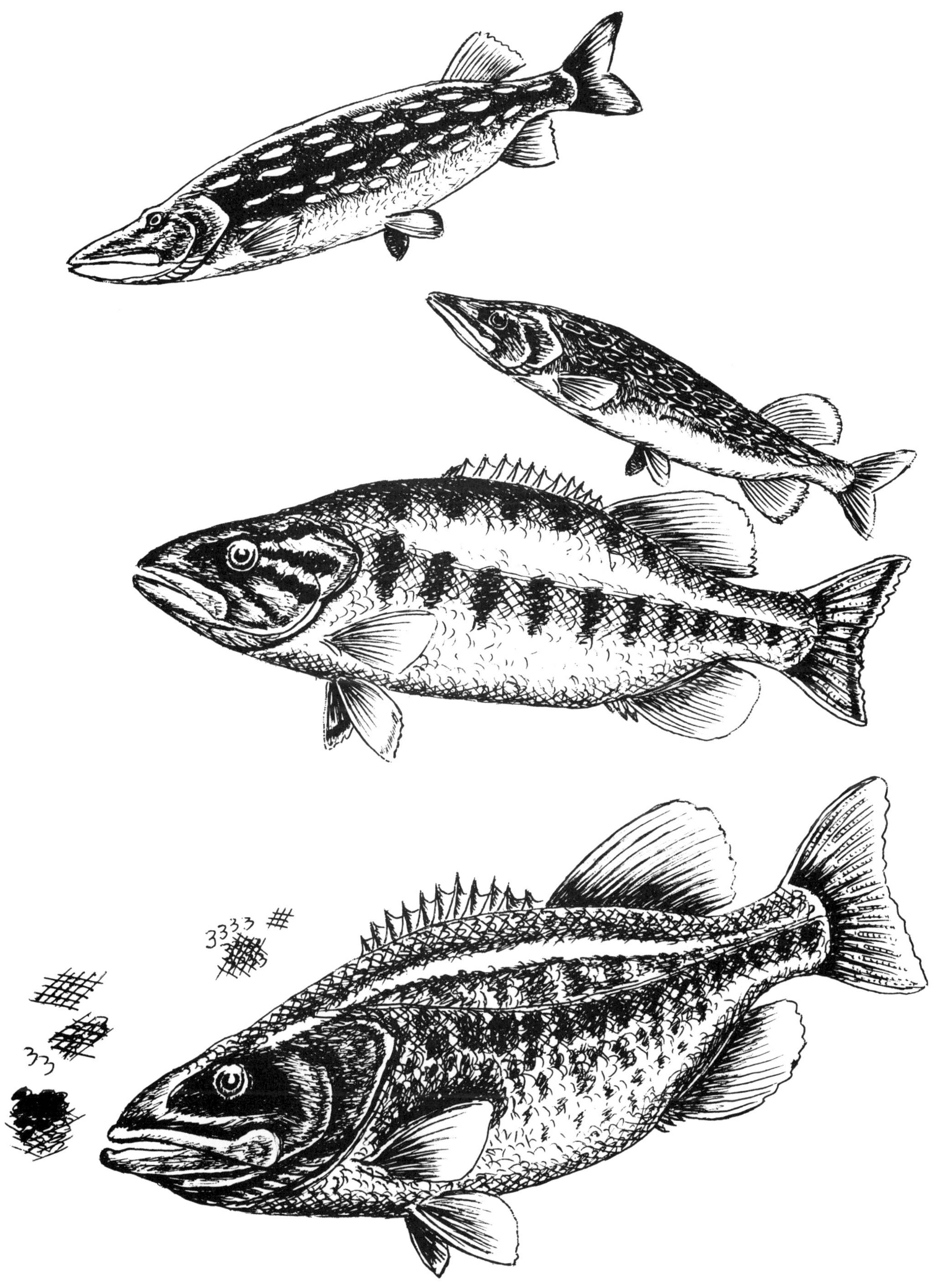

Figure 7.5 Some of our smaller and less glamourous fish make up for lack of drama by their very unusual color. The white perch, for example, is a bouncing, ever-changing mother-of-pearl mix of colors, and you can create a veritable rainbow here without straying from the truth. Actually, the fish is white, or yellowish-white, with green and olive overtones on the back. The fins are sometimes light lemon yellow or even slightly tan, but again note the rainbow colors near their tips.

The crappie is a myriad of black spots amid mother-of-pearl, with basically a green or olive base to work from, slightly darker in the head markings.

The little bluegill is a real charmer in the aquarium or as seen in the pond. Bluegills rival the expensive tropicals of collectors and are easily kept in a home aquarium. Usually caught by kids, bluegills will reward the artist too. Hold a fresh-caught bluegill and move it slightly to watch the rainbow colors scintillate; get this effect in your picture.

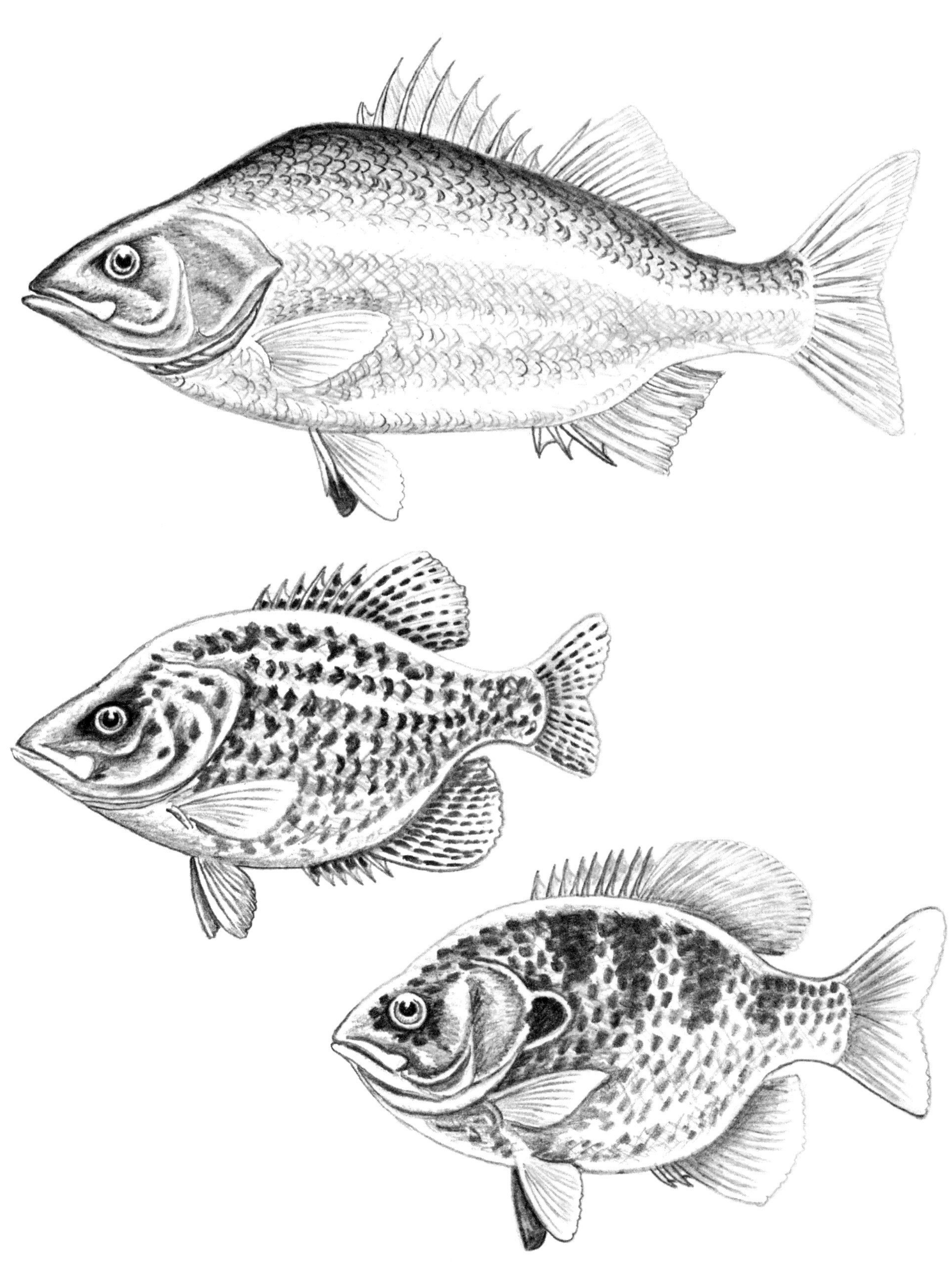

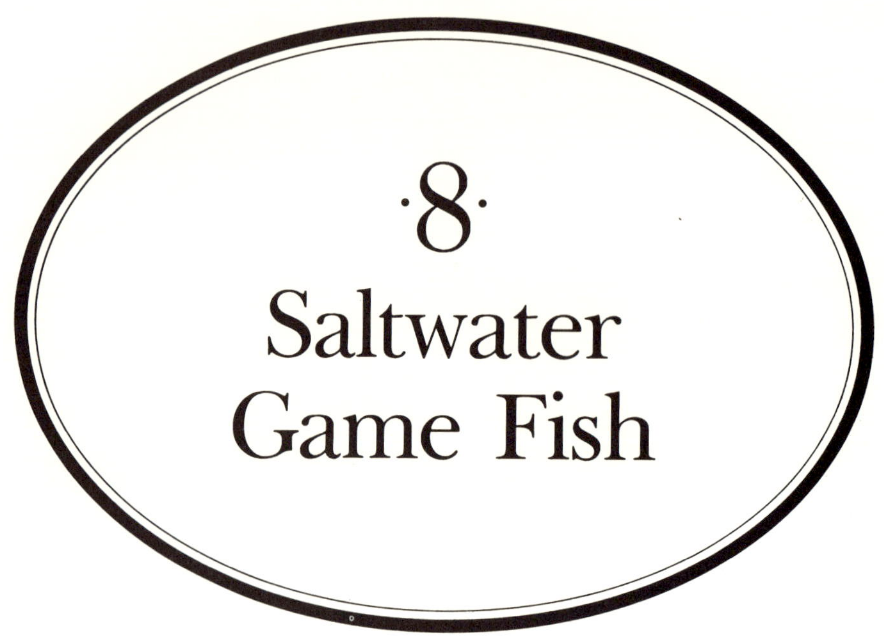

·8· Saltwater Game Fish

Saltwater game fish are one of the biggies of the sporting scene. Shown here in this chapter, for our work, are some prime examples of these strong and beautiful specimens of the saltwater domain. They are a little easier to render than the more detailed trouts and panfishes, but they make up in form what they lack in complicated markings.

The Atlantic sailfish and its near cousin the marlin are the biggest and most dramatic, usually painted in a jump while attached to an angler's line. Although the form of the fish is relatively simple, the trick is in capturing the motion and action of the fish as you attempt to stop it in midair. It takes a lot of "thumbnails" to arrive at a really good rendition of such action. Good photographs are needed here, unless you are quite familiar with the species from actual sightings. But again, imagination is a prime ingredient. The saltwater species selected here each have definite characteristics that you can bring out for an explosive and exciting picture.

The International Game Fish Association is the official keeper of record catches of all fish taken by rod and reel, under the stipulations of tackle specifications for each species. What actually constitutes a "game" fish is largely a matter of semantics as far as the fisherman is concerned. If he can play the game of entice-and-catch with a little flounder or a small kingfish, or even a chub, he could consider it good game.

Since saltwater sport fishing has grown into an international sport, the list of fish classified as "game" has expanded. The bonefish, for example, has become popular as a highly rated sport fish only during the past thirty-five years. The ladyfish, a smaller and not-so-sporty fish found in the same waters, is now considered to be "game."

Many food fish once considered not to be sporting have also become game fish, such as the pollock of the northeastern seaboard. Some game fish are considered inedible, such as the tarpon and the sailfish (to some extent), although delightful meals can be had with smoked sailfish on the menu. The barracuda, at times considered to be poisonous, is certainly a delicacy. The Jack cravalle is one of the hardest fighting fish in its class, but hardly table fare.

There are many ways to study these fish and their habits. One is to fish for them—from a dock, jetty, bridge, mudflat, inland waterway, brackish water bay, or on the wide ocean. One can wade, or fish from a rowboat or small fishing craft with outboard motor, or one can fish from a party boat with many fishermen aboard. The big game species are fished from a charter boat, which can be had for a day or more at quite some expense; the cost can be shared by a party of anglers.

By angling one can get to know the species, their feeding and seasonal habits, physical makeup, and, of course, their table taste. The fish market is another place of research, where whole fish can be seen on sale.

There are also public aquariums and entertainment centers such as the Marineland and Sea World attractions on both coasts, which exhibit many types of fresh and saltwater fish. A visit to a taxidermist shop will find mounted specimens that can be studied or purchased for a collection. For the serious student, contacting marine biologists and federal and state conservation officials can produce invitations to observe experiments and aquatic research.

Atlantic Sailfish (*Istiophorus albicans*)

Possibly the most popular of the big game fish, the sailfish is a junior edition of the marlin. Much smaller than the marlin, it is no less sporty or glamorous, displaying a beautiful, broadsail dorsal fin. When seen mounted, one wonders how in the world such a fish can jump as wildly as the sailfish does. But when hooked in the water, it puts on a show of aerial acrobatics second to none, especially on light tackle.

The sailfish has a blue back with silver sides, a blue-green dorsal fin, and blue-black tail. The Atlantic variety is technically the same fish as its Pacific cousin, although a bit smaller. The Atlantic weighs from 40 to over 200 pounds, whereas the Pacific can weigh even more. Annual fishing derbies, such as the Palm Beach Sailfish Derby, attract anglers from as far as Montana.

For many years great quantities of these fish were taken off the coast of Florida, but with conservation measures taken in its behalf most fish hooked are returned to the water. These measures have their admirers and attackers. Some claim that the sailfish returned to the water is exhausted and easy prey for sharks and that the damage to the fish will kill it eventually anyway. Many fish have been tagged by sportsmen and then recaught later, however, which to some degree refutes the "antis."

Palm Beach and Miami see the sailfish at its height from January to April, the top of the tourist season. They also range off Cuba and into the Bahamas on the other side of the Gulf Stream. Once in a while they are taken off Cape May, New Jersey, and Cape Cod. Though not as well publicized, good schools of these fish are found on the Gulf Coast offshore from Texas, Mississippi, and Alabama. This fishing is best in the summer.

Many anglers believe the sailfish to be more spectacular than the marlin, jumping more frequently, waving its big "fan," and tail-walking across the ocean waves. Techniques for fishing it are the same as for all big game ocean fish. Baits are trolled with the line held by high outriggers so that bait rides naturally in the water. When the fish hits the bait, the line is then in direct contact with the angler's rod—and the fun begins.

Blue Marlin (*Makaira nigricans*)

The blue marlin is the most popular of the big game marlins. All marlins are dazzling fighters, running deep one minute, only to surface the next and dance on their tails across the ocean as they try to shake the fisherman's hook.

From a distance it is sometimes difficult to tell the difference between a blue and a striped marlin. The blue is much less common than the striped or the white species. It is found chiefly in the Atlantic off our shores, from the lower latitudes of the Caribbean all the way north to Long Island, following the Gulf Stream. There is also a Pacific blue marlin, considered by some biologists to be a separate species. The silver marlin, thought to be a subspecies, is found well south of our borders.

Blues weighing over the 760-pound mark have been recorded often, and harpooned specimens are said to reach over the 1000-pound mark. Usually, they average out from 225 to 550 pounds.

The blue marlin is dark blue and sometimes even purple on the back, with lighter blue or whitish vertical bands from tail to head. The blue's dorsal fin is different from the other marlins—the anterior lobe is thinner and sharp. The others sport a broader spar on the dorsal fin. (See Figure 8.1*b*.)

The blue's habits are similar to all marlins. It roams the high seas, feeds on schools of bait fish, and is found at certain times along the shallower currents or along the drop-offs into the big deep. Tagging and, of course, angler's trophies help to record the movements, sizes, and environmental conditions of the marlin.

Tarpon (*Megalops atlantica*)

Resembling a colossal herring or shad, the tarpon lurks in southern waters from the Carolinas clear around the Florida peninsula, over into the Bahamas, and down through the southern islands including Cuba and

Central America. It is caught for sport only, as tarpon meat is not on the preferred list of ocean edibles. Tarpon are taken in the open ocean waters, but unlike the marlins and dolphins, they prefer bays, inlets, and brackish water, and even venture into freshwater estuaries and streams.

The large scales, oversize upper lip, big eye, and long, hard body show a build for a spectacular fight, even on heavy tackle. When hooked they jump hard and high, many times, making them an angler's dream of action. They feed on baitfish and will tackle all manner of lures, from cut and rigged bait to artificial flies and plugs. They inhabit the narrow waters of canals where salt and freshwater bass, snook, and jacks are also found.

In the shallow waters of creeks small tarpon from one to ten pounds abound, with some weighing more. Tarpon from 200 to 300 pounds can be taken in shallow inlets or in the open ocean. Their basic color is white with mother-of-pearl shadings.

Although they are taken all year long, May and June seem to be the top months in Florida. The Annual Tampa Bay Tarpon Derby is a must for tarpon lovers. The Gulf Coast through to Texas depends on the glamour of the tarpon to support its recreation industry. (See Figure 8.2*a*.)

Striped Bass (*Roccus saxatilis*)

Striped bass, the New Englander's favorite, are the prize sporting and eating fish of northeastern waters. The striper is also taken as far south as Florida and has been successfully stocked in the Pacific, where it is faring in Washington, Oregon, and northern California even better than in its native eastern seaboard waters. The Gulf States also enjoy the striper.

Basically an inshore fish, it seldom ventures into the open sea unless attracted by a wreck or shallows. It is often taken in bays, inlets, and estuaries, where it occasionally ascends into freshwater to spawn in the spring. Sometimes striped bass travel many miles upstream to spawn and so are caught in company with freshwater bass, channel bass, and other game and food fishes. In the Gulf waters and Florida, March is a good month; striper fans in New England are out for them in strength from summer through late fall. On the West Coast the striper is all-year fare, with the largest concentration during the spawning runs in the spring, along with various salmon, steelhead, and cutthroat trout.

Striped bass feed on anything from school baitfish to mollusks and crustaceans, eels, sea worms, and the rest. Consequently they're found in all kinds of places from surf to bays, to inlets, and even to brackish ponds. Frequently it is found in company with channel bass in southern waters. Tarpon are also taken in and around concentrations of stripers in the Florida waters.

With greenish tinges and dark green-brown stripes, it is an easy fish to identify. It does not have the tail spot found on the channel bass, and though its scales are large it cannot be confused with the tarpon. Because of its shape and fin arrangements, it also cannot be confused with the snook. (See Figure 8.2*b*.)

The striper is a coveted prize among game fishermen, and striper derbies are legion all along the coastal waterway. All manner of tackle is used, but fly fishing with rods designed for long casts and heavy runs is also used. Stripers jump readily, almost like a salmon, and thrash the surface. They are also known for dramatic runs where there is enough depth. As spectacular table fare, they rival the bluefish and snook for first place.

Bonefish (*Albula vulpes*)

"Fiery ghost of the flats" is the fitting description of the bonefish. The bonefish comes in from the big deep to feed on crustaceans, crabs, and worms—the scourge of the shallows—then it's off again to the ocean. Easily spooked by the presence of a boat or foreign movement in the quiet flats and shallows, the bonefish bolts away at the slightest movement or strange vibration.

Bonefish are most popular as sport fish and give the angler an unbelievable thrill with a long and spirited run when hooked. Preferring not to jump, they will rely on their powerful tails to propel against the pull of the line.

The bonefish is a comparative latecomer in game-fishing circles, having become popular about fifty years ago when anglers began to search in earnest for interesting species to fish. The Florida Keys and the Bahamas are prime grounds because of almost limitless shallows and ground where bonefish like to feed. At first, they were taken on conventional light boat tackle and baitfishing gear; later, on spinning rigs. Nowadays, bonefish have become a prize for fly-fishing addicts.

The bonefish is a distant relative of the tarpon, though it has few true tarpon-like qualities. Although most fish have a longer underlip than overlip, the bonefish has a much shorter chin or underlip. The extended nose is designed for digging in the mud to uncover crabs, worms, and other delicacies. Schools of bonefish can be found in the gin-clear tropical waters simply by observing little puffs of cloudy water caused by their digging and tail flapping.

Their color is a chalky, light blue-green with some specimens having a golden hue. Their scales are rather large and their tail forked. (See Figure 8.2*c*.)

Although the island natives prepare bonefish in a delectable manner, the fish is not considered particularly edible. Its flavor is reminiscent of bleached blotting paper, somewhat like tarpon meat.

Bonefish is also selected as a prime bait for marlin and other game fish. Since it is strong and fleshy, it makes a good fish to sew on hooks for the necessary trolling rig used for bigger fish.

A six-pounder is a good, big bonefish, worthy of mounting in the sportsman's den. Though they are quite rare, fish over ten pounds have been taken. Despite their small appearance, they more than make up for their lack of weight by their abundance of fighting spirit.

Blue Shark (*Prionace glauca*)

Both a game fish and the curse of game fishermen, all sharks spell action, trouble, and sport, depending on how the angler feels when he hits one. All are taken while trolling. Some anglers go after sharks exclusively, chumming for them by emptying buckets of blood, fish guts, and meat entrails over the side in order to attract them. The shark battles long and hard, actually offering a stronger battle than most big game fish such as the marlins, though their fight may not be as dramatic.

The blue shark is no exception. It is a tough "fish," a curse when the angler is out for marlin or other game. Sharks will wait until the angler has his marlin almost aboard, then come in for the kill, chomping off half the fish or tearing the entire fish loose from the hook, leaving the angler *mucho* frustrated.

The blue is a large shark weighing upwards from 100 pounds, and sometimes reaching the 1000-pound mark. It abounds on both coasts offshore and is found along the New England coast and as far south as Florida. Though not considered as hard a fighter as some of the other sharks, the blue does put up quite a battle, jumping wildly, and is especially dangerous if it jumps near or over the angler's boat. Like all sharks, it is long in dying and only the experienced boatman-angler should attempt to carry one aboard. The coloration is a blueish-gray above, shading to silver underneath. (See Figure 8.3*a*.)

Hammerhead Shark (*Sphyrna mokarran*)

The hammerhead is unique in all fishdom because of its hammer-shaped head with its eyes at the ends of the "hammer." The great hammerhead (*Sphyrna mokarran*) is the largest variety, reaching a length of fifteen feet. Common in the Atlantic as far north as Cape Hatteras and in the Pacific up to Point Conception in California, it can reach a weight of 1500 pounds.

Surf and even bay fishermen out for their favorite game fish often catch ten-pounders inshore, much to their surprise.

Although classed as fish, hammerheads have cartilaginous skeletons rather than bone skeletons, and like all sharks, they do not have scales. Hammerhead sharks are gray, grayish-brown, or brown with pale or off-white bellies and broad pectoral fins and high first dorsal fins. (See Figure 8.3*b*.) Although some sharks lay eggs, most are born live after hatching from eggs within the mother.

Figure 8.1 Here is the sailfish—a really big fish, massive in power and electrifying in beauty of line. I have drawn it here in a rather stereotyped pose, but you can find photos to study in sporting magazines that show the sailfish in many dramatic poses as it fights hard to get away from that hook and line. If you are lucky enough to be out on the water to witness one jump like this, you will see violets, blues, purples, soft greens, silver mother-of-pearls that will burn themselves into your memory. You can show it best in color, of course, but this wash is not so bad either. Even pen and ink is a good medium, especially for an unusual pose with sea and seagulls in the background.

The blue marlin is also a raider of the deep, and a beautiful blue-green it is. Although lacking the dramatic sail of the sailfish, you can twist the marlin into some spectacular poses, as it tail-walks on the water, charges across the surface, or jumps toward the heavens. Any angler who has ever tangled with one will admire your picture, for it will bring back to his memory that magic moment he experienced. Again, look through the magazines for good research and then ad lib from there. These big fish demand a big picture, even though they might appear relatively small in it. The sea and the sky create a big backdrop that a small picture just can't fulfill.

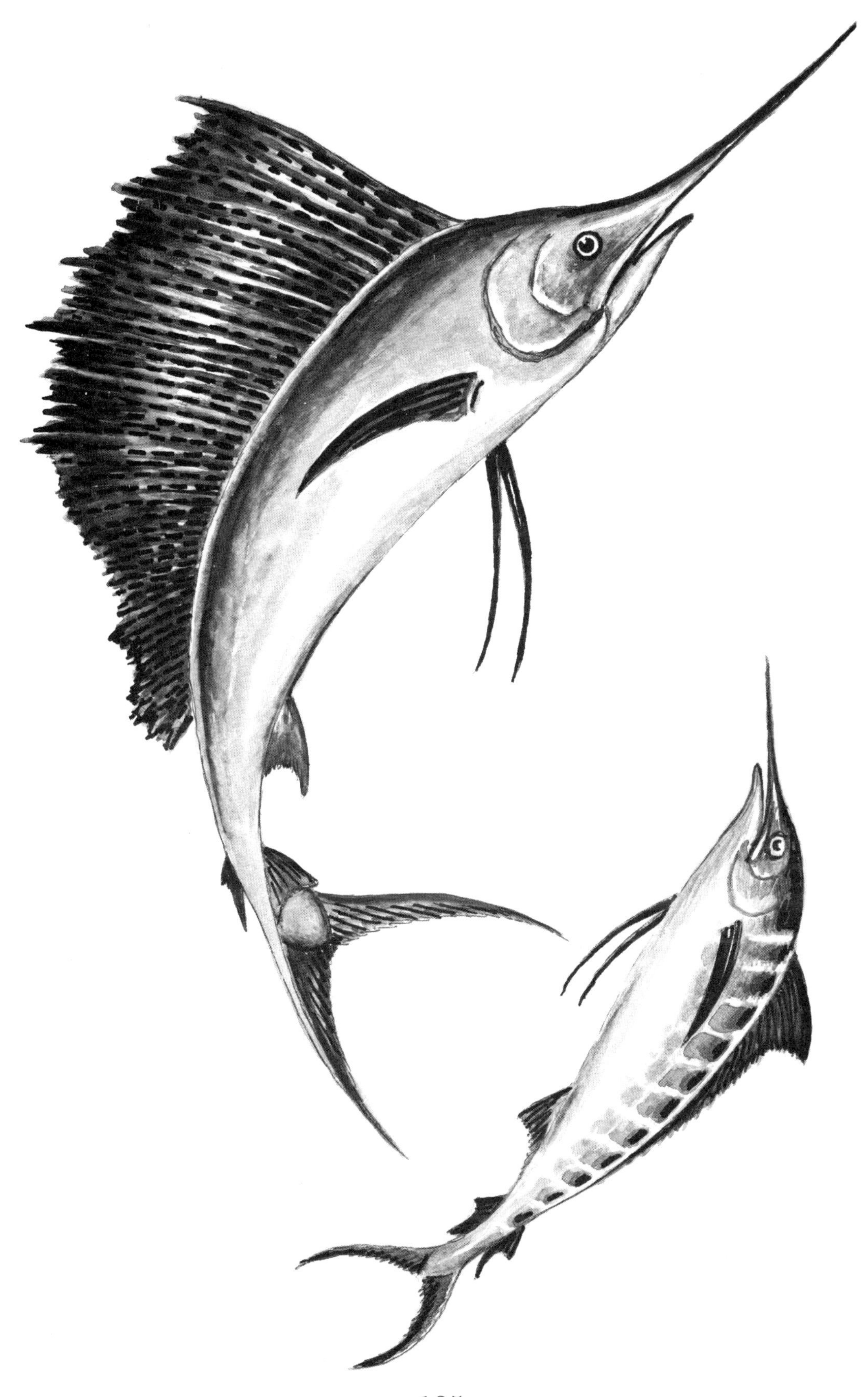

Figure 8.2 Here we have the striped bass, tarpon, and bonefish. Striped bass find their way to the market, so you can see them first hand; if not cleaned with their heads off, you have all the research you need. They are pictured often in sporting magazines, and a good book on fish will have fine illustrations. The pictures on this page are all done in wash for contrast, just to show the subtle sculpturing you can perform on a simple fish. The texture of the fins, their arrangement, the ovalness of the body, all must be brought out in order for the fish not to appear flat and uninteresting.

The tarpon (shown as a head in closeup, center of the picture) is, like the Atlantic salmon, a strange character. My, what a fighter! So make the tarpon look as if it were about to gobble you up. The small version is almost done in cartoon style, if you like to play around with character.

The subdued-looking bonefish is this way most of the time, as it rests on the southern flats waiting for food to swim by. Once scared, however, the bonefish takes off at lightning speed with a powerful switch of that big tail. Show this; make your bonefish explode out of its doldrums. It seldom jumps but will thrash the surface unmercifully when hooked, so that is another way to present it.

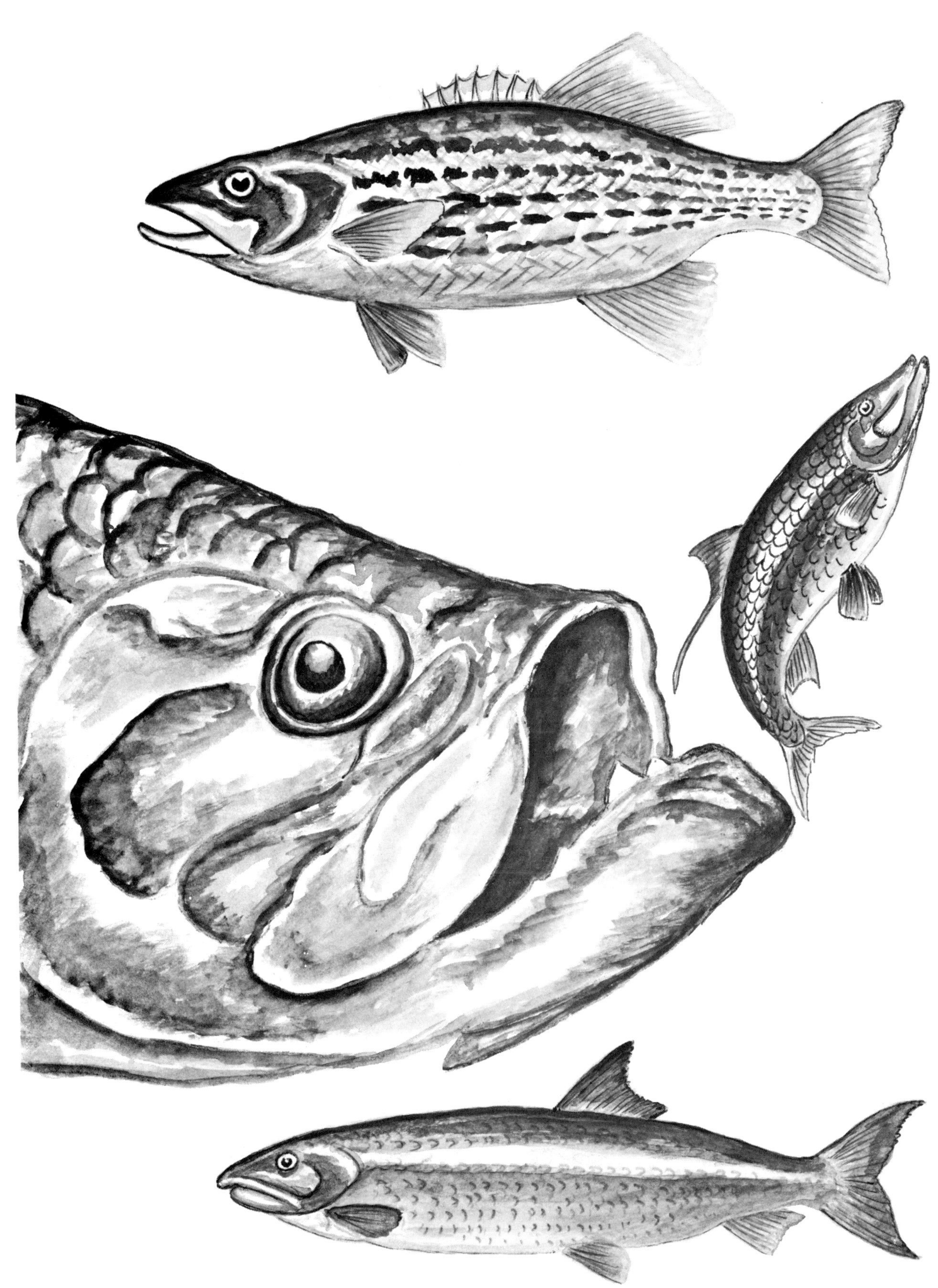

Figure 8.3 Finally, we come to the sharks. Best do these in half-tone, because they are soft in texture—with no scales, of course. They are a dull-gray color sometimes reflecting the green or blue of the ocean in which you picture them. You can also make them jump, either hooked by an angler or to thrash at the bait fish they are after. Be dramatic here. Frightening. People like to be frightened by sharks.

As for the hammerhead, this is a truly strange subject. The eyes of this beast are stuck out there at each end of the "hammer" like the wing lights on a plane. The hammerhead's for real, though, so have fun creating its bizarre shape.

Keep your sharks light and bright. They do not glisten when underwater, but you should try to imply dark against light here, as always, to show form and indicate motion. When hauled out of the water they do, of course, reflect the sunlight, as any wet object does.

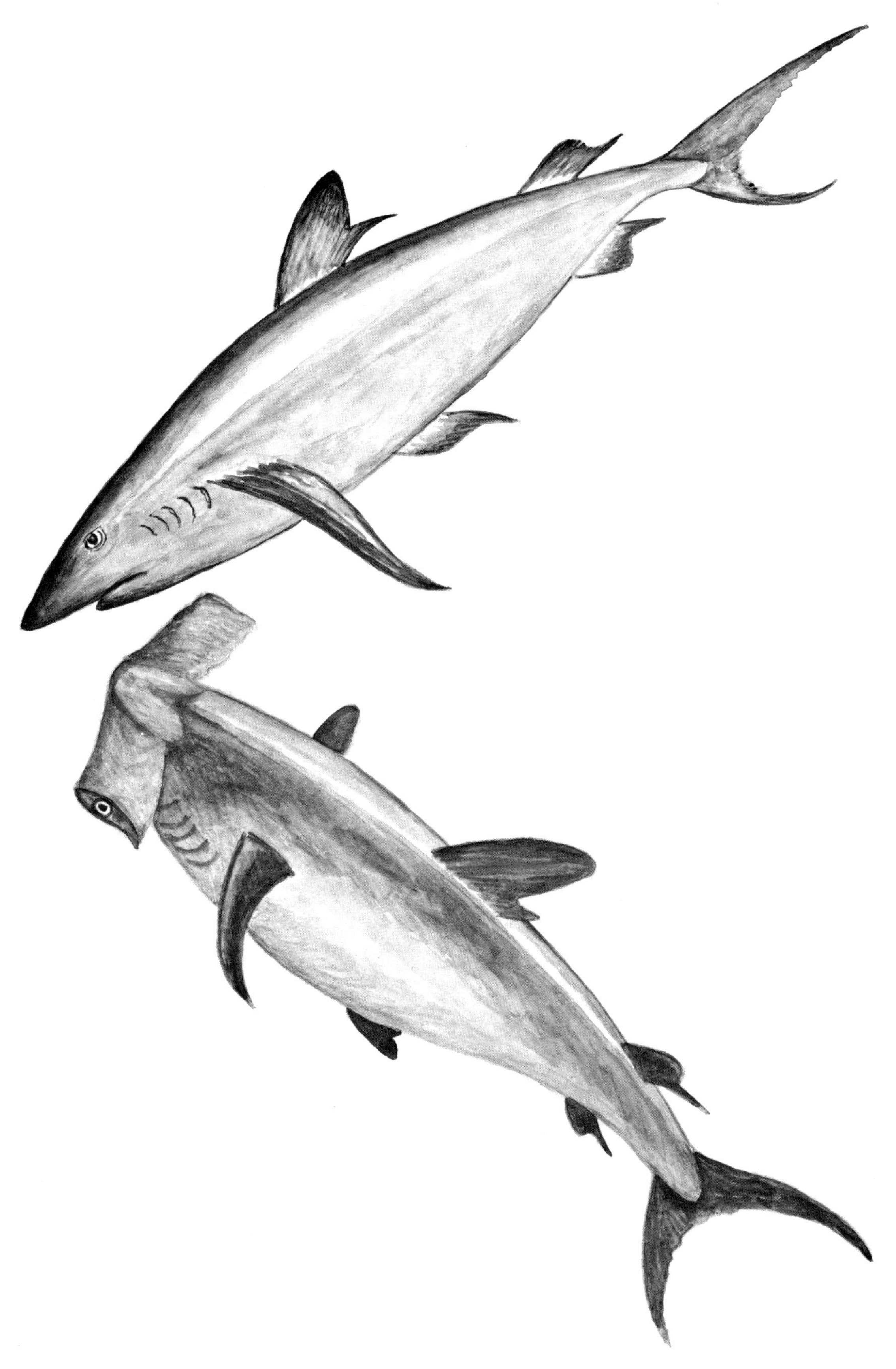

·9· Drawing and Painting Your Backgrounds

Obviously the backgrounds for our pictures of game birds, animals, or fish must be as authentic and believable as the subjects. Next time you walk in the woods or fields, along a trout stream, or along the beach, or take a ride in a boat on a lake or the ocean, open your eyes and scrutinize (with real attention) what you are looking at. You will have an entirely new experience outdoors, beginning to see like you never have before. You will see lights, reflections, shapes of shadows, forms of old knotted trees, the featherlike leaves of spring alders and willows, or the crisp, almost artificial foliage colors found in the fall of the year. Your whole outdoor world will take on new interest as you poke around, looking for background ideas for your game-painting subjects. You may meet things you never knew existed!

The main thrust of this book so far has been on rendering the actual specimens so that they are accurate, active, and interesting. Now you must place your specimen in a typical background. This need not necessarily be as detailed as the specimen itself, but it should reflect the nature and feeling of the surroundings.

Much background can be indicated rather than photographically represented. In fact, try to guard against having your background rob your subject of its interest. Work in the elements of the background easily and slowly, holding the picture out in front of you often to help your eye judge and direct the balancing of the background against the subject. Again (as always) it is light against dark, dark against light, as you form waves, wind-driven reeds in the duck pond, white birches against the darker evergreens, the rocks and cliffs against the faraway mountain tops. All these backgrounds can be rendered softly and in balance with the subject, but they must have inherent accuracy. Know how to draw a birch tree as contrasted to an oak tree. Know the different evergreens. Should there be smooth rocks or jagged ones? You can use old fences or stumps. You can capture, for example, a moss-covered windfall tree vibrating in the sunlight beside a resting grouse; you can render a cactus of a specific species in the desert behind your quail. Backgrounds are the meat of the picture and a joy to research in the photos and sketches you bring back with you from outdoor walks. Your camera should be worked hard in taking strictly background pictures for your files. You never know when you may need to refresh your memory of a woods scene or of the ocean waves.

Executing your backgrounds starts with the all-important thumbnail sketch. Granted you have the specimen outlined in the picture. Now you must give it something to stand upon or fly up from, something that is the key part of the background. From there, adding little incidentals can go on indefinitely. You can draw in flowers, weeds, odd-shaped rocks, crooked branches, seaweed, seashells, whatever. But these details are all secondary to the actual "something" your subject is leaving, or landing upon, or standing in or on.

Beyond the foreground and the immediate, closeup background lies the opportunity to give depth to your picture. The sand dune beyond the beach, the cove that extends down the shore, the far-off ledges against the crashing surf, the waving grain or reeds on the opposite shore behind your rising ducks, the birch grove or swampy area into which your woodcock will fly, the far-off hills or mountains. And even beyond that, a soft rendering of forest, fields, clusters of rocky cliffs, or a far-off point of land—all these are placed in the picture in perspective until you finally end up with sky. And sky, too, can have depth and added perspective if you include clouds in the picture.

You have worked from subject to immediate area of attention and then have backed off and indicated several perspective and depth features to your picture. Stand back from it now, visualizing just how you will shade the given areas for depth and feeling.

When you are ready to begin, start with the lightest note, whether it be the sky or something in the foreground. You gently sketch in the guidelines you will be using. Sketch in lightly so they can be erased as you work into the areas.

You can even shade in the ideas in your mind, to be accentuated later and darkened or deepened. It is quite all right to make your entire picture in very light pencil. You may decide to finish it in pencil, or may go to the pen or brush. But with the pencil shading, the indications of light against dark, and the perspective and depth areas noted, it is now a matter of gradually filling in.

To do this you can decide the major color of a given area and lightly indicate this. If you are working in color and wish, for example, to have a grove of birch trees in the fall foliage: wash in a swath of light yellow into the area and then a dark green, to start off your evergreens that will be standing there behind them. Blotch in light and dark yellows later. Block in your colors. By blocking in your colors, you will begin to see the nature of the picture you are beginning to create and can gradually add detail as you work forward, paying strict attention to your main subject so that you will know, when you get close to it, which way to go—light against dark, or dark against light.

Try not to concentrate on any specific area of your picture yet. Merely block it in, beginning the suggestion of shading of shadows and highlights, and add elements such as downed trees, fences, rocks, or whatever, as your mood indicates, making sure you can represent them without too much attention being drawn away from the main subject. Some background suggestions are given in the following pages. (See also Figure 2.9.)

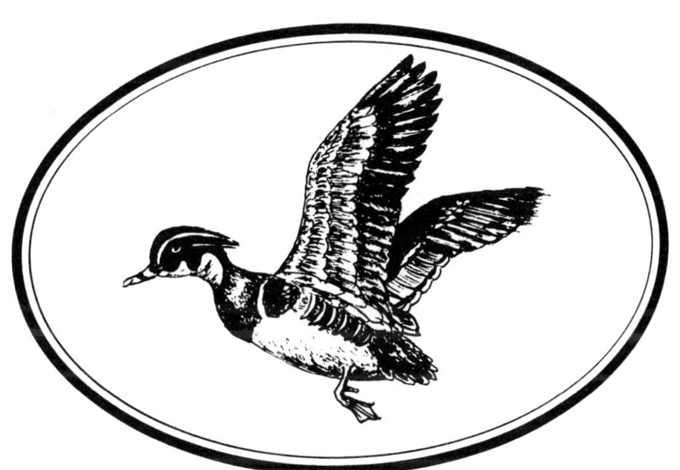

Figure 9.1 Here are several glimpses of the outdoors from my notebook and picture file, all suitable to use as backgrounds for our drawings and paintings. These are good for any of the upland game birds, a lake scene for ducks or geese, or with deer.

If you walk in the woods, take along a sketch pad or a camera and catch some views like these for future use. They will be authentic, typical, and real—because *you* have recorded them. When you make your thumbnail sketches, include one or more interesting "props"—an old stump, for example—for your subject or subjects. You can detail the prop if something is on it or if it is in the foreground. If, however, you choose to use the prop in the background, put it in lightly so it will not distract attention from your central feature.

Use your nature walks for sketching sessions and you will build a file of outdoor pictures that can well live on their own merits, even without a featured animal or bird.

Also, you can concentrate on the background and create a landscape, merely including a deer or other game as a minor feature in the overall picture. It is not always necessary to have your subject big and prominent. Many fine artists simply include a bird or an animal for minor interest.

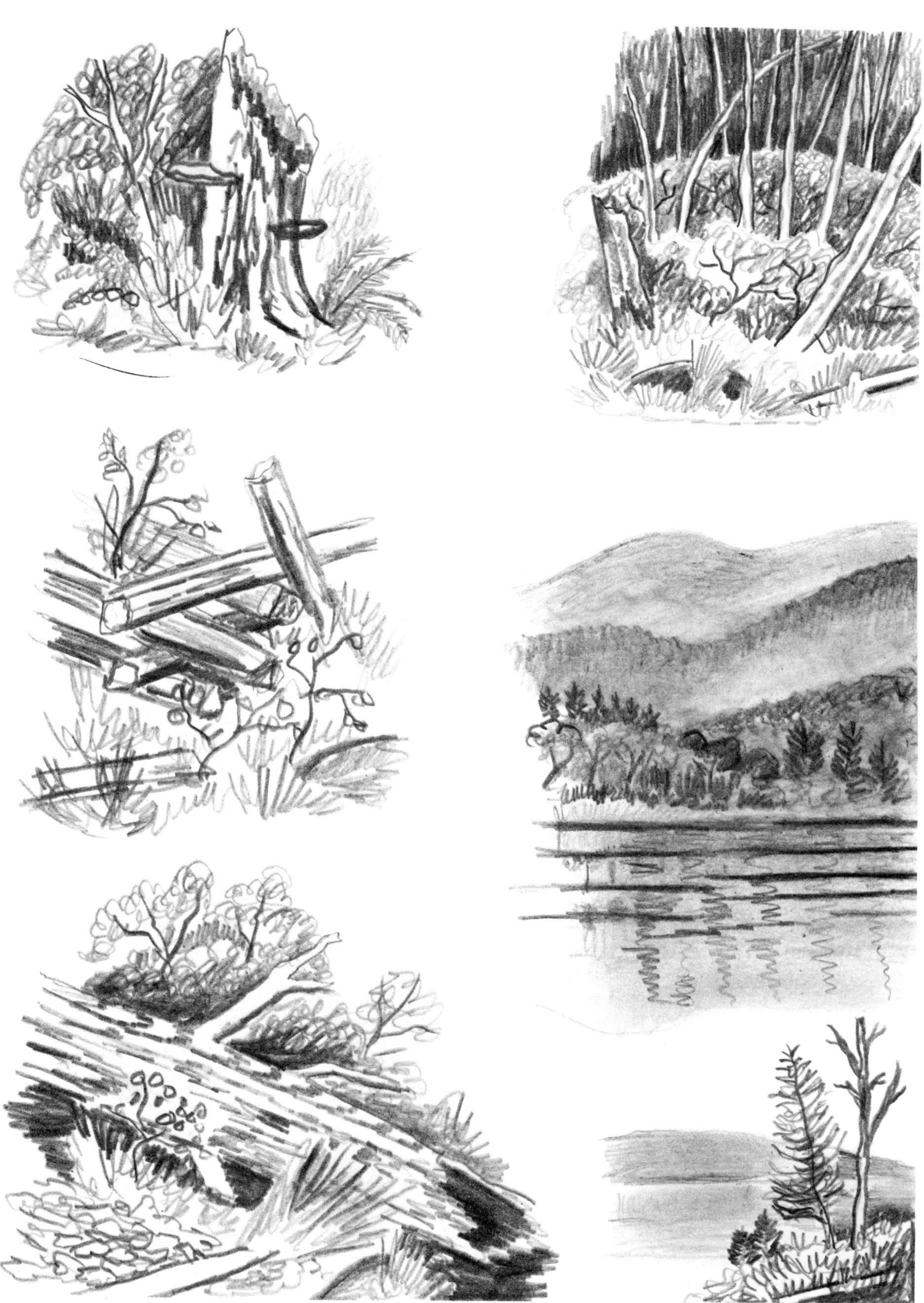

Figure 9.2 These backgrounds are typical of water sources where trout, bass, and panfish are found. You will have to study reflections from the water's edge and note the mood, speed, and action of the water on the reflections as it flows along the shore or is broken by midstream rocks.

In the upper drawing are several good backgrounds for your leaping trout. Or, if you like, have your trout or bass rising out of the wash behind the rock in the middle picture.

The splash a trout makes coming out of the water is a strong effect. Shown here is a conventional "hole" left by a rising trout. It comes out switching its tail and raises a fuss in the water. Try and keep the rising water and spray somewhat subdued. Avoid the look of "frozen" motion you would find in high-speed photography; it will seem unnatural in a piece of art. Try for the *impression* of rising water, not its actuality.

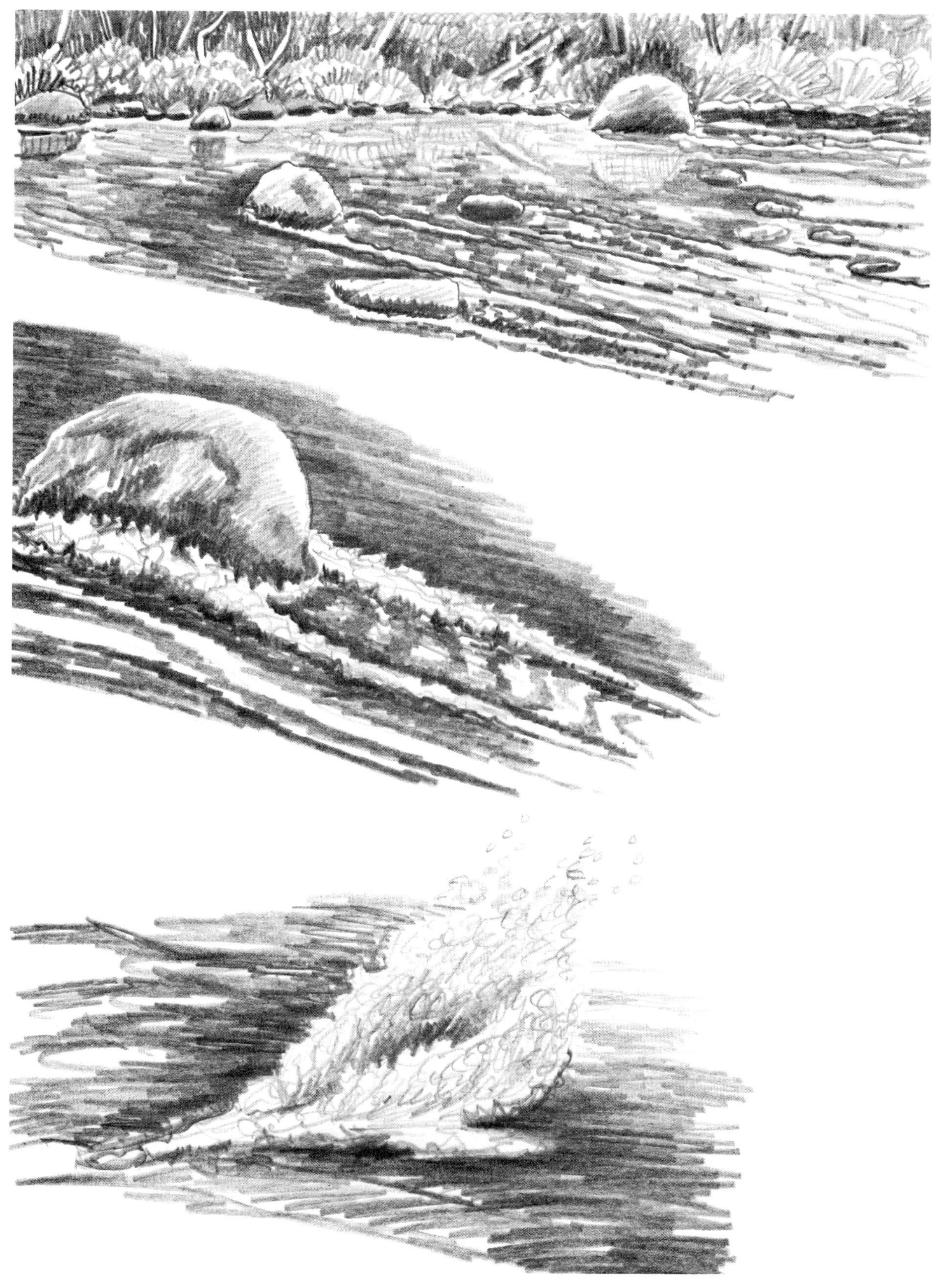

·10· Masking, Matting, and Framing Your Pictures

The worst painting cannot be made to look good by a fancy frame, but a very good painting can be downplayed and made to look uninteresting by being in the wrong frame.

I learned this several years ago when I knew a framer who had hundreds of frames available in his shop. I would take my work into the shop and pick out at random a dozen or so frames, placing them over my picture. I was surprised at how each frame made the picture "say something"—or say nothing.

The conventional way to frame a pencil drawing is to use a white or off-white mat and then frame it in an undecorated black or brown frame. Some modern artists like to put their pictures in metal frames, but metal usually seems inappropriate to game art, the capturing of natural subjects after all. Try and keep your frames in harmony with the subject. The outdoors says "wood," of some tint or other—old distressed barnwood being most compatible. Pen and inks are also matted, generally in white, and then framed in a black, narrow-edged frame.

The mat dimensions really depend on the strength of the picture. Some art looks better with a narrow mat, other pictures look better and, in fact, demand a very wide mat. I have seen very small pen-and-inks matted in wide-bordered mats, and the effect is quite startling. The conventional mat is the same dimension on three sides, with the bottom side a hair wider than the sides or the top.

Black-and-white washes in half tone are best matted and then framed by a narrow black or dark brown frame. The mat should not be too wide for most subjects. Practice with a few pieces of paper you have cut out, to judge the size you will order from the framer or cut yourself.

Commercial frames come in standard sizes and are far cheaper than custom-made ones, and it's unnecessary to go to exotic sizes in this work. When you make your first thumbnails and arrive at the approximate size of your painting, bear in mind the proportions, allow for a normal sized mat (give or take a quarter of an inch), and you arrive at the frame size. Or you can work backwards: from the frame, to the mat, and then to the size of the proposed picture. When you find this dimension, allow yourself about an inch more of finished picture. You may later want to mask it a bit to shift the accent higher or lower or from one side to the other. The added area all around also gives the framer some latitude to work with in cutting and fitting.

Framing and matting is an art, and so is the actual design of the size and shape of the picture you are contemplating. Very small pictures can be made to look exquisite, and large pictures badly balanced can be an abomination.

Your watercolor pictures should be done on heavy-grade paper, such as used in those pictures in the color section done on Bristol-weight board, or on good-quality watercolor paper. I am also fond of doing watercolor and half wash, and even, yes, pen and ink, on mat board—the white board that is generally used for matting pictures. It has a rough surface, lending itself to dry watercolor very well, and offers a rigidity for mounting into a frame.

I also like to work on rough-surfaced colored paper, such as used in some of my head portraits of game birds in the color section. There is no limit to the type of paper you can use, but it must be mounted in a mat that will help your picture literally "bounce" out at the viewer.

Very often I prefer a wood frame and no mat, the way oil paintings are traditionally mounted. If the picture is strong enough, a simple wood frame is enough. There are frames that include a white or off-white matlike area in the profile that butts to the picture, and others with the same idea but including a very narrow brown or black strip between the white area of the frame and the picture itself. Experiment with these. Don't choose a frame that overbalances your picture or detracts from it, but rather find one that makes the picture "bounce" out from it. There is no law that says you must mat a watercolor, so try the matless frame idea and see how it appeals to you.

In the following illustrations are some basic framing and matting suggestions for you to follow. Again, your artwork is an experience in learning to see, perhaps for the very first time in your life. Little did you know what was there outside your eyelids! You enter an exciting world when you become a creative artist, and framing and matting is one aspect of that art you should never take lightly.

Figure 10.1 Although you can usually arrive at a well-balanced picture when you develop your thumbnail, there is always room for improvement through the subtle art of masking. Even a thin slice off the picture on any one of the four sides can cause a change in impact for the viewer. This is why you work larger than needed, so you can cut later if necessary. Leave a good margin between the prime subject and the edge of the picture. The frame or mat will absorb at least a quarter inch of your paper, so don't find yourself losing vital elements of your picture under the mat.

The series *a*-1, *a*-2, *a*-3, *a*-4 shows four ways of masking a given picture. Note in each case how the mood and attention change. To try this out, take four sheets of paper and frame a work, adjusting each page to try out various sizes and shapes.

Matting can vary, too, as shown in *b*. (*b*-1) Indicated here is the black or metal frame line. (*b*-2) This is a narrow mat, 1″ to 1½″ wide all around with a quarter-inch more width at the bottom as indicated by *b*-3. (*b*-4) This is from 2¾″ to 3¼″ wide all around with a quarter-inch added on the bottom as indicated by *b*-5. (*b*-6) This is an extremely wide mat that can be quite effective with or without the black margin, done either on the art or on the mat edge.

(c) A cross section of frame construction is shown.

(d) This is a simple narrow wood frame and narrow mat.

(e) This is a simple flat-wood frame with a screen molding edge to hold the painting—a very simple but effective frame I use often.

(f) Here is a formal frame, a multirelief wood and concave mat used with flat mat.

(g) This is a simple driftwood or barnwood frame.

(h) Rope edging over the frame, for that outdoorsy or nautical look.

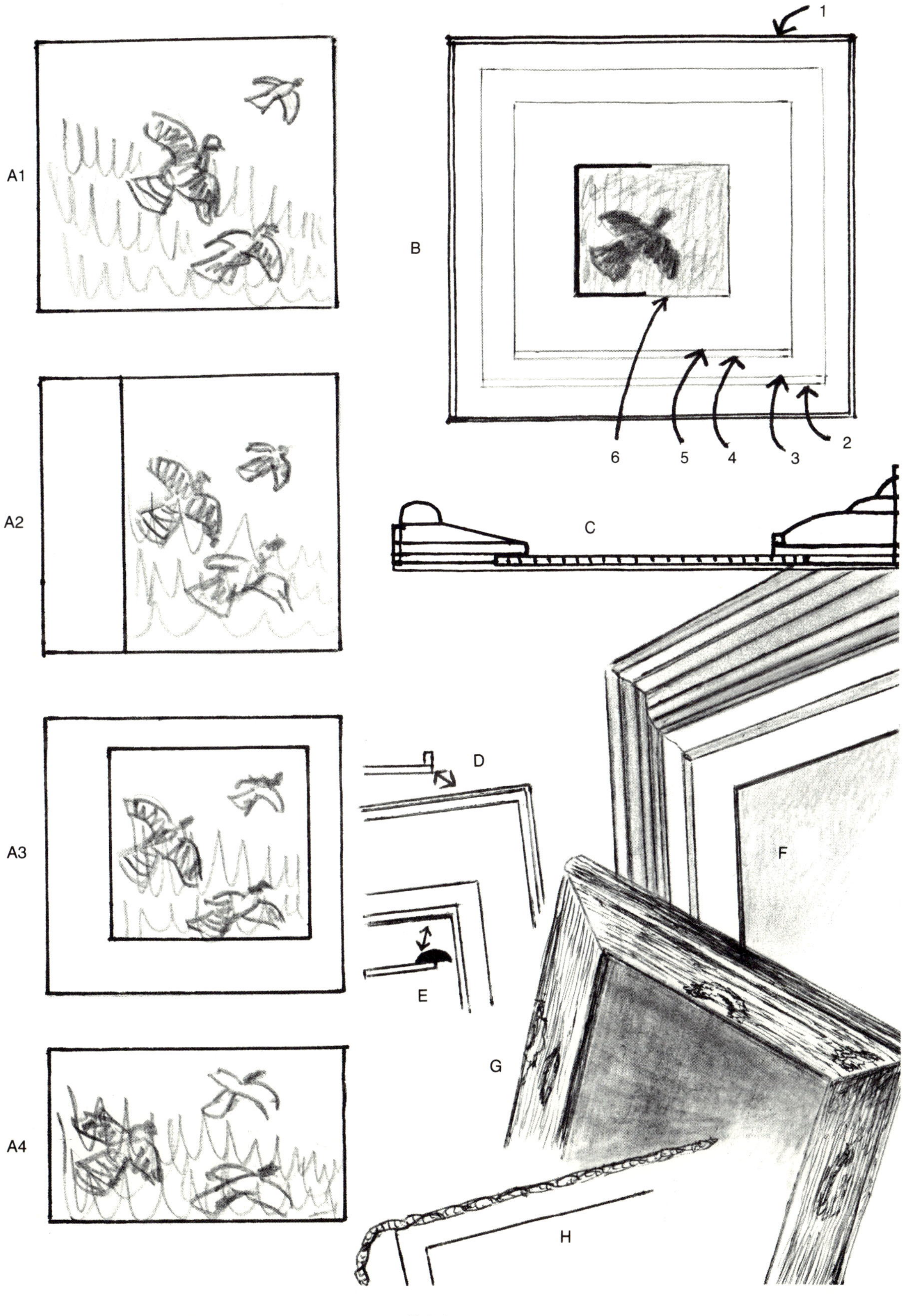
A1
A2
A3
A4
B
1
2
3
4
5
6
C
D
E
F
G
H

Index